DADDY, DO YOU BELIEVE IN

GOD?

DADDY, DO YOU BELIEVE IN GOD?

*The story of how we lost our faith,
and how we might find it again.*

JOHN HUNT

BOOKS

"Lead me from the unreal to the real.
Lead me from darkness to light.
Lead me from death to immortality."

THE UPANISHADS

"Buy the truth and sell it not."

PROVERBS 23:23

CONTENTS

CONTENTS

CONTENTS

ACKNOWLEDGEMENTS

There is nothing original in this book, I am simply indebted to the many authors I've read and the friends I've had conversations with. I'm grateful to a couple of evangelical friends for commenting on portions of an earlier draft, though I won't mention them by name as I doubt they'd want to be associated with the end result. When I'd nearly finished I came across the *Sea of Faith* network and e-mail discussion group. I haven't had the courage to contribute yet, but have come to appreciate more fully the difficulties in trying to define what we mean by "God." Also thank you to Ruth McCurry and Nick Fearn for reading through a later draft, and to Christopher Norris for copy-editing. I'm indebted to all in the office for putting up with my absence and inattention over the past year. But above all thanks to Ros, for putting up with the hours spent at the computer, and with me for the last 20 years.

Quotations from the Bible are from the Authorized King James Version except where mentioned. Apologies to English readers for using American spelling, but the market for Christian books in the UK is so small that it's just the way I've come to think.

PREFACE

This book was on its way to the printers when news of the shocking terrorist attacks on the United States was broadcast.

The reference to "warring fundamentalism" on the back cover seemed a bit "over the top" before these tragic events. So did the suggestion, in the penultimate chapter, that the next century might be one of warfare between the Muslim and Christian worlds. Today it doesn't seem so improbable. I haven't made any changes to the book itself. But to let it through without comment in the light of what has happened seems inadequate, insensitive as it may be to intrude so early on the grief and anger of others. Words like "evil" and "insane" may seem the only ones to use in describing the events we have witnessed. But it's also dangerous to act in direct response to those feelings; and this is a world issue, in which we're all involved. If there's any comment to be made, however tentative, now is the best time.

The talk from the US and UK governments of a "worldwide crusade against terrorism," a "global battle" of good against evil, is even more alarming than the events themselves. Maybe we're starting a war that is straightforward and just. But we don't seem to understand clearly why it began, or who we're fighting against, or how it will be best conducted, or how it will end.

Belief in God has been a comfort for many of the victims' families, and a source of strength for the US nation. It was also the inspiration for the attack. Islamic terrorists (assuming they are behind it) do not contravene the teaching of the Koran against suicide because they feel jealous of Western living standards, because they hate freedom and democracy, because they are cowards, or even because they are uniquely evil individuals. They do so in the belief that they are acting in a holy and righteous cause approved by God. Religion is part of the problem – it will have to be part of the solution.

The West will never defeat Islamic terrorism by military means. It may well have some initial success, but martyrs feed on death and war. Islamic terrorism represents the extreme end of a view increasingly held by a good proportion of the Islamic population worldwide, a view that has grown in strength over the last century, that the West is anti-Islam. Cheap oil supplies and company profits are seen to be of more importance than respect for the integrity of Islam and its sacred sites. Muslims feel powerless to influence the West by usual diplomatic or military means. Increasingly, individuals resort to terrorism. And, as we've seen in recent years, they are increasingly prepared to die.

Up till this month they have been relatively unsuccessful. That has now changed. Whoever planned the attacks on the US are probably years ahead of our game. They *want* the West to respond violently. They want to radicalize the moderate Muslims, to sow the ground for a multitude of martyrs, to turn the world into a larger-scale Israel. They *want* a battleground defined as "good versus evil", fuelled by anger, despair and bigotry. It's a battle they believe Muslims will win, because God is on their side.

We need to understand what we might be getting into here. We risk entering a cycle of revenge that is infinitely harder to stop than it is to start. It's not the Western educated elites of some Middle Eastern governments we need on our side, or even the anti-Western fundamentalist governments, or the ex-Communist ones. It's the billion or so Muslims who resent those governments, who might overturn them and create a world far more difficult to deal with than the one we have now. The battle against Islamic terrorism will only be won in the hearts and minds of the global Islamic population.

The century that has just ended will be defined as the century of the first world wars, largely between the Christian nations of the West, that left up to 70 million dead. Please, let's think twice before we risk starting a new one, with an added religious dimension. Think of the trauma caused by Vietnam, a small war of little purpose against a small people on the Asian coast. Be aware of the numbers of Muslims, their achievements and their history. Despite the interdependence of Christianity and Islam in so many ways the two civilizations have spent much of the last two millennia in conflict. Our appreciation of this has been dimmed by the economic and military superiority of the West in the last couple of centuries. A global war between the two, fed by the darker sides of triumphalism and the claims to exclusive truth that both contain, could dwarf the casualties of the last century.

This is not to say we should do nothing. But, even if military action could be effective rather than counter-productive, would it be the "right" thing to do? If a psychopath up the road killed my family I'd want to burn his house down, with him inside. But I'd go to prison for it, because we live by laws painfully developed over generations to enable national societies to function. We're now a global economy, and in many respects a global community. So why don't we have international laws and structures that would enable us to bring terrorists to court, and try them?

We could, if the will were there. But rich and powerful nations don't want to surrender their freedom of action, their short term interests, their sovereignty, to less powerful ones. So the present US government for example has rejected an International Criminal Court, continued to refuse to implement United Nations resolutions on Israel, wrecked a decade of negotiations on the enforcement of the global prohibition of biological weapons, insisted on going ahead with the missile defense plan which involves breaking previously signed treaties, refused to sign the Kyoto agreement to combat climate change, and rejected an International Convention on the Rights of Children, to mention just a few. The US and the West cannot continue to be the main beneficiaries of the world economy and the planet's resources, dictate the terms of the game, intervene to enforce them, and not expect a growing groundswell of resentment.

I never made it as far as Afghanistan on the hippy trail in the 70's, but I heard many reports of a beautiful country and a wonderful people. It's been reduced to rubble and fundamentalism by two decades of war against Russia and subsequent infighting, in which the West has played its part. We should remember that just a few years ago the Taliban were perceived as valiant freedom fighters, whom we funded and armed. Can't we be a bit more consistent? If we are to fight terrorism, shouldn't we start by working out what part we have played ourselves?

Perhaps we could broaden our outlook here. Terrorism can be carried out by individuals, by movements, but most suffering and deaths are caused by governments terrorising their own civilian populations. If you added up the deaths caused by terrorism over the last few decades, from the death squads of El Salvador to the genocide in East Timor, what figure would you get to? 10 million? 20 million? Have we cared enough to count? At times we've simply ignored terrorism when hundreds of thousands or millions have died, as in Cambodia or Rwanda, when it didn't directly affect our interests. At times we've promoted the cause of democracy when it helped us, as in Eastern Europe. At others we've supported tyrants, dictators, even been involved in the overthrow of legitimate democratic govern-ments, as in Chile. Large sections of Latin America and Africa have slid into chaos, at least in part as a result of superpower destabilization. The only consistent thread in our policy has been self-interest. We may not have pulled the trigger on all these deaths ourselves, but then we don't apply this reasoning to the supporters of Osama bin Laden. The death of 5000 in New York is a drop in the ocean of suffering, and we don't have the high moral ground. The threads of good and evil are mixed, in societies and in our own lives.

Let's be wary of demonizing other governments, movements, even individuals. Our judgements are likely to come back to haunt us. I remember when Nelson Mandela, now a virtual world saint, was a terrorist in the eyes of most Western governments. Is Yasser Arafat any more of a terrorist than the prime minister of Israel, Ariel Sharon? Perhaps some of those Palestinians rejoicing in the immediate aftermath of the news of the attack on New York had lost family members when thousands of men, women and children were butchered by Christian militia in the Sabra and Shatila refugee camps in Lebanon in the 80's. Responsibility for that action was laid by the government of Israel itself at his door.

Perhaps we should broaden the perspective further still. Let's also be wary of exalting our own society as a model for the world. Perhaps the larger issue here is that countries like the USA and those in Western Europe cannot be truly "Christian" or "civilized" whilst 60% of the world's population in a global economy lives on under $2 a day in a kind of economic serfdom, and millions of children starve to death every year. The increasing dominance of the West over the last two centuries has been accompanied by an ever-increasing gap between the richest nations and the poorest. Maybe today it's only rogue Muslim billionaires with a Messiah complex who can attack us, but future generations will face different threats. There could be dozens of Afghanistans to come, mostly countries we've barely heard of. Terrorism is part of the world we live in. It's an outcome of the world we have created. It can only be defeated permanently by seeking justice for all. No country can be an "island" any more on our small planet, any more than we can be as individuals.

Perhaps forgiveness is a word we can't use yet. Repentance, for our own actions, is one that we can. Perhaps we could use this moment of grief and awareness to create a better world, rather than make it worse. To find common ground and solve problems, rather than drop bombs on people from a great height who suffer as a result, probably don't support the terrorists anyway, and are already starving.

But where are the defining values to guide our actions going to come from? The thrust of this book is that the religious masters still have something to tell us, that all of human life is sacred and of equal value, everywhere. They often sum up these values in a description of God. But belief in God can be equally directed to good and evil ends. It's our choice. Certainty in belief is often achieved at the expense of love and tolerance. A 21st century belief in God must be based on our understanding that the universe itself is uncertain, that absolute knowledge is unattainable. We exist in a narrow strip of potential, between existence and non-existence, black and white. God appears in many guises, but ultimately He is our acknowledgement of our limits, our belief that it is in the process of exploring uncertainty that we find meaning for our lives. The best kind of religion embraces the interests and concerns of everyone, recognising that in our different insights we all have something valuable to share. Much of what we know and value in the West today, for instance, was transmitted to us through Islam in the early Middle Ages. The worst kind is represented by fundamentalism, whether the apocalyptic, anti-social Christian fundamentalism of Timothy McVeigh (the Oklahoma bomber) and others, the Jewish fundamentalism of the Zionists and their dream of a greater Israel, or the Islamic fundamentalism of the suicide bombers. All believe in the same God of Abraham, and that they alone have his ear. All, like Abraham himself, hold the purity of their conviction as more important than the lives of children. All are likely in the near future to have access to nuclear and biological weapons. God help us.

The kind of God we believe in will determine the kind of planet our children live on. The Koran is clear: "If anyone murders an innocent person, it will be as if he has murdered the whole of humanity". If there are Christians in Western governments let them encourage Muslims to follow the Koran by themselves following the teaching of Jesus. Surely, if being a Christian means anything, it means taking his words seriously. These are equally clear, though I haven't heard them yet in all the comment of the last few days: "But I say unto you, that ye resist not the other's evil: but whosoever shall smite thee on the right cheek, turn to him the other also."

September 2001

INTRODUCTION

"Theology is an attempt to explain a subject by men who do not under-stand it. The intent is not to tell the truth but to satisfy the questioner."

ELBERT HUBBARD

To Matthew and Simon

"Do I believe in God?"
"Yes, but...."

I guess part of the reason you asked me is because I publish chil-dren's books that often mention God – the stories of Noah and the nativity seem to crop up anew every year. Some of our adult titles cover the subject too, but it's more difficult to make them work. Publishing on this subject seems a bit like coalmining. You dig harder every year for less return, with the seams running out and new energy sources coming on stream all the time. A century ago most of what was published in this country was "Christian." Now orthodox Christian books represent 1% or so of the book market, still heading south. Few people make a reasonable living out of sales in the UK, which is why, of the million or so books our business prints every year, most are sold overseas.

After publishing all these books I should be able to give you a straight answer to your question. Let me try again. If you mean,

"Do you believe in God as opposed to being an atheist?", the answer is, "yes." If you mean, "Do you believe in the orthodox Trinitarian Christian God?", or to phrase it in fundamentalist language: "Are you saved?", the answer is "no."

Lots of Christian believers, probably most of them, would say this means I'm not one. I've lost my found faith, not found it. Or found another one. As some local market research, I gave this manuscript to your grandmother to read and the conversation went something like, "You write like an atheist."

"I'm not an atheist, an atheist doesn't believe in any spiritual reality, I do."

"But you don't believe in Jesus."

"I do believe in Jesus as someone whose teaching we should try to follow, that's what being a Christian means. I just don't believe he was the Son of God."

"But the Bible says he was the Son of God."

"The Bible is a selection of writings compiled by people you wouldn't call Christian. It's not clear from the Bible that Jesus believed he was the Son of God. I think the balance of evidence shows that the first generation of Christians didn't think of him as God."

"You talk like an atheist."

So why bother writing this book when it will offend my best customers and stand as much chance of selling as Viagra in a nunnery? (Ask your mother what this means.) As well as writing for you two, I'm writing for people I know, trying to explain why I'm in this odd business, dwarfed as it is by the sales of vitamin C pills. There are two groups of friends I'm not going to please. One is made up of those who are pretty certain of their Christian beliefs. Most people I know in the States and most of my relatives in the UK are in this group. In the idiom of some, I'm in the power of the Great Deceiver. I'm hoping they will exercise charity and that I can get them to stretch their definitions of who counts as a

Christian, even re-think what it means. I also have friends who think of all God-language as nonsense. Something the gullible haven't managed to grow out of. I'll have a go at arguing that you don't have to put your brain on hold to believe in God. If you're not convinced, and find God absurd, I'll suggest that even if you take Him out of the equation Jesus still gave us the best model we have of relating to the world. I don't expect to have much luck with either group.

But most people I know are "in-between" these two positions, believing but not entirely sure what they believe in. They might not call themselves Christian but they wouldn't call themselves atheists either. I'm writing for them more than anyone. This might at least help give some shape to their uncertainty (and my own). It means I'm skirting around the questions rather than answering them, but maybe uncertainty in this area is no bad thing? I don't think "truth" can be captured easily in words, any more than "beauty," or "love." You might know it if you see it, you wouldn't deny it exists, but it's hard to describe. This doesn't mean all truth is relative and of equal value. But perhaps it's that, as in science, formulas work for a while but then get overtaken by better ones. Perhaps it's the process of discovery that matters, enjoying what we find along the way, rather than arriving at the destination. Perhaps there is always a better formula to be found. Anyway, what I believe is nowhere near as important for you as what you believe, and everyone has to find that out for themselves. Maybe this will get you started, help you think.

A difficulty in answering the question is that, when it comes to talking about God, we've lost our common language. The last time I looked the word up on the Internet there were 22 million web pages linked to "God," second only to "sex." But flicking through some at random, I found they mostly each seemed to mean something different by the word. So which God is this exactly? The God who sends lightning and earthquakes to strike the wicked, the God we pray to as a friend, or the God that we think of as the sum of our values? The God "out there" of Christians or Muslims, Jews or Sikhs, or the "inner God" reflected more in Eastern religions, and New Age beliefs, in the positive self, or in the vague sense of principle that most people try and live by?

Up till a generation or two ago few would have questioned what you were talking about. God was the holy, personal, Christian one who redeemed us from a wicked world and our sinful selves through sacrificing his Son. But today this kind of "salvation history" is little more widely understood than "astrological psychology" or "cranial-sacral therapy." This common belief that we've lost is described in theology. Theology is the science of God. It was once thought to be the queen of the sciences because it concerned itself with the highest truth. Now we barely associate the word with "truth" at all. It's a minor subject slotted in somewhere between history and philosophy.

It used to be different. The Christian idea of salvation was worked out in detail by the Church Fathers in answer to the challenges of their times. Augustine formulated a new vision of God that bound Him together with Church, society and the individual. He was prompted to write *The City of God* by the collapse of the Roman Empire, when the barbarians were at the gate, pillaging homes and raping daughters. People wanted an explanation for why bad things were happening to them. The framework of ideas developed in this crucible of fire and suffering lasted us for a thousand years. But today there's no one remotely comparable. In world events in the last century, can you think of a single major figure from the Church? The outstanding political and spiritual leader was a Hindu, Gandhi, who liberated a subcontinent from a Christian empire (ours) by non-violent protest. It's hard to think of any Christian leaders today who shape world opinion and events in the same kind of way.

It's not that life is less dangerous or exciting than in Augustine's day. In the last century we've had two world wars, Hitler and the Holocaust, Stalin and Communism, the threat of nuclear destruction, the worst ever famines, huge advances in knowledge, the exploration of space, but the Church has had little to say that anyone has noticed. We no more listen to the Archbishop of Canterbury today for the truth about life than we read Hippocrates for the truth about medicine. There are no best-selling books on theology as on cookery, or gardening. No prime time TV programs, or pages in the color supplements. Books on subjects you might find excruciating at school, like physics and biology, sell in far greater numbers than books on theology.

Which is odd. Science sells today because it describes the world we live in and in everything we do through the day, it's shown to work. But it's not going to explain everything. It doesn't pretend to, mostly. We still feel in our hearts that there's "big stuff" around, the things we can't measure, that we can't even prove are "real:" love, purpose, faith, evil, meaning. Not so much the "how" as the "why." Why are we at odds with the world? Why can't we be happier? Why is nature beautiful? Even a barren desert? In what sense would it be beautiful if we weren't around to see it? Why do we feel the need for meaning? Is there meaning without us? Why is there anything at all?

It's not stupid to ask these questions. Armadillos specialize in body armor, cheetahs in speed, we specialize in thinking about what we see. To be fully aware of life and enjoy it we reflect on it, question it. Science advances the same way, as much by intuition as reason. The drive to find meaning, to create it, to see life as a whole, whether we use science or religion, art or music, this is what we "do." All these are different kinds of crayons we use to draw our map. We grope around the edges of our lives, wondering who we are, who we can share them with, whether we can change ourselves, where we are, where we're going, where the horizons are, whether there's anything beyond them.

This "need for meaning" may even be something "hard-wired" into the brain. After thousands, tens of thousands of generations of believing that there's more out there than we can see, that we're part of a larger reality that is not just material, you can't completely lose it in one or two. Agnostics, communists, humanists, atheists still believe in some of the ways that their grandparents did, and great-great-great-grandparents – ever since their ancestors came down from the trees and started burying their dead. And theology is to belief like cookery is to eating, like love is to sex; these basic activities that go back to the beginning of time developed around the cave fire together. We have a hunger for meaning like we have a hunger for food and relationship. Indeed in most religions these are linked in sacrifice and ritual meals.

When it comes down to working out the meaning in practice – how to live, how to relate to each other and the world – science is neutral at best, dangerous at worst. Art is descriptive, but doesn't direct. Music can be sublime, but doesn't answer. We tend to look to religion for guidance because all the great questions are religious or philosophical ones, and have been thought about for millennia. To work out answers for yourself is like reinventing the wheel. It can be done, but there are thousands of solutions already on the table, in different religious systems, summing up the experience of billions of people. Mind you, religion can be as destructive as science, and more damaging to your sanity. Perhaps we can work with both, balancing one with the other. Perhaps art too should be part of the equation. Maybe it's Fra Angelico who will still seem relevant in a thousand years' time, long after Augustine has stopped pressing our buttons.

So where can we start in talking about God? We all have beliefs. I've never had a problem with "belief" as such. I don't really think there are any genuine 100% atheists, any more than there are genuine 100% Christians. No one is that certain of the bottom line. We're born to believe. Given half a chance, we'll believe anything.

And if that seems too easy we'll invent some beliefs that are more difficult still. And there's the trouble. There are over six billion people in the world, some of whose beliefs stretch back over six millennia. Some for much further back still. They have a vast range of beliefs about "God," or a world of spirit that is "beyond" the material. Most people reject all other beliefs as wrong, though all are minority positions. So are most people fools? Or liars? Is all belief a fault in our wiring? I start, hopefully, from a position of respect for other people. Not only their right to say what they think, but the possibility that in a subject as indeterminate and subjective as religious experience they might be right and I might be wrong.

So do all people have a percentage of truth? Are there many aspects of God? Where do the different beliefs fit on the scale of probability? Is Christian belief any more credible than all the others? Today it revolves around the trinity of a personal God, a fallen humankind, and a unique Jesus as Savior. I believe bits of this in part, but not as a package. I think it's a package created by the Church in the first few centuries AD. Adequate maybe for a time, but not for today. In so far as beliefs can be packaged we can create better ones. People do. The best seem to me to revolve around two simple ideas, which Jesus sums up as the central thread of his teaching:

"Thou shalt love the Lord thy God with all thy heart, and with all thy soul, and with all thy mind. This is the first and great commandment. And the second is like unto it, Thou shalt love thy neighbour as thyself."
(MATTHEW 22:37-39)

Most people agree with the second commandment, in theory anyway. Our problems have always been with the first, with the definition of God. Is this a God "out there"? And if so what kind?

Or is He something we've imagined? Doesn't this best explain why there are so many versions of Him?

But if God exists only in our heads, what's the incentive to follow the second commandment? Is there any basis for moral behavior other than one we can collectively agree on? And what if we can't?

Whether seeing God is looking through a window or into a mirror is hard to say. The world is split roughly 50/50 on this issue. If you live in Washington or Teheran you probably see God as "out there." If you live in Paris or Peking you probably see this God as an illusion, and seek reality by going deeper into yourself, or into the physical structure of the universe. I can't help you much on that one. Either could be true, perhaps they both are. What I am sure of is that if a belief in "God" doesn't result in a compassionate life, it's worthless. That seems to be the main thrust of the teaching of Jesus and virtually every other spiritual master that we know of since the year dot.

I find living a compassionate life hard, so to avoid overburdening myself further I try and keep God simple. My understanding of the verses is that we know who our neighbors are, and God is everything else. I see Him as a kind of collective coded response, a means of growing in love rather than despair or anger. In positively living through the questions of life we increase our understanding of its bitter-sweet beauty. But when we try to load specific descriptions and meanings on to "God" we talk at cross-purposes, or abstractions that end up as word games, or get into arguments. Then we waste the compassionate moment.

I think most people would agree with this so far, though they would want to be more precise. And perhaps we can take it further. Perhaps we see only what we are able to see. Just as our senses only experience the tiny fraction of the world they are able to. Just as our thoughts are largely shaped by our bodily needs, our choices by our genes. But we have created something that adds up to more than this. We have each developed our own sense of "self," our personality. Everyone we know relates to that personality differently. Similarly we can describe the universe in terms of its body: atoms, stars, galaxies; and its laws: theories of gravity and relativity. But we mostly believe that the universe adds up to more than this as well. Each level of description is more than the sum of its parts. Life is more than molecules. Mind is more than brain. The universe is one of purpose and meaning rather than an increasingly complex assembly; it has its own "self," which we call "God."

Maybe God is not what's "left over" once you've explained how the universe works, but how we describe the whole shooting-match. He relates to everything there is in the same kind of way that our personality, our self, relates to our bodies. We can even think of Him as personal to us. But we all relate to Him differently. He is bigger than any description of Him we can give. It's a way, if you like, of seeing the world as 90% consciousness and meaning, with 10% matter. Rather than 90% matter with 10% consciousness thrown in. In describing this world of consciousness and what it means for us I think Jesus probably got it more right than anyone. But a measure of the power of an idea is the extent to which it gets twisted into something different. Which is why many no longer think of Jesus as a spiritual teacher, but as God Himself.

Is this too broad to be meaningful? We've already excluded a billion or so sincere individuals who think that there is no "self" anywhere, at any level. But we mostly need tighter definitions still, we need something to relate to. The trouble is we're aware of many belief options today. In past centuries there was less choice. You believed what you were taught to believe, or you were liable to be burnt, or crucified. So many crimes have been committed in the cause of particular beliefs that today many hesitate to admit to having any, even if they do. There's less to direct you now. You have to search beliefs out for yourself, in the same kind of way you experiment with different foods from the supermarket rather than

)uy your local produce from the corner shop.

This book might help as a guide. It's still ivory-tower stuff, it won't help you on the street, but I hope it's not too theological. Specialists in any discipline will say it's simplistic, and they're right. I'm a waiter, not a chef. Pointing out the options, not creating the cuisine. I haven't studied in any of the areas covered here. I find most specialists, particularly theologians, as obscure as they would find me naive. When it comes to words like "transubstantiation" I go blank. But then I'm more concerned about getting through the day without fouling up than learning another language. Most people are the same. Seems to me the great spiritual teachers always used simple language, or no one would have bothered to listen. If we can't describe what they said in the same way, we're getting it wrong. More to the point, if we don't try to live it like them, our words are just wasting space.

I've also got to admit I'm no great shakes at the "God-stuff," not any better than I can paint or do math. The grand experiences – visions, prophecies, salvation, speaking in tongues, enlightenment – pass me by. Having hands laid on me makes me embarrassed, as does public prayer, or dancing in circles. I love trees, but I can't hug them. Preaching turns me off. Meditation sends me to sleep. But believing in God has been a part of my life for nearly forty years, and here's where my thinking has got to. Not that thinking has much to do with religion – less than 10% maybe. It's perhaps as relevant as it is in cooking. It's the taste buds that matter. But I'm coming at it from that angle, trying to frame personal experience in a broader perspective. If you want to read exciting stories of how people found God, there are thousands of books to choose from. This one is not that. It's sketching out a starting line, not the finish, the bottom rungs of the ladder rather than the heights.

I jump around subjects a lot. I think if theology, even pop-theology of this kind, is to make sense today it has to relate to all other subjects in the way it used to. I find most Christian books frustrating because they mostly talk about Jesus, or doctrine, as if nothing has changed in 2,000 years. Some talk knowledgeably about how we can see God in the universe we know today, but then they don't relate this back to Jesus, or the doctrine. There's this 2,000-year gap which we have to bridge if we're going to make any sense of Christian belief.

If religious belief ignores knowledge, it's irrelevant. If it contradicts it, it's on the way to superstition. There's a point, though, beyond which knowledge doesn't take us, where we jump off and say, "I realize that this may not be true, but it works for me, and I believe it." I think that's what "faith" is. It's believing hopefully. We do this all the time, every day, in relationships, trusting people that they will build on what we've developed rather than beat us up or cook us for supper. It's what being human is about – having faith, risking love, making deeper connections. The trick of having faith that the world is one of love and meaning without switching off your brain seems to be a question of knowing for yourself where that point is. Being aware you're jumping off into the unknown, but that you're going to do it anyway. This is my attempt to sketch where the point is for me. It's different for everyone.

As for the "details", I don't know, for instance, whether the universe is 10 or 15 billion years old, whether Jesus thought of himself as a son of man or the Son of God, whether the Koran or the Bible is the more inspired book, whether dowsing works or not. What I am sure of is that the age of the universe is measured in billions rather than thousands of years, or the stars wouldn't yet have got around to forming. It's difficult to know exactly what Jesus meant by certain phrases, or whether he even said them, which is why there are so many Christian denominations. Well over a billion people believe with equal conviction that either the Koran or the Bible is uniquely inspired, and there's no way of getting an answer from God that both sides will accept. Dowsing may work, but drilling is more reliable. That's good enough for me. I want to know what the probabilities are, how they tie together, if they do.

I've tried to keep it short. I know it's far too long, but that's the problem with writing, editing and publishing the damn thing myself. There's no one to stop me waffling. Feel free to skip the boring bits. I think all the facts are broadly right, though I'm sure I've made a number of mistakes, and anyone who knows anything in any one area can argue over interpretations. There's nothing original here, no big new idea, nothing controversial, which is why I haven't bothered with footnotes. It's just chucking out the net to see what comes in, and making a few connections. I've tried to take a rough consensus of what the majority of the best-qualified people who specialize in a particular subject seem to think. And because our knowledge is always changing, and I'm changing, the perspective will change. On seeing the proofs of this book I want to rewrite it. But let's leave it with the idea that it's "work in progress." And that sums up for me what religion is about; there is always a tomorrow. And in the meantime the story of whether and how we relate to God is the biggest there is.

So let's stick to the big picture. And if there's anyone out there who comes across this and can draw me a better one, I look forward to hearing from you. This has taken too long, and I'm short of books to publish. Contact me on jthunt@freeuk.com. But please keep it rational.

PART 1

DEFINING GOD

1 How we got to where we are

"Even if you were the most sinful of all
sinners, you would cross over all evil
by the raft of knowledge alone."

BHAGAVAD-GITA

You may have a clearly defined view of God. Maybe you think it's the only right one. The Christian Church does. God may be almighty, omniscient, the ground of all being, but He also has a Son, a Church that interprets Him through a cartload of Capital Letter Doctrines, and a book called the Bible that He inspired various authors to write. This book details the history of His involvement with His favorite tribe in the Middle East, mainly from about 1500 BC to AD 50.

In the first two chapters I try and sum up the difficulty with the Church's view of God, with a couple of snapshots. The first is of the way the Hebrews saw the world. The Hebrews started as an insignificant group of nomadic sheepherders of the Middle Bronze Age, scratching a living on the margins of the great Persian and Egyptian civilizations. They adopted beliefs from the people around, adapted them, added some of their own, and developed their own world-view. Their thousand-year plus history, written in the light of their beliefs, came to form our Old Testament. The God that the Church describes originates with them.

The trouble is their world-view was nothing like the one we hold today. The Hebrews saw the earth as a flat table, about the size of Brazil, created a few thousand years ago. It is fixed "immoveable and firm" (Psalm 93:1). The underworld, where the dead went, is below the table. When they looked up to the sky they saw a thin sheet a few hundred yards up with the light of heaven shining through holes (stars). It could be reached by a ladder, or tower. It's a world where animals talk, chariots drive across the sky, iron floats, where God will stop the sun in the course of its circling the earth so the Hebrews can finish slaughtering their enemies (Joshua 10:13).

This view underlies the Old Testament, and the New. You can see it in the Book of Job, for instance, worth reading in its own right as one of the finest prose poems in world literature, written maybe in the seventh to third centuries BC (date very uncertain). It may be a variation on a Babylonian story that circulated in the previous millennium. God is a king up in the sky, holding court with his various sons (more about them later) and retainers. He asks one of them, Satan (not yet a separate force of evil), what he's been up to.

> *"Going to and fro in the earth, and walking up and down in it."*
> **(JOB 1:7)**

The two of them decide to run a bet on how far God's favorite servant on earth can be tormented and still remain faithful (Job incidentally is not a Hebrew at all but a foreigner from the land of Uz). God wins, sort of, and finishes the book boasting:

> *"Where wert thou when I laid the foundations of the earth? declare, if thou hast understanding. Who hath laid the measures thereof, if thou knowest? or who hath stretched the line upon it? Whereupon are the foundations thereof fastened? or who laid the cornerstone thereof; when the morning stars sang together, and all the sons of God shouted for joy?"*
> **(JOB 38:4-7)**

It's sublime language (at least it is in the Authorized, King James, Version. I gather it's great in the Hebrew as well). The Old Testament has many wonderful passages (as well as many that are not). If you want to curse or praise, top yourself or jump with joy, there's little to compare with the Psalms.

But as a world-view the Hebrew one was already past its sell-by date. If God had gone hiking like Satan He could have learnt some answers from the Greeks, a few hundred miles away. In Greece, a series of brilliant thinkers were starting to develop a different way of looking at life, measuring the world and experimenting on it. Today we call what they did "science."

The Greek philosopher Thales has been described as the world's first scientist. He put forward the idea in the early sixth century BC that the universe runs to fixed natural laws that could be worked out by observation and reason. He predicted an eclipse of the sun in 585 BC. His pupil Anaximander created the first "world map" in about 500 BC and speculated on the origins of the universe as a whirlpool in space. Aristarchus could have told the writer of Job in 275 BC that the earth didn't have cornerstones, that it wasn't even flat, but a sphere that circled the sun. Shortly afterwards Eratosthenes even "determined its measurements." He calculated its diameter to within 75 miles of the true figure (7,923 miles). Euclid's *Elements* remained the mathematician's Bible up till the twentieth century, when deep space conditions and added dimensions came into the frame.

Epicurus left us stunning letters reflecting on the nature and motion of atoms, the infinity of the universe, the nature of our senses, our soul, of language, of religion and society, and the happy life. And we could go on and on. In the sixth to second centuries BC the Greeks developed the first complete world literature, the most beautiful buildings ever, astonishing sculpture, the beginnings of democracy. Our philosophy, the process of understanding through reason, goes back to them. We've scarcely had an original thought since Plato (and he used to complain about the ignorance of the Greeks compared to the Egyptians).

The Greeks weren't perfect, and their legacy was not all positive. It could be argued that Plato's metaphysics missed essential truths that some older societies took for granted, and that science is rediscovering today. For instance, that body and spirit are not separate, that the genius of humankind lies in each person's creativity, that consciousness is more than rational thought, and that in looking at the world we change it. But in terms of understanding the physical world and describing it, they were in a different class to the Hebrews.

So does it matter to Christian belief today that in Job God has to ask the devil what is happening down there on earth? Should we drop the Hebrew God along with the Greek Zeus? Does knowledge affect belief? Many Christians (and most other believers, of all kinds) think not. Many Christians, for instance, don't take Job literally. Perhaps it's a parable rather than a real story, maybe a subversive one at that. It challenges the idea that God's blessing brings wealth, or even that He will be on your side if you are faithful to Him. It's not trying to say anything about how the world was made.

But we can't slide away from the question that neatly. The intent of the Book of Job may not have been to describe the world, and Christians may no longer think of God as a king living in the sky, but they still believe that the underlying thrust of the story is true. There is a God who thinks as we do. We are made for Him, and the universe exists because of this. God still intervenes on earth in the same kind of way. What the Church teaches today is still recognizably part of the same world-view.

How credible is it?

2 HOW BIG IS GOD?

"It is only in the microscope that our life looks so big.
It is an indivisible point, drawn out and magnified
by the powerful lenses of time and space."

SCHOPENHAUER

How did the Hebrew and Greek views of the world come down to us? Both peoples (the Hebrews now called Jews) were absorbed into the Roman Empire. The Romans were more interested in getting from A to B than in where Z was. Christianity, an offshoot of Judaism, began to spread through the Empire in the first century AD. By the second century leading Christians, known today as the Church Fathers, were investing vast amounts of time and energy in constructing a belief system which reconciled Greek and Jewish thought. Just before the Empire began to fall apart in the fifth century AD, it adopted Christianity as its official religion. Europe then entered a period described as the "Dark Ages." The light of civilization in this part of the world – of knowledge, tolerance, concern for the common good, was restored in the various dynasties of the Golden Age of Islam of the ninth to twelfth centuries (the Ummayad in Spain, the Fatimids in Egypt, the Abbasids in Mesopotamia). By pillaging some of these more advanced societies (in a series of invasions known as the Crusades), the Christian barbarians of the north began to recover Greek knowledge in the Middle Ages. This led to a further synthesis of Greek and Christian thinking, particularly as expressed in the philosophy of Aquinas in the thirteenth century. Since then the Bible and the Greek classics have been at the very foundation of our English culture, perhaps reaching their peak in the poetry of Milton and the plays of Shakespeare.

This is a very simplistic picture. The Muslim dynasties weren't peace-loving democracies, the northern barbarians were great cathedral builders. But most historians would agree with the broad outline. The Renaissance followed the Middle Ages in the fifteenth century. The Enlightenment came in the eighteenth century when Europeans started to think and experiment outside the world-view they had inherited from the Hebrews. Two millennia after the Greeks speculated on the earth as a round ball whizzing through space Christian Europe began to catch up. Today we may still pray like Hebrews, but we think like Greeks. Our view of the world is no longer that of the Hebrews. It has changed out of all recognition. Does how we see it today make a difference to belief?

Let's look at just one aspect of the universe, its size. The Hebrews believed in a God who was not only in our image (or the other way round), but was "personal" to them. That wasn't difficult when a horse and rider could cross all the land in the known universe in a few weeks, when heaven could be seen with the naked eye, and God could physically shout down from it and be heard. The heavens cuddled the earth like a warm blanket. It's not difficult to have a close relationship with a God like that. It's hard to avoid Him.

Today we see the world differently. The heavens are not cuddly. They're remote, dark, empty, fierce, beyond our imagining. Above all, they're vast. They're so vast that the idea they were created so we could cosy up to God leaves a wry smile. How vast? Imagine our sun on the table in front of you, or on the page of this book, as a spot so small you can't see it without a magnifying glass. It's much smaller than the full stop at the end of this sentence. The earth orbits this sun, but you would need a microscope to see that. The area covered by the earth circling the sun is the size of a pin-head. Now pick up this pinhead and throw it outside your window into the garden. Could you find it again?

The God described in the first book of the Bible, Genesis, had trouble finding Adam and Eve in the Garden of Eden, let alone a pinhead. If a beetle treads on it, it's gone. Why should what happens on this pinhead be the point of the whole universe we know today? Of course it might be. That's always a theoretical possibility, however remote. Maybe it takes 15 billion years and a universe this size for complex life forms to emerge, and we're the pinnacle of creation. But how could we know? To begin to be confident that that was a reasonable assumption, we would need to know what was going on everywhere else. And we're never likely to know that, as the nearest galaxy is moving away from us at a billion miles an hour.

So did the God of this universe really have an only Son who He sent on a once-only mission to this single planet? This made sense when this planet was a couple of thousand miles across and was all there was, when gods had sons, when they and their messengers commuted from heaven to earth. But would we give it a moment's consideration if it were put forward as a new idea today?

Actually the true scale of the comparison needs to be of a different order. Imagine the garden stretching for miles – tens, hundreds, thousands of miles in every direction. To measure the invisible sun and its orbiting earth against the size of our galaxy you would have to drop the pinhead into an area the size of the Atlantic Ocean.

And it gets worse. At the beginning of the twentieth century astronomers thought our galaxy *was* the universe. The latest, most accurate measurements came in the 1990s via the Hubble space telescope. Astronomers pointed it at one pinhead-sized area over a period of 150 orbits, collecting one picture a day, and then superimposed them. The result was a photograph called the Hubble Deep Field, an eyehole into deep space through which they could see 2,000 galaxies. Extrapolating this figure for the rest of the sky gave a figure of 40 billion galaxies. In 1998 this estimate was increased to 100 billion, each with 100 billion stars. The latest estimate is that there are several hundred billion galaxies. You would have to reduce the Atlantic to the size of another pinhead, and drop it back in there again to get an idea of the size of the universe. And keep on doing that. There are a million stars with their circling planets for every grain of sand on earth.

We also haven't stopped to consider that the universe is not conveniently frozen while you hunt for this speck of a planet. It's a seething mass, changing at speeds we can't comprehend. Individual jets of light hundreds of light-years long shoot at nearly the speed of light from black holes with a mass equivalent to billions of our suns. And human beings have only existed on this microscopically small speck for the relative blink of an eyelid. If this pinhead in the 5,000-mile-wide Atlantic, itself a pinhead in another Atlantic, and another, were to disappear tomorrow, smashed by an asteroid, would the point of the whole universe be over? Isn't it like an ant telling us the world was created for its benefit?

If you think that's enough, there's more. Recent developments suggest that the picture may be vastly bigger still. The consensus of scientific thought is moving toward the inflation theory, which holds that our universe is just one of many sprouting from black holes. The "multiverse" could be bigger than our universe by millions of powers of ten. And it may not exist in just four dimensions (one of time and three of space) but many. If our sun, our solar system, our whole galaxy of 100 billion stars disappeared tomorrow the universe wouldn't notice. If our universe disappeared tomorrow the multiverse wouldn't notice. And the multiverse itself could be one of an infinite number. There may be no limit to the universe. Can we really believe it all exists for our benefit? Because God wanted our company? The scale of the physical world that we can see around us is so unimaginably huge that it seems a kind of madness to assume we have any significance in it.

It's hard to hold this knowledge in your head and believe that the God behind all this is adequately described in the Bible, or by the Church, or by any single religion. It's ironic that having passed on to Christian Europe the learning of the Greeks that then kick-started us into the modern age, many Muslims today have regressed to beliefs more characteristic of the Dark Ages. Amongst various medieval *fatwas* (something like papal encyclicals), for instance, that have come out of the Muslim world in recent times was one in 1993 from the supreme religious authority of Saudi Arabia, Shikh Abdel-Aziz Ibn Baaz. It says that anyone who believes the earth is round is an atheist and should be punished. In many parts of the Muslim world a conviction for atheism carries the death penalty. In August 2001 a Dr Shaikh in Pakistan was condemned to death for saying in a university class that neither Mohammed nor his parents could logically have been Muslims before Islam was revealed to him. Today these kinds of statements and actions seem shocking in their ignorance and cruelty, as they would have done to many educated Muslims of the tenth to thirteenth centuries, and still do to many today. Before the Enlightenment the Christian Church thought and acted in much the same kind of way.

But perhaps the Church hasn't really changed that much?

There aren't many Christians who still think the Hebrews got it all right. We don't believe, for instance, in the world as flat, apart from a few thousand members of the Flat Earth Society. We know it's round, we can take a plane and in a couple of days end up where we started, with jet lag. We can't yet travel in time in the same way, though, and most Christians have as limited a view of time as in the past they had of space. After all, though the Bible doesn't provide measurements for the universe, it does provide a chronology for all the main events since creation. So most Christians, if you count them worldwide, still believe the world was created about 6,000 years ago. According to a Gallup poll last year two-thirds of Americans believe in "creationism" rather than evolution. Only a staggeringly low 9% believe that "man has developed over millions of years from less advanced forms of life." But then about half believe the sun circles the earth rather than vice versa (compared to a third in the UK or China), so perhaps the proportion is not that surprising.

But the view that the universe (or the earth, or man) is a few thousand years old is just as ludicrous in terms of our current knowledge as the idea that it is a few thousand miles wide. It turns everything we know in biology, geology, physics, anthropology, history, virtually any subject you can think of, into an illusion. It says the ink on this page was created instants ago, relatively, rather than being made out of fossil fuels (coal) that were laid down 200 million years back. On this reading God becomes a cosmic Joker who created the world to look old, to deceive us.

A minority of Christians (who in the UK are in a majority) find these beliefs frustrating. It reduces the credibility of Christianity to the level of that of the Flat Earth Society. That life really has evolved over millions and billions of years is beyond all reasonable doubt. All the problems that creationists put forward, like what's the use of half a wing or half an eye, have been answered many times over. There isn't a reputable biologist in the world who would dispute the time frame or the broad processes involved. The questions are on the mechanics, like whether it's "gradual" or "punctuated."

But then the minority of Christians who recognize this still broadly accept the beliefs arising from the world-view of two and three millennia ago. They have moved on, but not very far. They may not think of God as living in the sky any more but He still sends representatives to earth. He still took on human flesh in the form of a baby 2,000 years ago, lived and died, came back to life, went down into the underworld, up to the surface, and then rose up to heaven through the sky.

Some will pick and choose here. For instance, maybe Jesus didn't go down into the underworld, and didn't rise up through the sky. But most would say you do have to believe that Jesus physically rose from the dead. His body got up and walked away. That part of the journey is literal even if the other parts are not. We come back to that subject in part 5.

The line from seeing the earth as an over-sized beer-mat to the way we see the universe today is a long one. There are many positions of Christian belief along the way, each of which involves some re-interpretation of older teaching. What may have been originally intended as fact gets re-interpreted as "metaphor" or "spiritual truth." The more you accommodate knowledge the more of these "facts" you tend to jettison. Ideally we might say, "OK, let's throw away the assumptions of belief, the world-view it arises from, start with what we know, and see where we get to." The Church tends to work the other way. It says, "This is what we believe, let's see where we can fit knowledge in." And it does that exceedingly slowly.

The Roman Catholic Church took 400 years to admit in 1992, after a commission managed to spend ten years looking at the question, that it might have "misunderstood" Galileo (who looked through his new telescope and found that the earth wasn't the center of the universe). After bitterly opposing the new insights of astronomy, the Church fought in turn against geology and biology in the nineteenth century, psychology in the twentieth century, and most of all against a better understanding of its own Bible. Other subjects that don't seem to immediately impinge on its own teaching, like anthropology or physics, it ignores. It is not so much generations out of date as centuries, or even millennia. Today our knowledge is increasing at an exponential rate. But the Church as a whole isn't even prepared to consider that all beliefs have to be seen in the context of the knowledge of the time, and that to continue believing in them when our knowledge has changed is not to respect them, but to make caricatures of them. The map of possible belief the Church draws for us is no better than the maps Galileo had at school.

This is all very over-simplistic, we're just tracing out the territory.

The rational and religious are not always in opposition, you can argue that it was the Christian emphasis on an understandable God that allowed science to flourish in Europe. Way back in the sixteenth century the great Protestant reformer, John Calvin, accepted that the Old Testament reflected ideas about the world that were no longer possible to believe. The idea of God as an infinite, omniscient, only necessary reality is more Greek than Hebrew. And Greeks didn't walk around all day talking philosophy. Plato believed in demons as much as anyone. And at a deeper level, the Book of Job and the searching of the Greek philosophers came from the same kind of enquiring mind that around that time began to rethink our relationship with the world. The one explored suffering and purpose, the other matter and physics. But our idea of God today is a mix of the two Gods, the metaphysical almighty God of "thought" or "being" beyond space and time, and the friendly wonder-working local God who intervenes on earth and will help us with our exams tomorrow. He is also the Persian God of Zoroaster who is coming again in judgement and will send the wicked to hell. His image has been formed over three millennia, with each generation adding something and interpreting Him in their own way.

It's hard to believe in the literal description of God that the writer of Job gave 2,700 years ago, and not much easier to believe in the one the Gospel writers gave 2,000 years ago. Since then mainstream Christian thinking, as understood by most believers, has scarcely progressed. Science and religion have gone their separate ways. But maybe if we could think 400 years forwards, rather than 400 years backwards as the Church does, we could find a way of believing in God again that made more sense?

3 WHO IS YOUR GOD?

"I don't know that atheists should be considered citizens, nor should they be considered patriots. This is one nation under God."

GEORGE BUSH

Over the last couple of millennia the Church has often set the culture/knowledge agenda, sometimes followed it. But over the last century or two our knowledge has simply developed too fast for it to keep pace. Most Christian believers in the UK find it difficult to accept how marginal their beliefs have become, and the reasons behind this. It's not because of secularism, or consumerism, or any other "ism." It won't be reversed by brighter presentation, more dynamic leadership, better management, or returning to a more biblical line. Indeed that last point only highlights the problem. Taking the Bible or Church teaching literally provides the certainty that we're all tempted to reach for, but it also distances the group from the larger number of people who can't believe in it.

But in one key respect nothing has changed since the unknown writer of Job looked up at the heavens. When we think about the scale of the universe as described above we feel a little of what he or she felt; thrilled, humbled, scared. Many of us feel the universe is so astonishing that it just didn't happen by chance. We may go further. If there's a meaning behind all this, then we want to be a part of it, experience it. After all, however insignificant we are, we're here. We are the only starting point we have. But we need a different way of describing "God." We can't believe that God really lives just up there in the sky, or indeed anywhere. He didn't really speak in thunder in John 12:27-29, or from a cloud in Matthew 17:5, or in any kind of weather. He didn't open a trapdoor in heaven to speak and flutter down in the form of a dove, in Matthew 3:16-17, or take any shape on earth. And what the head cannot believe the heart cannot worship.

So around 75% of the population in the UK say they believe in God, but attendance is less than 10%. Regular attendance is around 5%. On a typical Sunday, worshipers in the national Anglican Church are under 2%. The figures depend on whether you ask people in the street or count them in the pews. About twice as many say they go as actually do. It's as if they would like to, but only maybe get around to it at Christmas and christenings, weddings and funerals.

This loss of a common religious language and practice hasn't happened suddenly. Church attendance as a percentage of the population in the UK started dropping a couple of centuries ago. There have been ups and downs in the graph, and there are always pockets of enthusiasm, but overall the decline has been fairly constant, speeding up a little in the last few decades. It dropped from 5.4 million in 1979 to 4.7 million in 1989 and 3.7 million in 1998, a rate of decline of roughly 100,000 a year.

In the next generation or two numbers will probably level off at around a million. The gap then between the Church and society at large will be much greater than now. People over the age of 50 today were brought up in a time when half of all children went to Sunday School, even if their parents didn't go to church. Now that's around 3% and falling. The next generation won't have the assumption that there is anything to hold on to in Christianity, even nominally.

It's the same in most of Western Europe. In North America it's the other way round. The average family goes to church (40% of the total population). Which is surprising. In the 1750s America had a smaller proportion of the population going to church than any nation in Christendom, about 7%. But attendance rose throughout the nineteenth century. The new flood of immigrants held on to beliefs that their contemporaries back home were abandoning. They were then strengthened by the strongest revivalist movements of modern times. For them "America" and

"Christianity" came to be identified as pretty much the same thing. Today around 96% say they believe in God, and 90% believe in heaven. This proportion is only found in similarly violent societies (the USA has 5% of the world's population but 25% of its prisoners) where faith and fundamentalism are strong, societies like Iran, Northern Ireland and South Africa.

The USA may be the "greatest" country on earth, but it's different. Having largely exterminated the previous inhabitants, they've started off with a relatively clean sheet. The blending of incoming traditions and cultures gave it vigor. Americans invent religions like they start businesses. If your church isn't anticipating the coming of the Lord eagerly enough then start your own: Mormonism, Christian Science, Christadelphians, Seventh Day Adventists, Jehovah's Witnesses, to mention a few.

Now the country is large, powerful and can afford to be insular in a way unimaginable a couple of centuries ago when it defined itself in relation to Europe. The East and West coasts are a little different, more open to other traditions. But as a whole Americans can find it difficult to envisage other ways of looking at the world. Indeed you can argue it's a country in slow decline (if I'm going to upset my best customers I may as well do this properly). The Founding Fathers consciously attempted to build a more rational, open society than the God-authorized monarchies they came from. Back in the 1750s the USA had one of the lowest rates of poverty and illiteracy in the developed world (excluding slaves and women). Today it has one of the highest. The mass media encourage a shallow engagement with the wider issues. Compare the letters written home by soldiers in the Civil War and those from Vietnam and you can see the difference in quality.

Christian fundamentalism took off in the States in the early twentieth century as a reaction against modern thought, and grows in strength every year. Europe is less prone to religious fundamentalism of this kind, though we've had more than our share of its political counterpart. We've had millennia of overlapping and conflicting cultures, several centuries of increasing contact with other religions and beliefs and a century of reducing influence. Our reliance on the God of seventeenth to nineteenth-century Christianity has decreased as that of North America has increased.

But in the UK today, when people say they believe in God, what do they mean? Imagine a line across this page, representing the population. On the left hand are 2% or so conservative Christians, half Protestants, half Catholics. For them it's simple. The Bible (or the Church) tells us who God is and how we should live. Everything it says is basically right and true. Maybe even Job was a real person. God spoke from heaven then, even if he doesn't now.

Maybe the conservatives are right, even if they're only 2%. There's no correlation between numbers and truth. Their strength is that they know where they stand. In practice though they don't take the whole Bible literally, they select. No one on earth today tries to follow all the 600 and more commandments in the Old Testament. Many are also fuzzy on whether particular events and stories really happened in the way they are said to happen. But this is the first step on the slippery slope. Maybe God doesn't live up there in the sky any more, but then why did Jesus ascend from the earth like a space rocket? If he didn't really do that, why believe he physically rose from the dead? If hell is not a burning lake of fire, why should heaven be a real place? If the devil is not a real, personal entity, why should God be? Once you start to qualify it's hard to know where to stop.

Moving along the line, we come to the liberal Christians, roughly another 2%, who are more able to live with ambiguity. Jesus didn't really ascend to heaven, and maybe he didn't rise from the dead either. He is a representation of the divine rather than God in human flesh. The resurrection is spiritual rather than literal. In committing ourselves to a life of service and worship we realize the best that we are capable of and triumph in spirit over materialism and meaninglessness.

The liberal experience of God is expressed more in terms of metaphors than creeds. But it's difficult to distill this into a simple "message." Does it account for the impact of Jesus on the people around him? Is the Christian imagery that much better than any other? At the extreme liberal end they will say there is indeed nothing "special" as such about Christianity. All religions provide different models that symbolize our relationship with what is ultimately real. But isn't it then difficult to remain in a Church that claims so much more?

There are also at this end of the line a small percentage of members of other religions, mostly Muslims and Hindus. I'm passing over them quickly but Muslims are the most vigorous practicing faith community in the UK, slightly ahead of the Catholics, if you measure by numbers of visits to a place of worship. Jumping to the other end of the line, we come, on the right, to many who are agnostic, perhaps humanist. Some are ex-believers, some indifferent, shading off into the last few per cent who are atheist. God simply isn't "there," we just like to think He is. How can we possibly describe ultimate reality when we are using language of our own invention? We come back to them later. But most people are in the large middle, neither convinced Christians nor atheists.

The majority of those in the middle may be described as nominal Christians. On statistical forms they're probably classified as Anglican, that convenient halfway house for the uncertain. Maybe, reader, this is where you are. Maybe you feel a sense of inadequacy at this, but then maybe doubt is a good thing. Faith, privately held, difficult to talk about, isn't the only uncertainty in life. "Love," for example, is another. It's not less real or important because it's hard to define. But at least with love there's a common language between two individuals. Faith is a relationship with the unknown, by definition. That's why there are many novels of love, very few of faith. Maybe it's a sensible position. After all, the word "religion" in

Latin, *religio*, has two meanings. One means "relationship," in the sense of "belonging," the other means "sacred." It's more an attitude of mind than a set of beliefs. Most people in the world still understand religion in this way. Maybe we can rewrite Christianity around these two words, and make it relevant for us again.

4 THE NEW GODS

"Truth's open to everyone, and the
claims aren't all staked yet."

SENECA

It's hard to evaluate individual belief, and so hard to come by reliable statistics. But the views in the previous chapter are probably held by about half the population. Conservatives and liberals argue amongst themselves about which approach is best. Conservatives accuse liberals of being wishy-washy and ineffectual; liberals accuse conservatives of leaving their brains behind. Both see the other as ringing the death-knell for the Church. The huge majority, the "nominal," can't see what the fuss is about.

Conservatives and liberals are equally sincere, equally bright. They both see themselves in the mainstream of traditional Christian thinking, because both streams have always been present. Conservatives point to the body of teaching authorized by successive popes, or the words of scripture itself, both reflecting the will of God. Liberals point to the diversity of teaching which the authoritarian Church squashed. Or to the interpretation of scripture by the Church Fathers, who see it as more allegorical than literal. Indeed this reflects a broader split between those who follow the "prophetic" tradition of rooting truth in historical events, and the "mystic" tradition of seeing truth as timeless. The former is stronger in the monotheistic religions, the latter in the theistic Eastern religions. Perhaps a lot of the difference simply comes down to how we think. Conservatives are attracted to hard definitions, verbal creeds, logic, hymns and choruses, mountains. Liberals prefer consensus, mystics, common sense, Palestrina, the sea.

Likewise the views of the "nominal" are no less sincere for being undefined and perhaps inarticulate. Perhaps they simply lack the qualities of conservative doggedness or liberal imagination to cope with the God the Church describes.

The archbishop of Canterbury needs to be a man (strangely this is still the case) of extraordinary qualities. He needs to match the conviction of the fundamentalists, the intelligence of the scholars, the subtlety of the politicians, the historical sense of the tradition-alists, and above all be a huge optimist. As many people suffer from schizophrenia as go to an Anglican Church on Sundays. It's unusu-al in our competitive market economy to find a "national brand leader," even a state-supported one, with such a low percentage of the market. But then a modern management MBA type might turn the problem around. After all, the percentage of people who answer "yes" to the question: "Have you ever been aware of or influenced by a power, whether you call it God or not, which is different from your everyday self?" actually increased from 34% in 1950 to 48% in 1987. Perhaps people leave the Church to find better ways of believing, not because they've lost belief. Perhaps we simply overestimate the degree to which there is a readily-accessible, clearly-defined ultimate truth out there and underestimate the role played in our conviction by culture, upbringing and personal temperament. Perhaps we're in more agreement than we think.

Just as sincere as the committed or nominal Christians are the many in the middle who are actively interested in spiritual growth but who positively reject the Church. In the '70s and '80s they were broadly described as the "New Age" movement. Now it's more often referred to as "Mind/Body/Spirit," or "Personal Development," or some such name. Some of them would say they believe in God, others not. Many believe in "God within," the "divine self," or spirit beings of some kind. This area of belief grows as fast as Church attendance declines. You can see it reflect-ed in book sales. Popular spiritual books are increasingly written from an Eastern rather than Western perspective. Chinese oracle books, roshis from Japan, lamas from Tibet, gurus from India, "channeled" writings, these outsell Christian writers. Overall the ratio of sales in the UK between "New Age" and Christian is now four or five to one. Today more people in the UK (11%) use practitioners in the mainstream New Age areas (homeopathy, acupuncture, herbal medicine, etc.), than go to church. There are more of these practitioners than there are GPs (general practitioners of orthodox medicine). Herbal preparations are used by 22%. If you think of formal Christianity as the elitist theater, New Age is increasingly the popular religious culture.

The "New Age" is not really new. There have always been threads of it throughout English history. A fierce Bible believer like the great scientist Isaac Newton spent far more time on alchemy than physics. The common ground between New Age and Christianity is much greater than either side tends to think. Many New Age practices have developed from a blending of cultures that include Christian roots. For instance one of the popular ones at the moment is Reiki, applying *ch'i* (the universal life force) to heal the body. This is based on the work of Mikao Usui, a Japanese Christian minister who, in the 1880s, became interested in the accounts of healing in the Gospels and in reconciling them with traditional Eastern medicine.

There are few New Age beliefs that have not at times been believed in some form or other by Christians down the ages, particularly in the first few centuries after Jesus. You could argue that Jesus himself and his disciples would have felt more at home in a modern New Age community than in today's Church. Their lifestyle had more in common with that of travelers today than with Christians in suburban churches (Acts 4:32-37). The New Testament is chock-a-block with practices many would now think of as "anti-Christian" if they were given the names used today: clairvoyance (John 4:18; Acts 5:1-11), etheric projection (John 1:48; 20:19, 26), receiving messages in dreams (Matthew 1:20), healing by touch (Matthew 8:3 and many others), by saliva (John

9:6; Mark 8:23), and at a distance (Matthew 8:13), astrological-type signs in the heavens (Mark 13:24-26), apparitions (Matthew 17:3), astral planes (Acts 2:31). The first disciples practiced divination (Acts 1:26). The Old Testament is richer still, full of practices that are now called shamanism, witchcraft, astrology, etc., sometimes condemned, at others not.

We can broaden this perspective further. "New Age" is a portmanteau term for pre-scientific beliefs from a variety of cultures around the world (often the more exotic the better). It's a misnomer. "Old Age" would be more accurate. The practices and beliefs found in the Bible, also developed before the age of science, are common to societies all over the old and new worlds. What are the ascension of Jesus and his walking on water other than masterful examples of levitation, high-ranking miracles in the Buddhist grades of achievement, and (so it's claimed) still practiced today? In this sense the Bible is the most significant "New Age" document we have.

If the Church had been more flexible, more open to differing interpretations of its own early traditions and texts, maybe it wouldn't have lost so much ground. New Age teaching and practice is more prepared to adjust, and meet people where they are. It focuses on "well-being" – health and healing, food and diet, sex and love, gender relationships. The clearest difference is that Christians can go to church for free (and it still struggles with low attendance), whereas New Age sessions cost you. People don't want to be saved today. They don't understand what it means. They want to be happy and healthy. And they'll pay for it.

So is this the religion of the future?

Here's a little example of the growth of New Age belief and decline in Christian thinking. About 12 million adults in the UK read their horoscopes regularly. The number roughly matches the number of adults who have stopped going to church in the last century. I'm not suggesting that everyone who stops going to church starts believing in astrology. Many only read their horoscopes out of mild interest in the same way that many go to church for reasons more social than spiritual. But a significant number live by them. Yet there is not a shred of evidence that the movements of the planets have any relation to events on earth – any astronomer would say it's laughable – and Chinese, Indian and Western astrologers use contradictory systems.

The idea of producing a daily horoscope was an invention of a journalist on the *Daily Express* in the 1930s. It struck a chord, and within a couple of years most newspapers around the world had one. Today there are far more professional astrologers than professional astronomers, by some estimates around 40 to 1. This is despite the fact that if you offer a free horoscope, and the same horoscope is sent to everyone who asks for it, over 90% will say on being questioned that it was relevant to them.

So why have people dropped one belief that they feel lacks credibility and personal relevance for one that has no credibility or particular relevance at all?

Reading your horoscope connects you with a feeling that there is a larger plan to life, that it's not just down to you. It advises you; it warms you. It speaks to you on your own level, when you want it. The Church used to provide this kind of assurance in the days when you could believe in the helping hands of innumerable saints, or that any Bible verse could be relevant to what you were doing at the time. But today very few people, maybe one out of a hundred, really believe in the active power of saints or read the Bible daily. Priests are few (the ratio of clergy to people in the UK is about 1 to 5,000) and remote, often preoccupied with repairing old buildings, church politics and ritual. Not many people, relatively, speak to them honestly and directly, or feel they could ask them for guidance. Authority in the Church is from the top down, and irrelevant to pretty well everyone as the base of the pyramid has disappeared. Even if we could recover a more meaningful

Christian language, there is not the right medium to express it in. You would need to turn the structure upside-down.

Much of New Age teaching draws on traditions that have been known to work for millennia, probably for millions of years; for instance, the healing powers of particular plants, or the therapeutic benefits of grooming and massaging. It's recovering the wisdom of older societies that we have lost. Equally there's a lot that's plain daft. If you go to a New Age product fair it's like stepping back into the Middle Ages. Crystals in place of relics, magical potions and lotions, charms and chants, fortune-telling. Perhaps the average level of superstition doesn't change from one millennium to the next. The most popular New Age teachings tend as usual to be the simplistic formulas for self-improvement. Follow these paths, or rituals, or horoscopes, tap into this force or that, find your inner self, or earlier self, or previous self, or other self, and you will realize your true potential. Change your way of thinking, your partner, your company, your color, the position of your furniture, what you eat, how you eat, when you eat, how you pray, who you pray to, and your life will be better.

New Age ideas seem to run seamlessly from the possible, through the improbable, to the impossible. Maybe our consciousness adds up to more than chimps with extra brain cells, but it's hard to believe that it was passed down to us from higher evolved beings from Atlantis, or space, or angels, or whatever. You have to stop somewhere. Christianity has at least spent much of two millennia wrestling with science and philosophy, attempting to reconcile Greek and Hebrew traditions, knowledge and belief. New Age ignores them. You can believe anything you want. But astroshamanic space maps are no more credible than God as a king in the sky sending messengers to earth. We need to do better than this, develop some kind of sensible framework of belief, or there's not enough reason for the lazier of us to get out of bed in the morning. So where do you draw the line?

The "New" Age has arisen out of the failure of the "old" Church to continue providing a sense of belonging to others and a sense of the sacredness of life. Like Hinduism seven millennia or so ago, it has emerged without a founder or a defining vision. Future historians of religion will look back and see the failure of the Church to accommodate the doubts of the nominal believers and the enthusiasm of the seekers as a mistake.

In summary, picture religious belief in the UK in the shape of a bell filling the page. You have the few committed believers on the left rim, atheists on the right, the bulk of the uncertain in the central body. These are mostly split between nominal Christians and seekers. The bell's center of gravity is moving across the page, left to right, at a rate of about 1% a year. But it doesn't seem set to carry on to the far end. Atheists and humanists, just as much as Christians, struggle with declining membership in their organizations. When people drop out of believing in Christianity they don't, as a general rule, drop out of belief.

This tour has been very sketchy, it's just trying to convey the range of possible approaches, which all overlap at the edges. In today's democratic society we start with the principle that everyone has a right to be heard. This after all was true of the first Christians. You couldn't remotely call the early Church a democracy, but every century or so, once they were in power, the bishops voted in councils on what they should believe. Bishops don't do this so much any more, the "point" of truth was fixed over a thousand years ago. Perhaps they should start doing it again. Because in the last generation or two we've drifted so far away from this point on the line that most don't even know it's there.

It's not as if the point hadn't moved before. After all, our own Christian tradition tells us that the truth about God is not static, but developing. In the second millennium BC Abraham's God was one for the family. Over the next few centuries the Hebrews enlarged Him to become their tribal God, then the God of the new nation. Over the following centuries He became the only God. The Christians enlarged Him further. He became not only the God of the Jews, but of all people. In about one and a half millennia God "grew" from a small spot in the Middle East to cover the earth. Then nothing changed much for another two millennia. In the face of new knowledge about the earth and the universe our image of God has shrunk and withered. Perhaps it's time for a fresh look.

A definition of God that excludes what most people today think about Him is too small. In the rest of this first section we look at a few directions in which we could enlarge our idea of who God might be, of what His concerns are.

5 OTHER GODS

"And if we reach, or when we reach, heaven's scenes,
we truly will find it guarded by United States marines. "
RONALD REAGAN

Belief doesn't disappear. It mutates. There's certainly more willing-
ness to believe than is suggested by the numbers who go to
church. But if we're to look at the question of God seriously we
need to range further afield still. Qualities like faith, insight, intelligence and sincerity are universal. There's no law that says we on
our particular spot in this particular time have got it right. We
know now that the great human achievements, advances in
knowledge, civilized societies, have been scattered all over the
world in place and time. Individuals who become Christians from
a no-faith background assume they've arrived at the only oasis in
the desert. But they're joining the huge majority of humankind
who have religious beliefs. We're a global village now. Our aliens
are from other planets, not other countries. Truth is not tribal.

To return to mainstream religion again, imagine the whole picture of human belief as, say, a house slowly being built over
millennia. The ancient pluralist world of spirits is at the bottom.
The time-line takes you up through the revealed religions, up
through to the monotheistic religions. Islam, the most recent
major religion, is in the attic. Christianity occupies a bedroom on
the first floor. But it's not a well-furnished room, it's stacked full of
cupboards and boxes. You would think that with one founder, one
Bible, one creed, one God, there would be one Church. Christians
would believe the same thing, worship together and live in harmony. Think again. An estimate that frequently appears is that there
are around 30,000 Christian denominations today, depending on
how you define them. Most tend to assume that its sinfulness or
ignorance that makes other people blind to their particular version

of the truth. But it's hard to escape the conclusion that Jesus did not set out a clear statement of belief. After a year (or three, depending which Gospel you follow) of being with him night and day, his own disciples had little idea of what he was about. Their incomprehension is a constant theme in the Gospels. The crucifixion and resurrection took them by surprise. Perhaps religions aren't as clear-cut as we like to make them.

Indeed it's only with hindsight that you can tell when a religion has become what it is. All religions begin as cults, or sects. A cult is still dependent on the charisma of its founder; a sect has taken on a life of its own. If it survives a century or two and gains enough numbers and traditions to be recognizably different it turns into a "religion," like a new species. This difference has been defined as around a million members. It took several centuries after the death of its founder for Christians to number a million; about a millennium to number ten million.

There are over 150 world religions today with one million or more followers. Often it's hard to tell where and when the old faith stops and the new one begins. Is the Church of Jesus Christ of Latter Day Saints (Mormonism) still a Christian cult or shaping up to be the fourth major monotheistic religious tradition? Hard to say. You might assume it's never going to amount to more than a cult, but then that's what the rabbis were saying about the "Nazarenes" in the first century AD.

To return to the analogy of the bedroom, as you explore the different cupboards you'll find many strands of Christianity, – strands developing under the influence of other cultures, for example, animism in Africa, or Buddhism in the Far East – that are moving in the direction of a different religion. To take one at random, the Church of Simon Kimbanya (who died in 1957) in Central Africa with a membership of four million has a better attendance most Sundays than all our UK churches put together. At times these strands definitely turn into something else, like

Voodoo in Haiti. Or there's the TV version of Christianity in the USA: a feel-good gospel of prosperity where God's blessing brings wealth. This may be in line with much of the Old Testament but seems about as far from the Sermon on the Mount as it's possible to get.

In some of Christianity's little boxes and cupboards there's an inverse relationship between numbers and exclusiveness. Often the more extreme the belief, and the fewer the numbers who believe it, the more fervently it is held. Tiny groups of Christians in remote corners and islands believe they alone, of all the people in the world who have ever lived, are the only ones to have got it right. Even in the larger mainstream churches most Christians suspect that most other Christians aren't really Christian. Some Protestant bookshops won't stock Catholic books; Catholics won't recognize the ministry of other priests. In the past these different groups have tortured and killed each other in the belief that God wanted them to. From the way some of them talk and write you get the impression they would still like to. In Northern Ireland some still do. The most compelling argument against taking Christianity seriously is simply to look at the societies that still do. For them perpetual conflict is better than peace if that means compromising the unique truth of their faith by going to school with the opposition. Listen to the recordings of sermons preached in Northern Ireland today against the Anti-Christ in the Vatican and you step back into the world of 400 years ago, into the wars between Catholics and Protestants that tore Europe apart for generations and left over a million dead. Christianity, with its propensity to define belief narrowly in creeds, is particularly prone to this sectarianism. Hinduism is equally diverse but historically more tolerant in that it accommodates belief in many gods. Instead, it internalizes division into the world's worst caste system.

Talking of Hinduism, we notice other rooms on the first floor of the house. In the past we all tended to assume that our religion had to be the only right one. I'm not sure what the word for this is – not quite racist, perhaps "religist," "religiously challenged." So 200, 100, even 50 years ago, people of different color and other faiths were, let's face it, not quite as bright as we were. Their religions were primitive and weird. But with global tourism and modern communications, our contact with these other religions has increased enormously. The Chinese invasion of Tibet in 1951 scattered Buddhist teachers in much the same way as the Roman destruction of Jerusalem in AD 70 scattered Jews and Christians.

Now the picture is very different. For example, we see Hinduism as the most successful religion in the world, in terms of being followed by the largest proportion of the world's population for the longest time. In its unity of matter and mind it seems to have taken for granted a level of truth that we are only just re-awakening to. Many are attracted to Buddhism as the most peace-loving and contemplative of all religions, apparently the most "advanced." If you're looking for an intelligently con-ceived monotheistic religion that makes few demands on credulity and focuses on good practice in this life, then Sikkhism is a good bet. Taoism at times seems closer to the teaching of Jesus than does Christianity itself; a good Taoist has few needs or wants and doesn't exercise power over others. Islam generates a level of sustained prayer and devotion across the whole commu-nity that puts Christianity in the shade. Confucianism demonstrates a stronger commitment to the family, the wider social unit and the principle of good government than Christianity has ever been able to get its head round. Shintoism is the most ancient and simple of all major religions practiced today, and perhaps the most beautiful.

These religions and many others have enormously rich, varied and complex traditions, literatures and rituals. This is not to say that that the grass is any greener on the other side of the hill, but their resources of spiritual and social capital are no less than those of Christianity. The level of personal commitment is unquestioned. Often their teaching can seem more intense and integrated than our own. Indeed the word for "religion" only exists in Western languages. In other cultures religion is more integrated into all aspects of life. There is not the same split between the spiritual and material, body and soul, sacred and secular.

Most of these religions are on the first floor; they are the "revealed" ones. In these God usually either wrote to people or came to earth and talked to them. The first religious founder to make this claim was Zoroaster, maybe some time in the second millennium BC (date very uncertain). I don't mean to underestimate the degree of difference between different cultures and religions, but as far back as the sacred writings of Zoroastrianism we can find common ground:

"Prayer is the greatest of all spells, the best healing of all remedies."

ZEND AVESTA

But it's important to keep the claims of revealed religion in perspective. Our assumption that religion is some kind of "revealed" truth doesn't make it so. And not all religious leaders claimed divine authority. Buddha, for instance, based his philosophy on observation and reasoning. Buddhism is the way to truth and happiness without God.

But what the first-floor religions do have in common is the idea that experience is more than the material. True reality is in the next, higher world. The key century, which set the pattern for this way of thinking, is generally seen as the fifth century BC. What the twentieth century was to technology, the fifth century was to spiritual thinking. Increased urbanization had led to the emergence of a new literate class, not only in Greece but right across the Old World. They looked with skepticism on the cults that celebrated fertility and survival, and developed more universal spiritualities concerned with personal conduct. If you were a long-living Marco Polo in that century, you could have paused on your journey to sit at the feet of individuals who have shaped the way we've thought ever since. You could start in Italy with Pythagoras, the West's first great mystic, who realized that the nature of the universe could be expressed in mathematics, and taught reincarnation and the sanctity of all life. Then there's Socrates and Heraclitus teaching their vision of the Supreme Good in Greece. Move on to Jeremiah and Ezekiel with their idea of a holy, just God and individual responsibility in Palestine, where the Old Testament itself was taking its final shape. In India you have Buddha's experience of Nirvana and the first readings of the *Upanishad*. Also Mahavira's religion of non-violence to all living things. In China Confucius and Lao Tsu were teaching the philosophy of the good and virtuous life. We would struggle to find a comparable group from the last two millennia.

But it's probably no accident that it was around the fifth century that "science" made huge strides as well. In the last few centuries science has stormed ahead, but religious ideas and language haven't essentially altered in the last two and a half millennia. That's why the twenty-first century may be one to match the fifth century BC – there's a lot of catching up to do. Maybe Christianity, having (however reluctantly) cradled the industrial and scientific revolutions of the last couple of centuries, can begin to change itself in two ways, if it's not too late. The first would be to draw on the cumulative wisdom and experience of everyone rather than a single tribe or tradition. Why shouldn't meditation or yoga be as natural a part of a healthy spiritual life as curry and rice is part of our diet? If it makes sense to be religious isn't it logical to accept the best practices from the broad range of traditions? Perhaps the Church should be providing guidance across a multitude of religious paths rather than spending its energies narrowing the options. Maybe it's through embracing diversity that we come closer to truth. It's clear that God didn't want us to be too sure of where it lies.

The second task for a new generation of leaders would be to come to terms with modern knowledge. Feature DNA more than the devil, look for inspiration to the stars rather than to saints. Return to the problem of how we conduct ourselves to enable survival as a species in this world rather than working for salvation in the next.

6 OLDER GODS

"There is only one religion, though there are a hundred versions of it."

GEORGE BERNARD SHAW

We're on the first floor of the house. Find the staircase, let's move down the timeline. Antiquity and truth are often associated. The most powerful criticism of new cults is expressed in the question, "How can you believe something as absolutely true that's only just been thought of?" By which criteria, the further back in time we go, the better a perspective we will get. How far back should we look?

Maybe you feel this is irrelevant to your own religious experience. But you can't really understand any religion, the framework in which you express your experience, without being aware of its debt to earlier beliefs. If you grew up alone on an island you wouldn't work out any of the creeds from looking around you, any more than you can be "English" without an England to live in. These things aren't written up in the sky. We always underestimate the degree to which our upbringing, culture, our very genes determine what we know and even how we think.

It's hard not to be skeptical when theologians, evangelists, gurus, ayatollahs, monks, masters or mullahs all explain with brilliant logic why their religion alone is "true" and why their beliefs should be the standard by which others are judged. Every revelation seems rational to the believer, and weird to everyone else. Hey, give yourself a break. In the bigger picture we're all weird. Of all the several billion species that have crossed the planet none is so strange as *homo sapiens*. We're all puzzled creatures, caught in the dim twilight zone between self and universal consciousness, much as our primate cousins are in the zone of dawning self-consciousness.

How do we get our particular belief picture? As a general rule we inherit our religion from our parents or adopt it from our peers. The Christian faith is something we learn. If a good Christian had been born in Saudi Arabia he or she would probably be a good Muslim today. So would Billy Graham. No one makes a totally informed, objective choice on the merits of one religion against another.

Our parents inherited their beliefs from theirs, and we can go back through the generations. Christianity has been around for enough generations – a hundred or so – to affect the very way we think, whatever we believe now. This is why it's more important than we realize, even if we don't accept its belief structure today. For instance, we see our personal rights as being of first importance. This arises from the notion of a relationship with a personal God. By contrast, in Hinduism your personal rights are secondary to your place in the caste system. We believe in our power to radically change the direction of our lives. In Buddhism change happens in increments over hundreds of reincarnations, not suddenly. We think of our own lives as stories in which we are the main players, moving from birth to death. Most of us find it impossible to take on board the insignificance of the self (indeed its non-existence). We think of history as a progression of events, of the world moving from a beginning to an end, and it's hard to understand the Buddhist idea of time as a wheel rather than a line, of the endless recycling of life, building up your karma along the way. We think of "God" in the singular, whether we believe in Him or not, and find it hard to embrace the Hindu idea that there are 330 million gods (oddly enough very similar to the number of angels that medieval monks believed existed).

Above all we think of the "self" as something separate, that's "me." We Westerners exist in our heads, emotional, calculating and solitary. We can't live in the same way as animist peoples who experience all nature as interconnected and sacred. Being stoned out of your head is not the same thing. This is one reason why we're not venturing far on to the territory of other religions here. It's hard enough to make sense of your own inheritance without having to get under the skin of a different culture. Very few of us have the time or energy for that. We can learn from other religions and societies, speeding up the regular process of cultural osmosis, but we can't change who we are.

But these significant religions and religious figures that we've mentioned did not appear out of nowhere. They were building on the insights of their predecessors. So to get a more complete perspective on the different belief options we need to get down to the ground floor.

Imagine further back, four or five millennia, to around 2000 BC, before the great "revealed" religions started to shape our common experience, creating structures of belief and hierarchies of gods. Looking backwards in time, our pictures of God start to converge in the Indo-European tradition. All European and Semitic languages (with the exception of Basque) can be traced back to a common Proto-Indo-European language that survives in archaic Sanskrit. Our Christian "Father in heaven" can be traced back to *Zeus Pater* in Greek, *Dios Pater* (Jupiter) in Latin. These derive from the ancient sky god of the *Vedas, Dyausa Pita* (sky father).

Is the male sky God the start of the line, our first religion? We've barely begun. One persuasive theory is that he came with the establishment of cities, when power was centralized in kingship. The king, emperor, or pharaoh was either a god or ruled by divine right, leading to the idea of monotheism, of one deity holding absolute power. Cities had emerged from villages, which developed with agriculture, bringing the gods of the seasons, and the weather. Prior to this there were the pastoral nomads, who carried carved images of their gods around with them. Still earlier we find the idea of God as Mother, which has existed for far longer than the idea of God as Father. She emerged out of the spirit world of the hunter-gatherer societies, which still exist, just. If it weren't for our chopping down their trees they would outlast our own civilization.

So how far back can we trace the experience of God? Where's the beginning of the thread? Fertility symbols (Venuses) go back 30,000 years (1,500 generations). Claims have recently been made for one such figurine (Berehat Ram) to go back more than 250,000 years. There's evidence of rituals being carried out in caves 250,000 to 300,000 years ago (about 12,000 generations).

Across all these traditions there are many different images of God. The number of societies that have existed on earth with distinctively different pictures of the human and divine world is estimated at somewhere around 70,000. How is it possible to begin to tell which one is right? Isn't it more likely that if religions have any truth in them they must all reflect it to some degree? And if we see a progression here, with beliefs advancing from the primitive to the more sophisticated, why should we call a halt with what we have today? There may be another 70,000 religions to come. We may in future look back on the religions of revelation as we now look back on the religions of spirits and Mother Earth.

But the experience of God, or the search for Her (or perhaps the two are the same), must go back still further than this, to a time before we had any societies. Because if you believe in God you surely must believe that He is an intrinsic part of the experience of all human beings, of whatever period. After all, in the first book of the Bible, Genesis, God is there at the beginning, with the first man and woman.

So when were the first man and woman?

7 IS GOD HUMAN?

"Body and spirit are twins: God alone knows which is which.
The soul squats down in the flesh, like a tinker drunk in the ditch."

ALGERNON CHARLES SWINBURNE

Here let's *really* use our imagination. Let's step outside the house. Houses after all are something we build. Surely the God of the universe we know today isn't confined to what we make Him, to how we think of Him. The first clue religion gives us to who we really are and who God is is in one of our oldest, deepest and most beautiful stories. In the Bible it's called Genesis. It's the Middle-Eastern equivalent of the Songlines of the Aborigines. Similar myths about how we came to be are found in every society. This one describes how we became self-aware.

The first human beings came to see themselves as separate. The world became divided into "me" and "it." They began talking. They began to describe this separate world. Naming things gave them power over them (an ancient, worldwide tradition). They began to manipulate the world around them with tools, and to clothe this distinct person that they became aware of as "me," to decorate it. They began to make choices, to call actions good or bad. They began to remember, to be aware of the patterns of the seasons, and to plan ahead.

Our ancestors began to wonder how they could not only survive the next winter, but survive death. They began to fear this prospect, to feel awe at the natural processes of life that seem to transcend it, to dream of immortality. They began to project these emotions back on to the world around them, fashioning them into images that they could worship and offer sacrifices to. These images represented the meaning that reunited them with the separate world. But when roughly did this happen?

The Hebrews put Adam into what we now think of as recent

times, about 4000 BC. This was arrived at by counting backwards through the generations. Being nomadic sheep- and goat-herders, with no written records, they confined themselves to a genealogy you can count in your head if you multiply the average lifespan by a factor of ten or so. The average lifespan of the ten generations from Adam to Noah in the Old Testament was 857 years. The nine generations from Noah's son Shem to Abraham reaches a more modest 333. We know from tombs of the period in Jericho (which was a walled town from at least 8000 BC onwards) that most people died before the age of 35, few lived beyond 50. It's ironic that of all the world calendars available, the modern scientific Christian West should have based its cosmology on one of the least accurate. In contrast the Persians believed the world was created 500,000 years ago. Further east, in India, the number of years in a cosmic cycle was reckoned as 8.64 billion, about two-thirds of the universe's real age.

Our understanding of man has changed over the last century as profoundly as our understanding of the universe. Both are equally fundamental to the religious picture of the world. It's tempting to think we are a unique and distinct creation, descended from Mr and Mrs Adam, who made love and quarreled and did wrong much as we do. But we now date the human race back to our first ancestors who separated from the chimps around five million years ago. They're called *Australopithecus*, or Archaic Humans. They're not one species, but many (*Australopithecus afarensis, africanus, anamensis*, etc.). There's not one straight line of development from them to us; there are at least a score of different species, maybe many more, with dead ends, branches, bits missing. New species are still being found. It's perhaps the most exciting search on earth today, piecing together our ancient ancestry.

Think of *Homo* as like the cat family. Today we have leopards, lions, tigers, cheetahs, panthers, etc. that have found their separate niches, territories and foods. *Homo* developed the same way, but their ability to control body temperature through clothes, their immediate environment with tools, and to mash food and cook, enabled them to spread up and down the food chain and through different territories. It brought the various human species into conflict with each other. Only one of them (us! *Homo sapiens*) is still around.

Were these early *Homos* really "human"? Take an example. The most complete skeleton of *Homo erectus* that has been found is 1.5 million years old. *Homo* had by then already been using tools for about a million years. *Erectus* lived until about 100,000 years ago, which in anthropological terms is like modern times. (Estimates of the ages of fossils, by the way, are accurate to around 10%.) Their brain was as big as ours, they built houses, worked wood, threw spears, drank from bowls. In the burials at Choukont'ien outside Peking, there are signs that they believed in an after-life. Whether a sub-branch of *erectus* developed into *sapiens* half a million years ago, or whether we came on to the scene more recently, we don't know. Either way we are very junior cousins.

Neanderthal Man (*Homo sapiens neanderthalensis*) is even closer to our own time. About 500 of their skeletons have been recovered, the latest dating to 34,000 BC. They had a stronger and tougher body than ours, designed to cope with the Ice Age. We don't know much about Neanderthal Man, but we know they buried their dead with ritual and ceremony, covering them with flowers, placing stones and antlers around the graves. They were undoubtedly around when our immediate ancestors came on the scene, and we may have killed them off.

What's the point of this ancient history (or rather anthropology)? It shows that religion is not something that only dates back 2,000 or even 20,000 years. It goes back to the dawn of our own history. And it's not even confined to our own species. Other species have also believed in an after-life. You can't do that without a capacity for abstract thought, the ability to conceive the idea that reality lies elsewhere, beyond this life, a "religious sense."

This is why religion will always be with us. The "sense" for it is so wired into our brains that some evolutionary biologists have claimed there are genes for believing in God. Some neurologists similarly say there is an area in the parietal lobe of the brain, nicknamed the "God-spot," that sifts incoming data to enable us to distinguish between the self and the world. But at times circumstances (which can be occasioned by our own efforts) suppress it, leading to moments of transcendence when the sense of "self" disappears. The changes in brain patterns this produces are the same across all cultures and faiths. In other words, experiencing Krishna or God has the same effect. We don't all have this "God-spot" equally. As with other genes, in some individuals this capacity is strong, in others weak. It's inherited, and so not completely under our conscious control. Epileptics can suffer from it severely. It can be triggered with electrical impulses.

An atheist might say this is a fault in our wiring. The brain pulls its plug and exists in a state of indeterminacy, uncertain what is real and what is not. The believer sees it in reverse. The brain plugs itself back into the real world, momentarily abandoning the temporary self it has constructed and returning to its natural state of spirit.

Whichever is true, we give the word "soul" to the part of us that perceives or imagines God. It's why we don't stop believing, and searching for spiritual truth. "He has made everything beautiful in its time. He has also set eternity in the hearts of men; yet they cannot fathom what God has done from beginning to end" (Ecclesiastes 3:11 NIV). The interesting question is not so much whether we have the right religion, as whether we have the right "soul" in the first place. Perhaps Neanderthal Man was more "religious" than we are. Perhaps Genesis is more deeply true than we imagine. Perhaps we are all the race of Cain, and have killed off our gentler brothers, cursed by our genes to fight to the finish, only intermittently able to grasp the principle that true religion is based on love not fear, awe not anger. God had His doubts about the Hebrews in the Old Testament, perhaps He still has doubts about us. Perhaps the intended purpose of creation is another million years away, or a billion. Perhaps it won't be realized till the universe ends.

8 IS GOD MAMMAL?

"I sometimes think that God, in creating man, overestimated his ability."
OSCAR WILDE

You see why a straight "yes" or "no" to the question, "Do you believe in God?" is difficult. It implies a belief in the orthodox Christian God as taught today. But let's leave to one side for the moment the question of whether any religion is true. In the sense of believing that life is more than we can see or touch, that there may be an after-life, maybe a God, religion has been a force in the development of humanity for hundreds of thousands of years. If we date it from the development of language (the date for this is much disputed), religion has probably been practiced in some form for more than a million years. Christianity has been practiced for about 0.02% of that time. In that brief period it's mostly been followed by 1 to 10% of the world population.

Think of year zero in our terms as 0 AA (*Anno Adam*). Did nothing of spiritual significance in the world happen after that till around 996,500 AA when Abraham made a covenant with God? And then nothing till 998,000 AA when Jesus burst on to the scene? God let 40,000 generations live and die in ignorance? And then threatened to come back any day in judgement? It doesn't make any kind of sense. It's why so many Christians cling to the idea that the world is only a few thousand years old. The salvation history of Christianity is written from that perspective. But even if we go back only to our immediate ancestors who came out of Africa about 60,000 years ago, and whose genetic tree we can trace in our bodies, the entire Christian experience only registers as a little blip. It's a thought that came a minute ago, as are agriculture, writing, and "civilization."

To believe in this kind of God, who has made such a brief and apparently unsuccessful entry on to the world stage, is like believing in a flat earth. Surely He must have been in the frame for earlier generations, and for other species. But that would mean a different kind of God. If, for instance, it had been *Homo robustus* (a vegetarian who dug for roots rather than a scavenger like ourselves) who had come out on top and survived to our own day, wouldn't we then have religions without the common theme of drinking blood and eating flesh?

But let's kick this ball further into play. Over the last few millennia the tradition has grown of seeing humans as the pinnacle of creation, so naturally we see God in our image. The Hebrews, Greeks, Hindus all believed that the gods were biologically the same as us. There was frequent crossbreeding, with the children usually being male and often larger and stronger. In Genesis 6:2-4, for example, the sons of God copulate with the daughters of earth to produce giants. Blue eyes, representing the sky, were also a common feature of these children. In Hindu stories the children of such partnerships were blue all over.

But a still older tradition sees gods in the form of animals rather than men and women. And if you think about it, why not? If religious consciousness, the "God spot," has been present in many different species of *Homo*, why should it not also be present in chimpanzees, dogs, gorillas, elephants, dolphins? They all show compassion to varying individual degrees, like people. We're far closer to other creatures than you probably realize. Look at your hand. It's a chimp's hand. And so are every bone and nerve in your body. We still have the goose pimples which raised our now nonexistent fur against cold and enemies. Genetically we're no more different from the chimps than two species of clam are from each other. For the first few weeks of life our embryos are indistinguishable.

And the likeness is not just physical. We care for our children in the same way, intrigue, make war, hug each other when afraid. We suck our thumbs when young, live together in groups but sleep separately at night, preferably one floor up for security, but not too many in case we fall out. Chimps feel happy, sad, have a sense of humor, can be brutal and caring, have a prodigious memory. They use tools and modify them, passing on behavior from one generation to the next. They are self-aware, and can recognize themselves in mirrors. They understand symbols and can be taught (by people) a computer language. The most experienced chimp-watcher in the world, Jane Goodall, has often seen them perform a kind of primeval rain dance in response to lightning and thunder.

Some biologists say there are basically three species of chimp today, separated by five million years (300,000 generations): the Common chimps (*Homo troglodytes*), the Bonobo chimps (*Homo paniscus*), and ourselves (*Homo sapiens*). Both we and the Bonobos split off from the Common chimps. The Bonobos were cut off by the River Congo; our ancestors may have been separated in a similar way by the Rift Valley. We know our ancestors were a small separate group because there is more genetic variation among Common chimps than among us. The consequence of being exposed in more open savanna led to the physical developments that superficially distinguish us from the chimps today: losing our fur to sweat, and walking on our hind legs, which freed our hands to use tools.

But though we have changed the most physically, socially we are more similar to the Common chimps than to the Bonobos. We're both competitive and aggressive. The Bonobo chimps developed differently. The Bonobo family groups are led by females who maintain their leadership through the use of sex rather than force. Let's speculate: if it had been the Bonobos who moved out on to the open plains on the other side of the Rift Valley and started walking upright, our society could have been more "moral." Our priests and presidents would be female. God would be Mother. Sex would be initiated by the female to reconcile and reward rather than by the male to express right and power. The

Bonobos would probably have been better at managing one of the main problems confronting the earth today – over-breeding.

The superficial differences between us and the chimps are greater than between us and other branches of *Homo*, but, again, most people who work closely with chimps say it's hard to say that there is a fundamental difference. It's a question of degree. And as we're the ones driving them to extinction, much as we have probably exterminated our other, more closely-related cousins, perhaps the degree is not that great. There are only about 200,000 chimps left now, gradually being killed off for "bush meat" in restaurants.

There's a joke about a man and his dog who had both died in a car accident. They were walking along a road and came to a high marble wall. In the center was a tall mother-of-pearl gate that glowed in the sunlight. Behind it was a golden street.

The man and the dog walked toward the gate. As the traveler got closer, he saw a man at a desk. "Excuse me, where are we?" he asked.

"This is heaven, sir," the gatekeeper answered.

"Wow! Great! Would you happen to have some water?" the man asked.

"Of course, sir. Come right in, and I'll have some ice water brought right up." The gatekeeper gestured, and the gate began to open.

The traveler pointed to his dog. "Can my friend come in, too?" he asked.

"I'm sorry, sir, but we don't accept pets."

The man thought a moment and then turned back toward the road and continued to walk the way he had been going.

After another long walk the man and his dog came to a dirt road that led through a farm gate. There was no fence. As the traveler approached he saw a man in a chair, reading.

"Excuse me!" he called. "Do you have any water?"

"Yeah, sure, there's a pump over there. Come on in."

"How about my friend here?" The traveler gestured to the dog.

"There should be a bowl by the pump."

They went through the gate, and sure enough, there was an old-fashioned hand pump with a bowl beside it. The traveler filled the bowl and took a long drink. Then he pumped some water for the dog.

"What do you call this place?" the traveler asked.

"This is heaven," was the answer.

"That's odd," the traveler said. "The man down the road said that was heaven, too."

"Oh, you mean the place with the gold street and pearly gates? Nope. That's hell."

Said the traveler, "Doesn't it make you mad for them to use your name like that?"

"No. I can see how you might think so, but we're just happy that they screen out the folks who'll leave their best friends behind."

So maybe God is not just the God of the human species – He's the God of the primates, too. We are no more the favored species than the Jews are the favored people. In 400 years' time perhaps we'll look back on our habits of owning and eating animals with the same kind of horror that we now view slavery and cannibalism. They will equally be the mistreatment and murder of creatures made in the image of God. We'll wonder how we could all have been so blind to our kinship, and why it took so long to take on board these insights from Eastern religions.

9 HOW FAR BACK DO WE GO?

"God is our name for the last generalization to which we can arrive."

RALPH WALDO EMERSON

Keep the imagination working for a moment longer. To talk about chimps in relation to God may seem just nuts. But what is really barmy is the assumption that we are the only life form in the universe that He ever planned to relate to. For most of our history we have been a microscopically small number, invisible on the earth's surface in relation to the numbers of other animals, scavenging a living under their noses. More prey than predator. We're an oddball species that through an evolutionary quirk funneled energy into the brain rather than into muscles or claws, and it's got to be said that the chances of our lasting for hundreds, or even tens, of millions of years, as some other species do, look slim.

Why should the universe have been set in motion to produce you and me, 12 billion years later? We're not the peak of an evolutionary pyramid even on earth, but a twig on a massive tree. Or perhaps it would be more accurate to say a twig in a forest that is periodically subject to huge fires. Over the last billion years half a dozen of these disasters have happened, and each time up to 90% of life forms have been made extinct. But this forest is continuous, always emerging again from its roots. Life has only started on the planet once. We are one of literally billions of shoots, 99.9% of which have come and gone. Only the bacteria survive indefinitely; they are the soup out of which more transient forms like us emerge and disappear.

So why restrict God's interest in conscious life to the primates? For instance, what about whales and dolphins? They're mammals like us who returned to the sea about 65 million years ago. The proportion of the brain's cortex (the intelligent bit) to body weight, which is the measure of how advanced the brain of a species is, is the same as ours. The fact that they don't have hands to hold tools doesn't make their brainpower any less than ours. Dolphins have been around in their present form for about 25 million years. Perhaps they've been seeing God in their image for millions of years before the primates and human beings were thought of. Who's to say? We don't understand the sounds they make. Perhaps dolphins have a more developed language than our own. Their language is sonar and so communicates in three dimensions, with the waves created by the sounds they make penetrating the flesh and bone. They may "see" the sound in a more complex way than we do, since we merely hear sound waves banging on the eardrum.

What if the world had turned out a little differently and there had been no land for the mammals to walk on, then surely consciousness in the form of self-awareness would have developed in the seas, in creatures without lungs? Octopuses are intelligent. Given another 10 million years, who knows what they might evolve into? What other forms of consciousness might develop in the next billion years?

We can follow our family tree back further. We've been developing in the direction of sociable communities since the evolution of the hominids (joint ancestors of the primates and ourselves) about 24 million years ago. But we can go back still further, back to the rodents, and see similarities. We still have our common fear of snakes, dating from when their ancestors pursued ours in tunnels under the feet of the dinosaurs. We still mimic a snake's "Shh . . ." as a warning to children. But it's more than physical. Young rats that are regularly and gently stroked with a brush function better as adults. Being "loved" makes them more relaxed and comfortable. They can actually work out problems better. Their brains get more wired up. This doesn't work with reptiles. It's taken a lot of scientific experiments here to prove what every pet-lover instinctively knows.

It's the same with people. Children from loving, secure homes grow up with more confidence in their abilities than children from violent or broken homes. Good relationships develop communication skills, which in turn lead to greater understanding and more complex responses to situations. As these children acquire greater sensitivity to shades of meaning they find it easier to develop symbols that summarize and convey attitudes. Love actually grows the brain, in a virtuous circle. A more complex brain enables deeper love, which in turn spurs the search for meaning. Life forms that are higher than human beings are likely to be more loving forms, or they would have destroyed each other (we hope).

"Love" is not the right word for this process. It's the crudest of words for an extraordinarily wide range of emotions. Think of it for the moment as simply the highest form of self-awareness that we know of. It has emerged, over a vast period of time, from co-operative relationships. These are fundamental to life. Half of all species are parasites – 90% of the living cells in our bodies are bacteria. We don't know what prompted the first cells to combine. We don't know what prompts each further level of complex organization. But it's taken 3.5 billion years for our bodies to reach the stage they are at now: a "co-operative." And in our bodies and brains we can follow the history of this little co-operative right back to the first seeds of the forest. Our blood is salty, combining elements of sodium, potassium and calcium in the same proportions as seawater, deriving from the time when the first circulatory system of sea creatures was just that – seawater. Our skeletons are still hardened with lime. We each begin our life in the tiny ocean of a womb. For half an hour or so we exist as a single cell, before embryonic development repeats the evolutionary stages, starting with gills rather than lungs. We can trace the development of self-awareness in our own brains, from the reptilian at the stem to the mammalian at the top. We are part of a community of life. Nature is so connected that every time we breathe in we take in about a thousand million molecules that Jesus breathed out.

So how should we think of God and ourselves? In the last couple of centuries we've found it convenient to divide nature up into categories: species, phyla, animal/vegetable/mineral, mind/body/spirit, etc. but the ancient perception that life is a whole is still true. These classifications are not "real." What we see now is that there is no absolute dividing line between body and brain, brain and mind, mind and consciousness, consciousness and spirit. Every society, every religion, draws these lines differently, and differently at different times. Christianity itself has at times disputed whether children, or women, or slaves, or colored people have souls. We still differ as to when an individual life begins. These are lines that we construct for our convenience, they are not "there" in our environment. If there is a clear line anywhere it's the one between bacteria and all other life forms.

Surely if God exists He has always been active, is always present, in every birth and death and every leaf fall, in every chemical reaction since the beginning of time. He didn't just become interested in life in the last millisecond, as it were. Think of life on earth as taking up a year. You're sitting in a chair, looking at the clock. The period of humankind's recorded history (5,000 years or so) flickers past in about 0.004 of a second, too short a period for our minds to register. It's equivalent to the layer of paint on top of the Empire State building.

Good religion is aware that we assume our own importance and draw these lines at the peril of losing our souls, as we are part of everything else. Maybe we don't need to go as far as other religions. Good Buddhists avoid stepping on ants. Jainism goes furthest, teaching the inter-relatedness of everything, including rocks, fire and water, to the point that adepts wear masks over their faces to avoid swallowing insects. But we need to learn something from them about the unity of life.

We started this section with the Book of Job. What Job says to us today is that when you strip away everything that we tend to think of as constituting our lives: possessions, home, health, family, friends, we're still not alone. Sometimes it's only when we lose everything that we find God. He is part of our genetic glue, like the need for warmth and companionship. As much as our "self" shouts to be separate, it longs to be reunited with Him. We're never entirely at ease with our separate selves. Trying to feed the self with more possessions or power or relationships doesn't work. Even the best that life has to offer is imperfect; we still have an image of perfection in our heads. We want to make sense of the world, to put it back together again. We yearn for the Garden of Eden, for the time before we realized we were naked, and invented clothes and fashion, work and worry, religion and psychology. At the heart of the experience of all religions is the feeling of reclaimed "oneness" with creation, of belonging to a "whole" that is both divine and beautiful.

> *"God in the depths of us receives God who comes to us; it is God contemplating God."*
>
> JAN VAN RUYSBROECK

But who is this God? An atheist would say there is no God, this is self-delusion. There is no spirit or soul at all. A believer today might say the universe is one of unity and purpose, God is behind everything. But maybe we have drawn the lines too narrowly. The fact that we read this unity as "personal" shows it for what it is: a personal effort at understanding. Individuals will therefore see it differently.

Maybe the "real God," if He exists, is as alien to us as we are to the chimps. We believe that God is like us and we form Him in our image because we couldn't picture Him otherwise. But it's like saying parrots are human because they can speak English. Maybe the houses of religion that we build no more adequately contain God than the house you live in contains the planet, or the universe.

PART 2

FOLLOWING GOD

10 WHAT DID GOD SAY?

"Truth did not come into the world naked, but it came in types and images. It will not receive it in any other way."

GOSPEL OF PHILIP

A twenty-first century understanding of God – assuming for the moment that we're talking about one local to this universe – is of a God who acts impartially across 50 billion trillion miles, over 15 billion years. He has delighted in the birth of several billion species on this planet alone. So what does my particular brand of religion that is Christianity have to say about Him? Does it work?

One of the root meanings of the word "religion," as mentioned above, is "to relate," "to belong." The Golden Rule of relationships is: "Do to others as you would be done to." We tend to identify this with Jesus, but it was a frequent theme in Judaism. Rabbi Hillel, a near contemporary of Jesus, used much the same language, and managed it without reference to God. Confucius said the same thing 500 years earlier. The key concept in Confucian philosophy is *ren*, which Confucius defines as "the love of man" (*Analects* XII, 22). The basic Buddhist precept is that you must consider all beings as like yourself. The same ideas are central to Jainism and Islam; in fact, all the major religions have the Golden Rule at their heart.

All the great spiritual leaders say that relationship is at the core of the universe. There is less agreement on how to describe the ultimate relationship called "Spirit" that is behind it, except to say that it's indescribable. But it is committed to our growth and wellbeing. In that sense it's a "loving" relationship. We're on the same side. And in a minimal sense at least, this must be right. We can live without the concept of God, we can live without poetry, music, but we can't live without love of some kind. And all religions agree that if this belief doesn't result in the outworking of love, in practical compassion, it's worthless.

How well does Christianity express this?

You don't need to be a fundamentalist to read the Bible and take it seriously. It helps if you're not. Learning it by heart is no substitute for understanding its context. In so far as it has a "message" it can be said to focus on the two commands of Jesus: to love God and to love your neighbor. But how do we relate this to the kind of language we read in other parts of the Bible? The psalms encourage us to "hate them [God's enemies and ours] with perfect hatred" (Psalm 139:22). God threatens the Hebrews with cannibalizing their children if they don't follow all the tribal laws of Leviticus (Leviticus 26:9). The Old Testament is full of stomach-curdling episodes and speeches of violence, revenge, hatred and vindictiveness, on the part of God as well as the Hebrews. Can all these be reconciled as equally inspired words coming from the same unchanging good God? To say all the words in the Bible convey the same message to all people at all time is not to be true to the Bible but to make it meaningless.

We understand the Bible by seeing it as a developing project. It's quite simply the most extraordinary record in world literature of a people's experience and understanding of God as it changes over a millennium. That's why it's still worth reading. It's the most exciting story we have. The only problem is that a few centuries after Jesus the Church became the most powerful organization in the Mediterranean world and called a halt to further development. It's like stopping work on a skyscraper at the third floor.

So what is the Christian message that we've inherited? John summed up what he considered to be the core of Christianity in perhaps the Bible's most famous verse: "For God so loved the world, that he gave his only begotten Son, that whosoever believeth in him should not perish, but have everlasting life" (John 3:16). It sounds wonderful. A Supreme Deity of Absolute Love rules the universe. He identifies with us to the point that He sacrifices his Son for our benefit.

But this immediately gives rise to some questions – questions that Christianity itself has wrestled with since it began.

Shouldn't God have sacrificed Himself rather than his Son? Isn't sacrificing your child more of a barbaric act than a divine action?

What does it mean for God to have an "only" Son? Does it imply He could have had two, or that He Himself had a Father? If we don't take this literally, what do we mean by the word "God"?

If everyone who doesn't believe is going to perish, why not make it a bit clearer? Give us more of a sporting chance? What happens to all the people who have never heard the message?

Does it sound right that a Christian who lives a bad life goes to heaven, but a non-believer who leads a good life goes to hell? How could heaven be "heaven" when you know that many of your family and friends are "perishing"?

Has this verse actually "worked"? Do Christians behave as if they believe it? What does "believing it" mean?

There are many other sons of God in religion, direct descendants, incarnations, avatars, the sacrifice of whom is a common theme. They are described in many sacred scriptures. Is only the Christian Son the real one, the others fakes?

How do we know that John knows this verse to be true?

These are just a few quick questions that come to mind. Most people conclude that the verse doesn't ring true any more. But Christianity itself has come up with many different answers. Here, for instance, is a quote from another John:

> *"John, there must be one man to hear these things from me; for I need one who is ready to hear. This Cross of Light is sometimes called Logos by me for your sakes, sometimes mind, sometimes Jesus, sometimes Christ, sometimes a door, sometimes a way, sometimes bread, sometimes seed, sometimes resurrection, sometimes Son, sometimes Father, sometimes Spirit, sometimes life, sometimes truth, sometimes faith, sometimes grace; and so it is called for men's sake."*
>
> THE ACTS OF JOHN

This seems to contradict John's Gospel. According to this other John our images of God are like a kaleidoscope through which we express in our different ways what we cannot fully understand. Words like "Son," "everlasting life," "resurrection" are ideas, not facts. Belief has to accommodate uncertainty and multiple options because God Himself does.

How do we know which John was right? Many biblical scholars today would say it's equally improbable that either John quotes Jesus at all at any point in their Gospels. Who were these Johns? We know very little about either. *The Acts of John* was accepted by parts of the early Church as canonical, but didn't make it into the New Testament. It was then "consigned to the fire" at the Second Council of Nicea in AD 787. But the decision-makers in this instance were as far removed in time from Jesus as we are from the twelfth-century French rulers of England.

The Church's decisions on the New Testament canon were made centuries after the time of Jesus. How do we know it chose the right books? The contradiction of Bible-believing Protestantism is that it accepts the judgement of a Church it regards as flawed, of individuals who were probably not "saved," on what the Bible itself is. All reasoning on this subject is circular: we believe in God in the way the Bible says; that way is right because God inspired the Bible. Those who submit to the authority of the Church use the same circular logic.

Perhaps we should follow the later John. The first one is already starting to shift the emphasis from love to dogma. "By this we know that we love the children of God, when we love God, and keep his commandments" (1 John 5:2). If you don't obey God the way I do, then you don't really love other people even when you think you do. Anyone who thinks differently about who God is and what He said are "children of the devil," "antichrist" (1 John 2:18-25; 3:9-10). It's the beginning of persecution and fundamentalism. It begins to explain how the rule of the Church replaced the Golden Rule. How Christianity became a religion that created division and barriers rather than broke them down, as Jesus did. This leads to distrust, which leads to hatred. Fundamentalism breeds evil like poverty breeds crime. It's possible to be loving and warm toward people you believe are essentially wicked and going to hell, much like it's possible to be honest if you're down-and-out in a world of rich people. But it's a lot harder.

"Authority" is the problem. Shared systems of belief are helpful in that they enable individuals to rise above their self-interest. But belief in the system needs commitment. In willingly making the commitment individuals tend to surrender their power of independent reasoning. Over generations, centuries, the system of collective belief hardens, writes teaching in stone, and reason disappears. It even defines itself against other systems rather than being open to further sharing. Every now and again it all needs to be pulled down and rebuilt, like Jesus wanted to do with the Temple. Each new religion starts as an act of destruction.

In Jesus' time the Temple was run by the priests, who belonged to the party of the Sadducees. They taught that you could only come to God by believing the right things and doing them in the right order. Our equivalent today is the clergy, the Church. The Pharisees were the other major Jewish group that Jesus struggled with. They believed that the only way to please God was to live in accordance with their interpretation of the written law. Protestants believe in the same way, claiming their interpretation of the Bible as true. In both cases they've stopped journeying, bottled the Spirit and put the stopper on.

Maybe there's another way of looking at Christianity. After all, Jesus answered questions with more questions, with puzzling parables, not rules about what you should believe or not. Maybe Christianity is not about knowing the answer, but knowing where the right questions are and living with the knowledge that the answer may be around the corner. The trouble is, the corner has no ending, in this life. The question we're left with is how to live in the light of best practice in the meantime.

Perhaps the two poles of truth and love provide an answer. Truth is the aim of the journey. Our lives have to incorporate what we know to be true. It's the principle we follow. Love is the measure of how far we've traveled. It's the basis of our practice. God is our best understanding of both. Jesus is our best example. The fascination of religious publishing is in seeing the different balances and compromises people reach between the two. Truth tends to exclusiveness; love to tolerance. Certainty in one is the enemy of the other. Everyone draws their own line, leaning this way or that. In what is now a global village maybe we need to draw a wide circle, one that includes everyone, if Christian holocausts are not to become the Christian Armageddon. Maybe this circle will be so wide that "Christian" becomes meaningless. If so, maybe we have to start again. Or maybe we can redefine the word, get something new going here. You can decide.

11 IS THE CHRISTIAN GOD "GOOD"?

"There lies at the back of every creed something terrible and hard for which the worshipper may one day be required to suffer."

E. M. FORSTER

Is the phrase "Christian holocaust" absurdly over-dramatic, a very lopsided view of history? Surely Christianity, as the religion dedicated to love, promotes democracy and human rights, representing all that is best in the world? Let me tell you a story . . .

About 500 years ago the majority of the world's population followed one of seven major religions: Christianity, Islam, Hinduism, Buddhism, the South American sun religions, and in the Far East Confucianism and Taoism. Each of these cultures had enormously impressive achievements in various fields – science, astronomy, architecture, engineering, literature, art, and so on. Numerically Christianity was probably the smallest of the seven faiths. The monarchies of Christian Europe were developing a technological edge, but its cities were like villages compared to the metropolises to be found in the Far East and Central America. The idea that white Europeans always conquer colored natives was still centuries away. Europe itself was still at risk from the Muslim Turks, who had penetrated central France in the fifteenth century and besieged Vienna in 1529.

In 1519 Cortéz and 314 fellow soldiers and adventurers beached their ships at Veracruz (the Rich City of the True Cross) in Central America and set out to conquer the fabled Aztec Empire. The odds against success were incredible: a few hundred against millions. The Spaniards were driven by a powerful combination of extreme greed for gold and glory – for themselves and God. They knew their lives were on the line, it was conquer or die. They took their chance with extraordinary courage and ruthlessness.

They needed these qualities, in abundance. The Aztecs were not peace-loving softies. Their Empire was built on the concept of tribute, much of it in the form of human sacrifices. To keep the sun turning in the sky, humans had to die on their altars, their priests ripping out their still-beating hearts; 20,000 were sacrificed at the dedication of the great pyramid of Tenochtitlan. They were a society geared to constant warfare, conquering territory to maintain the supply of sacrificial victims. At the time of the invasion, their emperor, Montezuma, was an aggressive leader and campaigner. Nor were they primitive. In some ways they were more advanced than the Europeans. From the Mayan civilization in the Yucatan peninsular they had inherited a calendar more accurate in some respects than the one we use today. The Mayans had made astronomical calculations extending over millions of years. A thousand years ago, they forecast the 1991 eclipse of the sun. We have a more accurate knowledge of the dates of their emperors than of the kings who were their contemporaries in the Dark Ages of Christian Europe.

Yet within a couple of years Cortéz was in power and the emperor was in prison. How did it happen? There were many factors, notably the defection to Spain of tribute tribes, but the main single reason may have been the confusion of the Aztecs as to who these strange god-like people were, with their horses, ocean-going ships and guns, which had never been seen before. The Aztecs had a god called Quetzalcoatl, Feathered Snake (inherited from the Mayan Kukulcan), who was the re-creator of the world. Born of a virgin, he had dived to the underworld to regain the bones of death. He was resurrected and saved the dead, whose bones he reanimated. He had a cross as a symbol, and had promised to return one day from the east to restore his rule and bring prosperity. The Aztecs mistook the Spaniards, also coming from the east in their feathered ships, riding extraordinary animals, killing at a distance with flashes of noise and light, for the gods in the story.

Montezuma is reported as saying, "This is the same lord for whom we are waiting." The Aztecs thought their gods had actually stepped out of the myth and arrived. Many Christians similarly believe that God is on His way to rule the earth.

With no prior contact, separated by 5,000 miles, quite different social structures and cultures, Christians and Aztecs had nevertheless developed the same doctrines of sacrifice and resurrection, virgin birth and second coming. Having the same psychological needs, we come up with the same kinds of answers. In the Aztec sacrificial system, the victims represented the gods, the priests consecrated the body and blood, and onlookers shared the flesh to identify themselves with the gods, in a similar manner to the Eucharist. Spanish priests noted the common practices and saw the Aztec religion as the devil perverting the truth. And in many ways it was a truly nasty religion, though it has to be said that many victims probably went voluntarily, seeing their death as a passage to Paradise.

The first point here is the similarity between religions, even those with no opportunity of directly influencing each other. Sacrifice is central to all religions. We fear the universe is hostile and we offer something up before we get eaten ourselves, like the lizard leaving its tail in the mouth of a predator.

The more important point, though, is that this story shows the dark side of religions that claim to be exclusively true and demand to be believed. The arrival of Cortéz was the first of the huge land grabs of modern times, when European Christian nations used superior technology to subdue and largely eliminate the inhabitants of entire continents. Sanction for it was given to the Spanish and Portuguese by papal bulls of the fifteenth century, and the Protestant Dutch and English followed in their wake. Within a century of the arrival of Cortez, the original population of what is now Mexico had been reduced from 25 million to 1 million. It has been estimated that within two centuries 90% of the indigenous population of the whole of South America had been killed off. Even the Amazonian rainforest was penetrated within a few years of the conquest, with a population of around five million reduced to the couple of hundred thousand natives that are still there today. The guns began it all; European germs counted for most of the deaths. Christian missionaries did their best to stamp out what was left of the original culture. The civilization of the Incas and of dozens of other nations was obliterated.

Catholics got there first, but much the same happened in North America and Australia with the Protestants, though the numbers involved were fewer, those areas being less densely populated. Africa escaped relatively lightly only because the Arabs controlled the north and the mosquitoes the middle. Even so, around 24 million were carried off by Europeans to work as slaves in the newly emptied lands of the Americas, with another 12 million dying *en route*. And we're talking here about a period when the population of a country like England was around five million. Over 70% of the migrants who were shipped into America between 1580 and 1820 were black. The reason North America remained predominantly white for several centuries is because their treatment was so inhumane. They died young.

Historical population figures involve a lot of guesswork. But best estimates suggest that the worldwide population in the sixteenth century was around 500 million. Christians amounted to about 10%, or 50 million. Over the next century or two, by means of conquest and colonization Christians killed off another 10%. By the twentieth century Christianity had increased its "market share" to around 30% of the world's population, where it remains today.

Christianity is now the number one religion, with the largest following in the world, though on last-century trends Islam is going to overtake it in this new century. Of the other six religions mentioned at the beginning of this chapter, the sun religions have been wiped out through Christian conquest. Communism, an offspring of Christian Europe, has made large inroads on Buddhism, Confucianism and Taoism.

Genuine Christian missionary effort, motivated by concern for souls rather than conquest, has had little appreciable effect on the other six religions. Today after extraordinary efforts by tens of thousands of dedicated individuals there are proportionately fewer Christians in the Middle East and the most populous countries of the world – India, China, Japan, Indonesia – than there were 500 years ago. Maybe in part this is because these people can see what Christians shut their eyes to. Their increase in the religious market share of the world's population from 10% to 30% was achieved through the greatest episodes of genocide, slavery, and forced mass-movement of peoples that the earth has ever seen. The result is that 60% or so of Christians today live in the Americas and Africa, compared to 1% or so in the sixteenth century.

Christians see their God as a God of light and love. Taking a global historical perspective, many more have seen Him as a force of death and destruction, of evil. An equivalent holocaust today to the sixteenth-century genocide in Central and South America would involve figures of around 600 million – nuclear war proportions. The Aztecs thought of hell as a period of time rather than a place, a belief they adopted from the Mayans. Their survivors dated it from 1519 when the Christians arrived.

12 ARE CHRISTIANS GOOD?

"I want you to just let a wave of intolerance wash over you. I want you to let a wave of hatred wash over you. Yes, hate is good...Our goal is a Christian nation. We have a biblical duty, we are called by God, to conquer this country."

RANDALL TERRY, USA EVANGELIST

It was in the sixteenth century that Christianity really started to motor. The Atlantic trade winds carried Cortéz's successors from Spain and other European nations around the world like a new Black Death (a fourteenth-century plague that wiped out one-third of the population of Europe), reshaping most of it as a series of warring Christian empires.

Christians prefer not to see it this way. In the manner of oppressors everywhere they can even think of themselves as the victims, the "persecuted Church." But at the beginning of the twentieth century the Western Christian nations, including Russia, controlled something like 90% of the world's surface and its manufacturing output. Here was an opportunity for the Church to create a new order for the world, to bring peace and justice and prosperity. It was the first and hopefully the last time that any one religion has had so much power. The moment was ripe for a new Augustine to articulate a vision for a new City of God, one that would embrace the whole planet, including the knowledge of the new sciences, to see us through the next millennia. We know what happened. The century will go down as the one where developing technology outstripped man's capacity to control it, leading to the first two devastating world wars, both generated in Christian Europe, and the Holocaust, humanity's worst crime.

Was this the fault of the Church? Christians will say Hitler wasn't one of us, though he was baptized as a Christian (Roman Catholic) and never excommunicated. Stalin, who was responsible for killing even more, was baptized as an Orthodox Christian, and was educated by priests at Tiflis Theological Seminary. The right-wing dictators Franco, Pétain, Mussolini, Pavelic and Tiso (Tiso was a priest who headed the German puppet state of Slovakia) thought of themselves as Christians. Hitler and Stalin may well have regarded themselves as atheists, though Hitler writes in *Mein Kampf* (1928): "I am convinced that I am acting as the agent of the creator – by fighting off the Jews I am doing the Lord's work."

But this is beside the point. The Holocaust happened because Hitler had the approval of the vast majority of the German people. The Christians in Germany overwhelmingly supported him. The racist German Christian Movement with half a million members praised him in church services. The SS had the words "God is with us" printed on their belt buckles. Of course there were exceptions, but what is astonishing is how few there were. There's no record of a Catholic or Protestant bishop speaking out strongly against Hitler. Archbishops around Europe like Cardinal Hinsley of Westminster and Stepinac in Yugoslavia referred to him as carrying out God's will. Pope Pius XI ordered the Italian and German Catholic parties to support Hitler and Mussolini. In 1933, Pope Pius XII signed a concordat with Hitler to gain favorable rights for the Catholic Church in the new German state. In 1941 he endorsed the anti-Semitic legislation of the Vichy puppet state, looking the other way as SS troops (with their fair proportion of Christians, and even more of doctors) rounded up Jewish families in Rome and drove them past the Vatican to Nazi concentration camps. After the liberation the pontiff requested that no colored Allied troops be stationed in Rome. The Vatican claims he saved hundreds of thousands of Jews in secret, but the evidence here is thin. Maybe he should have shouted it from the rooftops. And this anti-Semitic and racist individual, a man who believed in a conspiracy between Judaism and Bolshevism to destroy Christendom, is someone whom the present pope wants to canonize. The stark truth is that in the greatest moral crisis that Europe has ever faced the major Christian Churches were worse than useless.

The real problem for the Church, and Christianity, is that Hitler's views weren't a momentary aberration. Christian teaching down the ages has been anti-Semitic. Kant and Schleiermacher, the founders of modern philosophy and theology, were both anti-Semitic. Going back further, Martin Luther recommended burning Jews out of their homes, and then exiling and slaying them (in *On the Jews and their Lies*). Anti-Semitism is historically as integral a part of Christian culture as Bible reading or missionary endeavor.

We've looked at two episodes in the sixteenth and twentieth centuries. But you can find similar ones in every century. No other religion has colonized such large areas of the globe quite so brutally, with the possible exception of its monotheistic rival, Islam. No religion has so consistently persecuted a minority faith (the Jews) for such a long period.

Of course there's another side to the argument. For every Hitler there's a Bonhoeffer, or a Mother Teresa. But can one individual helping thousands undo the damage of another murdering millions? It's not the individual sins that are a problem, historically speaking, it's the collective ones generated by the delusion that my creed or country is better than yours. The question is not whether Hitler was "evil," it's why large numbers of Christians supported him, and why the Church has been happy with that way of thinking for two millennia.

Every good side has its dark side, too. It's easy to point to compassionate Christian individuals who achieved much to benefit society. In nineteenth-century England, for instance, William Wilberforce campaigned to end slavery and child labor. But then you can also ask why the 80 or so Christian generations before him thought that slavery was part of God's divine plan for society, and why it was accepted throughout the Old and New Testaments. The Franciscans cared for the poor in the same way as Mother

Teresa, but they also led the way in conjuring up hysteria against the Jews and other minorities. The Dominicans produced great learning and works of art and churches, but they were also involved in setting up the Papal Inquisition, a strong candidate for the most evil institution known to humankind. The papal document that launched the Inquisition, the *Malleus Maleficarum*, "Hammer of Witches," is up there with *Mein Kampf*.

And the Protestant historical tradition is little better. At the height of John Calvin's period of power in sixteenth-century Geneva, heretical prisoners were handcuffed together to prevent husbands killing themselves rather than face the brutal tortures they had seen inflicted on their wives and children. Over the next few hundred years, Protestants burned witches at the stake, numbers reaching to the tens or even hundreds of thousands.

Is this unfair on Christianity? It's not difficult to point the finger at other religions and show how badly they've behaved, and still do. Buddhist kingdoms have fought amongst themselves as viciously as any others, though it has to be said that none ever set out on a crusade in the name of Buddha. There's little record of Buddhists persecuting other religions; the same is true of Taoists. In Islamic tradition, Mohammed himself led dozens of military campaigns, but then this is a religion of obedience and justice rather than love. Hindus have their fair share of barbarity toward their fellow believers, institutionalized in the caste system with its 3,000 levels of status. But they don't generally try to convert people. To the Hindu all religion is ultimately the same and all end in the same identity of Being. It's true that most religions persecute Christians today to some degree or other, often more so now than in the past. Fundamentalism in all faiths is on the rise everywhere. In some cases it may be a reaction against the dominance of the Christian West. But whatever the ups and downs over the centuries, whatever the blame and counter-blame, at the beginning of the twenty-first century it's hard for Christians to claim any kind of moral superiority for their religion.

It seems unlikely that the next century will be much different from the last. On a smaller scale, many, not all, of the current trouble spots involve Christians: Protestant Unionists against Catholics in Northern Ireland; Orthodox Serbs against Muslims in former Yugoslavia, and Christian Maronites in Lebanon against Muslims. One of the most dynamic revivals of the twentieth century happened in East Africa, concentrated in Ruanda, a country with one of the highest proportion of churchgoers to non-churchgoers in the world. Yet in 1994 these Christians were egged on by their priests to carry out the worst genocide since World War II with over three-quarters of a million people murdered. Maybe with the increase in fundamentalism things will get worse.

Christianity is no worse than the other religions, and of course there have been many outstanding Christian individuals. Clearly much of the religious conflict between Christian sects and between Christians and members of other faiths has more to do with tribal hatreds than with religious beliefs. Maybe this chapter is too bleak, and in retrospect the Western liberal democracies of today will be seen as a golden age. Or maybe this will be seen as the worst of periods, the time when we built up our nuclear arsenals (in which case, if we use them, we may never be around to know). It's too early to make judgements. But from an historical perspective, you can't argue that Christianity is "better." It doesn't seem to raise people above the average level of quarrelsome behavior. But it should. It's the only religion that claims to be both one of love and of equal relevance for everyone. For most of the last 1,000 years Christians have been the overwhelming majority of the indigenous population in the countries where they've lived, with every opportunity to put into practice the teachings of their founder and to be "the light of the world. A city that is set on a hill." Logically, after two millennia of practice, history should show a steadily increasing gap between the morality of Christian countries and their pagan neighbors. It hasn't happened. The Church hasn't even shown the way. This is why there seems to be no necessary connection between the "Church" and "God."

Nor, as the next chapter suggests, does there seem to be any necessary connection between Christians and God. If heaven exists, perhaps Christians are in a minority there. If you think back through the last 10,000 years or so and figure Christians as a percentage of the total population, what number would you get to: 1 in 100?

13 COMPARING GODS

"If Christ were here now there is one thing he would not be –
a Christian."

MARK TWAIN

If you don't think of yourself as a Christian believer you might
want to skip the next three chapters. If you are, you're probably
thinking: "All this historical stuff in the last couple of chapters is all
well and good, but irrelevant. Maybe these people thought of
themselves as Christians, but maybe they weren't. What counts for
me is my experience of Christ. We may not live up to what he asks
of us, but it's true for me. You can't know what I'm talking about if
you don't believe. We live by faith, not knowledge."

It's not the point here to sell short the experience of God that
Christians have. For hundreds of millions it's the very foundation
of their lives. God is as real to them as anything else. Their faith,
expressed in prayer, studying Scripture, meditation, worship, service, is part of the way they think and act through the day. It's who
they are. It supports them in times of crisis, particularly illness and
death in the family.

It's more than this too. It's not just a vague feeling of wellbeing,
of assurance, of being loved and rewarded by a heavenly Father. It's
the magic moments of answered prayer, of "words of knowledge,"
of ecstatic praise. It's the times when your whole being is caught
up in worship, when the veil between this world and the next,
between your self and God, splits. The very experience of time,
space and nature is changed by it. Faith brings miraculous healing,
innermost thoughts are opened, childhood problems come to light
and are cleared away, demons are exorcized. The experience of the
presence of God is the single defining point around which the
world turns. Work, money, relationships, all are transformed in the
light of Jesus.

So, of course, the response to your objection is, yes. Believing in God in the traditional Christian way can work for the individual. Many people have been changed for the better through a commitment to Christ. They're happier, more stable and responsible members of society as a result. Christians do huge amounts of good work in helping others as an outcome of the way they believe God has helped them.

But all this applies to Buddhists and Muslims, to believers in all religions and none. Here's a sample description of a religious "turning-point" from a previously published book, by an English author we're publishing next year:

"At around 6pm on a calm, sun-kissed evening, I had the most profound spiritual experience. For what was probably only 20 seconds – although it felt like forever – I was engulfed in a brilliant white light which I could only describe as pure spirit. All sense of the world dissolved, including my body. As this light filled my consciousness, I was aware of being at its source, whose presence was both familiar and tremendously beautiful. In this subtle encounter I felt a soundless voice convey three things, for which these words are totally inadequate – 'Welcome home, your search is over' and, 'I love you.' There was an overwhelming feeling of meeting my oldest and dearest friend after a thousand years apart. I can never forget the intensity of the love that poured into my being. This experience altered the course of my life." (Mike George, *Discover Inner Peace*)

There are thousands of similar accounts in print. Often, maybe with the alteration of a few words, it's hard to tell in which religious tradition the experience takes place. This particular one is in the Hindu tradition. Is this experience inferior to that of a Christian? Or a Muslim? How can you know? Isn't it more spiritual pride than discernment to say it is?

Christians have no monopoly on goodness, insight or God. Believing otherwise can lead to pride and arrogance, however unconscious. It is hard to believe you are "chosen" by the almighty God of the universe and not feel a little special, that you are right and others wrong. And some Christians do not find that their faith makes their lives better. Their problems don't go away. They may be magnified rather than cured. Being a Christian can bring extra stress and breakdown. Driven personalities before conversion often remain so afterwards. Some become leaders and spread their problems around. With membership in overall slow decline some react by becoming more authoritarian. Many succumb to revivalist or millennial tendencies – they raise the stakes. Double the emotion. Revival or the second coming are around the corner. All the little problems and compromises of life get caught up in a dynamic vision of complete renewal or change, in turn creating a further multitude of little problems when the world disobligingly carries on much as before.

On the personal level the evidence one way or another is anecdotal. Some Christians seem very impressive. You can want what they have, and be persuaded into faith. Others are not, they can persuade you out of it. It depends on whom you meet. The same goes for other religions. I've known senior people in Christian organizations who have cheated on their partners, beaten their wives (they're mostly men), stolen, recklessly flouted company law, been convicted for child abuse and pedophilia. But mine is too small a sample to draw conclusions from. There have been very few surveys attempting to analyze changes in behavior after people have become Christians. In a 1991 Roper poll in the USA 4% of born-again Christians said they had driven whilst drunk before conversion and 12% had done so after conversion; 5% had used drugs before conversion and 9% after; 2% had illicit sex before they were Christians as opposed to 5% afterwards. There have been several attempts at analyzing comparable divorce rates in the USA, which all tend to suggest that Christians divorce more frequently than non-Christians – 27% for the born-again, 21% for others,

24% for atheists. You can't put much weight on these figures (maybe, for instance, more Christians get divorced because more of them get married?) but there seems little evidence to point the other way. Atheists live as rich and satisfying and moral lives as believers. In the statistics of suicide and depression there's no difference between them.

At the personal level, let's face it, people aren't stupid. If there were any clear evidence that being a Christian really made people noticeably better, happier, healthier, or more fulfilled, or that God answered the prayers of Christians rather than those of other faiths or of no faith at all, the churches would be full to the rafters. Everyone would be a Christian.

The same is true of organizations. Anyone who's moved from working in a secular to a Christian organization will understand the sudden shock that comes from the realization that these Christians are no better than a comparable group anywhere else. And that "no better" refers to the ordinary things like rubbing along happily and getting a job done, not the difficult stuff like really making a difference to the planet. Organizations established to promote peace or ecumenical relations can have the most damaging office politics. Those devoted to relieving poverty can have the largest bureaucracies and the most meetings. Those devoted to nourishing the spirit and evangelizing souls seem to need headquarters in large mansions in the world's most expensive real-estate areas. Individuals who can't sustain relationships of their own set up groups to explore deeper ones. The celibate priestly hierarchy of the Roman Catholic Church seems designed to encourage perverted sexuality. There is nothing unique about the Christian Church in this respect: it happens in all communities, secular and religious (Buddhists suffer scandals in their male priesthood). There are similar New Age counselors, therapists, and the seekers after truth who keep searching for the ultimate spiritual trip but who can't sustain a stable relationship. (Never take advice on sex or relationships from someone who enjoys neither).

In summary, if you imagine there's a more perfect religious experience, a better group of people, waiting for you around the corner, forget it. Stay where you are. Charismatics, conservative Catholics, evangelicals, hermits, Christians who combine their beliefs with Hindu practices or Buddhist meditation, teachers of Celtic wisdom, practicing Buddhists, crystal worshipers, followers of Hindu gurus, neo-pagans, humanists, whoever, there's little difference between them. Those you expect much from can deliver the least, and the most unpromising can be the greatest pleasure to deal with.

Why doesn't being a Christian help more? Maybe the devil attacks Christians harder. But the more obvious reason is that this experience of faith doesn't in itself tell you how to live. Christianity in this sense began as one of the least "thought-through" religions. It begins with a handicap. Jesus had one year of ministry (if you follow Matthew, Mark and Luke), or maybe three (if you follow John). By comparison, Muhammad had over 20 years between his revelation and his death. Buddha had 45 years. Confucius had maybe 50. They had more time to develop their teaching, try it out, pass it on to their disciples, to organize their succession. Jesus was a relative youngster. Maybe if he had lived longer he would have passed on his ideas more coherently and in greater detail. "Love your enemy" doesn't amount to practical advice. In contrast Muhammad gave Islam a blueprint for society as well as a religion. Muslims know that they *must* give to the poor: *Zakat*, the giving of alms, is one of the five pillars of the faith. Similarly Buddhists know they *must* practice non-violence, or they slip down the karma slope. Jains *must* be vegetarian, to be otherwise would be cannibalism. These are defining characteristics. In contrast Christians can give a lot to the poor or nothing. Join the army or not. Eat meat or not.

This is one reason why Christians argue over so many issues so intently – there are few clear guidelines. And of course it's not that rules necessarily make you better either, but they do make for some consistency. So when you begin to doubt the creeds that the Church laid down in the centuries following the death of Christ there is less to hold you, which is maybe one reason why Islam, for example, has been so much less affected by secularism than Christianity.

But the more basic reason is that no religion or experience of faith in itself makes you a better person. It can help, but that's your decision, what you do for yourself. Individuals can better themselves, develop maturity, improve relationships, come close to God through becoming Christian, or Muslim, or Buddhist, or by leaving formal belief behind. The "God-spot" in your brain is like a spot for music, or sport, or logic. It doesn't improve your character, any more than being a concert pianist does. Nor does it necessarily make you happier. Psychologists say that happiness is mainly a question of personality. Individuals who can manage stable relationships are in general happier than those who cannot. Those who can live without unreasonable expectations don't get disappointed when they're not met.

Religions are all essentially trying to do the same thing. They try to explain why the world is the way it is, and how we can become one with it again. They give different remedies because they describe the world from different perspectives, and the remedies change within each religion as fashions and knowledge change. But they all describe our sense of separation. At the heart of each solution is knowing and being yourself, reconciling your inner being with the universal law, with God or with a way of life described as Dharma, or Torah, or Tao, or whatever.

The superstructure of belief shifts to accommodate changing perceptions. The sense of the divine spirit is variously incarnated in animals, man, prophets, god-men, God, in "non-being." The many spirits of the native religions, for example, still exist in monotheism but are redefined as demons and angels, saints and trinities. The feeling of where divine reality lies moves from nature, to the heavens, to our own hearts. So long as it relates to where we are, it works. Believing in God can change your life for the better. So can losing belief in God. Because for everything that a religion gets right, it tends to get something else wrong. That's why they need to keep changing, or they die. To try keeping definitions intact is like the Amish trying to halt history in the seventeenth century.

So which Christian beliefs now hinder rather than help a belief in God?

14 A GODLY BELIEF

"If human villainy and human life shall wax in due proportion, if the son shall always grow in wickedness past his father, the gods must add another world to this that all the sinners may have space enough."

EURIPIDES

Here's an example of a belief that needs to go. The Church today defines the human condition as one of original sin. Adam and Eve disobeyed God in the Garden of Eden, and as a result of their rebellion we are all in a state of sin, or separation from God, prone to suffering and evil. The Christian definition of humankind is that it is "fallen."

Leaving aside for the moment how this stacks up against the definition that other religions provide of the human condition, is it "true" to Christianity itself? You don't find the words "original sin" in the Bible. It's a later interpretation of the Garden of Eden story. Even if you take that story literally the first reference to "sin" doesn't come till Genesis chapter 4, when Cain kills Abel. The story doesn't say Adam represents all of us, or that there is a new Adam (Jesus) to come who will redeem humankind. The Jews, whose story it is, see Genesis as a hymn to the greatness and goodness of God, not part of salvation history. The story is not referred to again in the Old Testament.

Of course the Hebrews had a concept of sin, but this was based more on the wrongdoing of generations and collective disloyalty to their deity than on the misdeeds of an individual. All through the pages of the Old Testament we read of horrible acts committed by the patriarchs, but there's little sense of condemnation in the text. The very idea of the individual alone, rather than the family or tribe, having responsibility for his or her actions, doesn't seem to appear in the Bible till around the sixth century BC with Ezekiel (Ezekiel 18:2-4, 20).

Jesus himself never mentions original sin, which is strange if the whole purpose of his life was to redeem humankind from it. He's happier in the company of children than priests. Indeed he said you have to become like a child to enter the kingdom of God (Luke 18:17). He seems to go out of his way to affirm people as good rather than bad. The people he condemns are the religious leaders who enjoy saying the opposite.

The idea of "original sin" first appears, obliquely, in the letters of Paul, who talks of "one man's disobedience" (Romans 5:19). He elevates this into an event of universal significance to provide a reason for the crucifixion and resurrection: "as by one man [Adam] sin entered into the world" (Romans 5:12).

The full doctrine of original sin was developed several centuries later by Augustine, an individual, like Paul, who was obsessed with sins of the flesh. For him Adam and Eve actually existed, they were the first two people, and they passed on their catastrophic sin to everyone else through the act of sex. Jesus escaped from this cycle of sin because he was born of a virgin, so his was the only possible sacrifice that could be made to God that would be acceptable – the unblemished lamb.

But there's an alternative Christian viewpoint. Many of Augustine's Christian contemporaries disagreed with him. His main opponent, Pelagius (from Britain), believed that people are born innocent. We later choose to sin, but can be good if we try. He quoted the Gospels to support his argument. It's not just a few who are saved, but everyone (John 1:17; 12:31-32; Mark 3:28; 1 Corinthians 15:21-22; Romans 5:18; 11:32; 1 John 2:1-2).

Augustine vigorously attacked Pelagius, who was tried three times for heresy, and acquitted on each occasion. Augustine eventually persuaded the Emperor Honorius to pressurize Pope Zosimus to excommunicate his opponent. Augustine was made a saint, and the writings of Pelagius were condemned. But was Augustine right? Original sin sits oddly with the idea of a good

God in whose image we are made. When in the last few million years of evolution did this original sin suddenly blight us? Perhaps more to the point, no one *believes* this any more. I've never met a parent who thought their babies were evil at birth. It's possible they may grow up that way, and we pray not. But we're all a mix of good and bad.

If you think your life is desperate, if you can't control your appetites, if you're miserable, you may feel that you're in a state of "original sin." In that case, you'll feel better if you are told you can enter into a state of grace. But it is Christianity that generated that definition of sin in the first place. There is no sin in nature, it just is. The lion doesn't eat lambs because it's sinful, but because it can't chew grass. There is no "perfect" creation to fall from because it is constantly evolving. Original sin is one of many possible, partial descriptions made to explain what we are and how we feel and behave. The trouble for orthodox Christianity is that if you say humankind is not irredeemably evil then you don't need a divine Redeemer (Jesus) to be sacrificed on the cross. Fundamentalists are right in that once you start to pull the thread it all unravels. Original sin, the virgin birth, the resurrection, are all of a piece.

Even today there are many variations within Christianity on the theme of original sin, and how to be redeemed from it – from Calvinists at one extreme to Quakers at the other. Each group sees their interpretation as obviously "true." Each has re-stitched the cloth that was painfully woven together over many centuries as the early Church worked out how to put labels on individual experiences of God.

If you repeat new understanding often enough it is laid down as a pattern in the brain to be found more readily again. Tell yourself over and over again that you're a sinner and you begin to believe it. Practice ritual confession and it becomes necessary for your mental health. Over time new insight becomes tradition, part of the way the community thinks. Tradition then becomes expectation.

Whatever it is that you see you can only interpret it in the expected way. So Catholics see the miraculous in statues weeping blood. Eastern Orthodox, with their tradition of disallowing statues, see it in stigmata, the imprint of Christ's suffering on the flesh. Protestants see it in the opportune arrival of cash; Hindus in the materializing of holy ash or jewelry. And so on. There's never real, objective evidence. The intensity of the expectation creates at least the belief of change if not the reality.

The idea of original sin has its usefulness. It encourages you to search your heart, see what you're capable of, to understand the evil to which you can sink. All religions have these steps which force you to see your self anew and to renounce it. Hinduism, for instance, describes our condition as a state of impermanence rather than sin. Not only are we insignificant, our very self is a fiction. There is no "I." We are part of the flow of creation. In reading and meditating on the sacred scriptures we recognize this impermanence, transcend the self and come to an understanding of what we are, why we are here, how we should act. If you've been selfish you can restore yourself to harmony with the cosmic order by offering everything up in a spirit of sacrifice. You then become one with the Eternal Reality and feel inner calm. It's described in the *Upanishads* as the "turning point in the seat of consciousness." The *Upanishads*, written around the time of the Buddha, led to the religion of the Brahmins. Brahmin is the inner reality of all things, to be known by the renunciation of action and desire. There is no self, we are part of everything.

> *"He who sees Me everywhere, and sees*
> *everything in Me, I am not lost to*
> *him, nor is he lost to me."*
> BHAGAVAD-GITA

This experience is similar to the new birth that Jesus describes. But, and here's the main difference with the Christian approach, the Brahmins teach that basically people are good, a teaching which is not just good for you psychologically, but makes sense metaphysically. If reality is truth and goodness, then lies and evil must be the illusion. Good must triumph. If, on the contrary, you believe that people are intrinsically evil, and you expect that of them, you're likely to get what you look for.

Buddhism takes the illusion of "self" even further. It developed as the "Middle Way" of the eight-fold path. There were two strands of teaching in Hinduism, reflected in every society down the ages. One was that a person's true self is eternal, and to be realized through asceticism and denial. The other was a more nihilist position that everything is impermanent and random, and the only happiness to be found is in sensual pleasure. Buddhism answered this by saying that we don't have a soul, as that implies something fixed, but we all have "Buddha nature" (as do all living things). We are not only impermanent, our true nature is *anatta*, no-self. We are made up of our choices, which change us and influence our future. Realizing this can lead us to enlightenment. This enlightenment can happen suddenly, or through a long process of deepening awareness.

Similarly in Taoist China if you've been a prodigal son and strayed from the right path, you can return to the fold by reconciliation with your family and ancestors. All these beliefs work for the people who think in those ways.

So free yourself from the idea that you have some kind of core of evil. It's not part of the teaching of the Bible, or of Jesus. Let's start with the idea that creation is good, that life is an incredible gift. Recognizing it and being thankful for it is the start of the road to happiness and wisdom. We are all in need of forgiveness and grace. But this is a virtuous circle between ourselves, our neighbors and God. Not a one track line between God and us. The point of believing in God is to expand the area of goodness in your life and the world, not diminish it.

15 WHY NOT TO BELIEVE IN GODS

"If God did not exist he would have to be invented."

VOLTAIRE

But perhaps there is no God at all. At the far right end of the line we've been traveling along in the UK (see chapter 3) we come to the atheists. They (and the humanists) say there is no God, nor any "Buddha nature" within each of us. And there is no existence apart from the one we have here on earth; anything beyond that is all imagined, in the head. Why should human life have "meaning," any more than a tree has meaning? Spiritual experiences (undeniable) are simply a part of our general psychology. They are a by-product of our ability to think rationally, to look for cause and effect. If we throw a stone, we see the splash. So if we see lightning, we invent a god who must be throwing it. Now that we've grown up we know better than this, and our religious genes are no more relevant than the male nipple.

Non-believers say that religion is all an illusion. We know how easy it is to deceive ourselves. We can believe we have skills that we haven't. We fall in love, think it's forever, and fall out again. We believe prayers are answered even though most are not, and though we know that on the law of averages some will be. We fantasize. On the scale from coma to ecstasy our minds operate at many levels simultaneously: we are often not conscious of what we are doing or thinking. So how certain are we of our "belief experience" that we can claim it as true, as the one and only God speaking to us? The intense feelings that religious experience can generate are a credit to the hormones in our bodies and the neurons in our brains, not because there is an external "spirit."

Any belief demands at some level a willing suspension of reason, a degree of wish fulfillment. Believers recognize this. Even John Wesley asked his mentor: "How can [I] preach to others, who

[have] not faith [myself]?" The answer: "Preach faith *till* you have it; and then, *because* you have it, you *will* preach faith" (*Journal* March 5, 1738). So how can we be certain enough of our faith to claim that most other people in the world are deluding themselves? Certain enough to go to war? To torture believers of a different faith? To cut the throat of our own child, believing that God is telling us to? This is what Abraham attempted to do, according to the Old Testament. Do we really believe that God was telling him to do this? If he tried it today we'd lock him up and throw away the key. Where's the line here between faith and madness? It's easily crossed. We look back at the witch trials of Puritan England and wonder how they could have happened. Then in the eighties there was a craze in the USA (which spread to Scotland) in which thousands of parents were accused of satanic ritual abuse, largely by evangelical Christians believing, totally unjustly, that they were uncovering the devil's work. The same kind of thing happened in the nineties with "recovered memory syndrome."

Maybe atheism represents a huge step forward in the development of humankind, being the ability to look at the world straight and true for the first time, without projecting on to it our fears and hopes. Believers point to the miraculous power of prayer, the ministry of healing, changed lives. But these are subjective matters, not "provable." Atheists will say these claims support their argument. After all, the success rate of faith healing, for example, is roughly 10%, no more than might be explained by natural remission and placebo effects. The odds of a miraculous cure at Lourdes are still less. The Roman Catholic Church has accepted about 65 healing claims as genuine though 150 million or so people have visited the shrine over the last century and a half. In any case, the divide between miraculous and natural is often artificial. It's known that the mind can cause disease, even fatal ones, and so can also cure itself. Belief in a cure sometimes makes it happen. This is true of religions everywhere. Faith-healing has been practiced in every society since time immemorial. Historically it's played a low-key role in Christianity compared to other religions, particularly in the East, where the body is more closely integrated with the mind and spirit.

Atheists could put the argument for their views much better than this. But they don't need to argue. It's not up to them to dis-prove the existence of a God they don't believe in, can't see any evidence for, and don't feel the absence of. Believers, if they want to argue, need to show some grounds for belief. The argument from revelation is the weakest – "Believe in God because God tells us to." The atheist only has to point to all the conflicting revela-tions to show the pointlessness of that. The argument from experience is no better – "Believe in God because He makes me happy/well," whatever. But what's candy for one person is poison to another.

At this level, atheism makes sense. Any beliefs we have can be seen as constructs of our imagination and our culture. But then is this a bad thing? We need the help of our imagination to get through the day as best we can, as enjoyably as we can. We're not wholly rational beings. But then the universe doesn't seem to be entirely rational either. Maybe in matching an irrational self with an irrational world we can reach a deeper level of reality, which we call God.

PART 3

PROVING GOD

16 THE UNCERTAIN LIFE

"In the beginning there was no death then, nor yet deathlessness.
Of night or day, there was not yet any sign.
The One breathed without breath, by its own impulse.
Other than that there was nothing else at all."

RIG VEDA

Belief in God survives the advance of science, the divisions amongst believers, the crimes they commit. Why do people turn to Him?

Sometimes it's the young, around the time they learn to stand apart from their parents and look at the world by themselves. They don't always like what they see and can get carried away by the idealism of saving the world or themselves. They can be uncertain in their first steps, and turn to religion like to a new home. But the need for a religious faith hits older people as well. Perhaps it's because there's more stuff to worry about. You get ill, or depressed, or are working too hard, or have been made redundant, or are fending off alcoholism, or drugs, or there's someone in your family or circle of friends that is. Or maybe everything's going fine, but there's a larger area of life that you're responsible for as your parents get older. You can begin to see where your boundaries are, how many dreams you might not reach, and wonder if that's going to be all there is. Or perhaps you're surging on and life is still opening out in front, but you're driven still further by curiosity, or desire, or discontent. That poster of a Pacific island, that nice house in the country, that happy-looking family – they make you think that there could be a better way of living around the corner.

We always want to know what comes next, and hope it will turn our lives into something better. In relationships when we're single we worry about finding a partner. When we're settled (hopefully) in a stable relationship we're worried about children.

When we have children we're worried about their future. When we've planned that, we worry about their happiness. And we worry in the same way about money, about promotion.

But these are never-ending spirals of relative non-achievement. If we're measuring success there's always someone higher up the ladder to be chasing. And even if we've got what we want, can we really enjoy it when there are beggars on the street and most of the world can't get a drink of clean water?

When we've got to a reasonable level of success, if we're lucky enough to recognize it, we can still worry about whether that's all there is to worry about. And even if we're not the anxious kind we still need to make sense of life beyond the daily business of making a living, falling in and out of love, beyond our little defeats and triumphs. There's occasional sheer delight at the astonishing fact of life. There are moments of inspiration or insight, and gratitude at being loved. We have twinges of transcendence, through nature, or music, or literature, or meditation, or sex. Our "God-spot" may not be strong, but at times we all feel the pull of something else, something "out there," that we accept gratefully.

Then, as we get older, what seemed important seems less so, and we wonder, "Was that the point?" The brute facts of life and death loom larger. At births or christenings there's the optimism of new life to carry us forward. Maybe the young ones will be able to work it out even if we can't, and anyway, they've got time. But the scythe swings closer – grandparents, parents, we're next in line. When someone we know dies, we ask: What's a funeral for? Is it a celebration of a life lived or a passage to the next world? Do people just live on in memories? What kind of encouragement do we offer the family? Is there some sense in which the individual life carries on? Are we happy in what we believe? Can we see life as a whole, including its ending? It's difficult to handle the important bits of life without religion.

The best kind of religion, though, is not the type that proceeds from needs. These can be prompters, but they can also lead to a religion that's a kind of addictive pain-relief. We assume that if these pills have helped us, they'll work for everyone. But some people need different remedies, or don't need pills at all. A surer path in religion seems to be that of "recognition." This is the awareness of ourselves as spiritual as much as material, of the world reflecting God in all things, at all moments, rather than in occasional highs. The best religious teachers all seem to say that an awareness of ourselves and the world as spirit, looking to what we can become rather than back to what we have come from, is one that can be cultivated. Most of the time we are too consumed by the concerns of the self and the business of living to be aware of it. But by following certain practices – which can be Christian, but need not be – we can enlarge the area of spirit in our lives, and this spills over into a love for others.

This "works," or we would have given up on it thousands of years ago. In itself, that is not proof that it is true. It doesn't seem to improve the odds on God existing. But maybe all belief reflects an awareness of a greater consciousness than our own, which we interpret according to our culture and temperament. Maybe matter can organize itself into systems of greater complexity that we call "spirit." Or maybe the "spirit" came first, and organized itself into matter. Perhaps consciousness and the capacity for religious experience are just two manifestations of this. The theologians may have little to say, but perhaps the scientists exploring the edges of what we know about space, time, matter, and our own brains have taken their place.

17 THE NATURE OF EXPERIENCE

"Do we, holding that the gods exist,
deceive ourselves with unsubstantial dreams
and lies, while random careless chance and change
alone control the world?"

EURIPIDES

The idea that you can "prove" the existence of God died in the eighteenth century with the philosopher Kant. No serious thinker has attempted to do so since. Today there are several main perspectives on the Christian God that exist as possibilities. One is that of conservative believers (also held by Jews, Muslims and many others) that God exists "out there," and we are His creation. Another is the more mystical tradition that God exists "in here," but is still "real." A third, held by some liberals and humanists, is that God exists as an idea we've created, but it's a useful idea and worth working with rather than against. At the very least people who live in hope tend to live longer and lead happier lives, whatever their religion. A fourth, that of atheists, is that God only exists as an idea and we're best ditching it. There's another approach combining elements of these that has been put forward in Europe since at least the seventeenth century, though it's more commonly linked to Eastern religions today. This is that God is both an external reality and a human creation. The distinction is an artificial one. Not only is what we create in our heads real but everything material is "created" by a process to which we give the name God. We are part of the process. We don't originate it, nor are we its product.

This is not a belief that depends on historical events. In this respect it has more of a philosophical flavor. Schopenhauer probably expressed it best in the nineteenth century. Following Kant he divided reality into what could be experienced and what could not. We can't understand reality without experiencing it, so "independent reality" remains a closed book. Independent reality is "will," though not in any personal sense. The nearest we come to it is in exercising choice ourselves. During the course of Schopenhauer's life some of the major Hindu and Buddhist texts were published in translation in Europe for the first time, and he discovered that these ancient traditions had come to similar conclusions.

The question of how we "see" reality, and what it is, is a difficult one. To the non-believer it's obvious that God doesn't exist. To the Hindu or Christian it's obvious that He does. At first sight atheism makes sense. You can't prove "God," there's no "evidence," so why bother? Isn't belief just a fault in our wiring? The Christian might retaliate that you can't "prove" anything that matters. Isn't living more important than logic?

Let's start with the idea that atheism is 100% right, and see if we can find some better odds.

The divide between the world and the self is not clear-cut. For babies it doesn't exist. Young children believe that objects can be moved by their thoughts, that they have invisible friends. Even as we get older we find it difficult to sort out the signals in our heads, unlike animals that don't have to think about them. As many as one out of every four people suffer from mental illness at some time. With one out of ten it gets more serious and can turn into schizophrenia, which mixes up signals between the world inside the head and the world outside. A smaller number lose all sense of the distinction, and live in their projection of what is real. Or worse, they can have split-consciousness or multiple personalities, believing different things are real at different times. Those who work in medicine know that the brain can believe anything. The brain can override what is obvious to the eyes.

Is religion simply a reflection of our inability to see the world straight? We're animals who, over millions of years, have developed in ways that improve our chances of survival. A part of our brain has acquired the ability to question and think. But even the thinking part is not really designed to analyze the world, but to interpret it. We see what our brain chooses to see. This isn't our choice alone, but one we've inherited over thousands of generations. When adults who are blind from birth recover their sight they don't see trees, houses, people, but a confusing jumble. Sorting these out into pictures that make sense is a process they learn.

Most of us are fortunate enough not to suffer serious mental or physical illness. As we age and "learn" we exercise control over our surroundings by reading significance into what we see. We name things, and question their purpose. Is it a piece of wood? Shall we use it for a stick? For making a fire? For building a table? For getting that snake shape out of it? For making an altar? We build up layers of meaning, making symbols, images, imagining possibilities. Humankind has learnt these patterns over millions of years. This has turned into our cumulative wisdom, instinctive and cultural. Out of it we create art, music, religion, politics, everything that makes us what we are. The "self" doesn't figure all this out on its own. It can't be understood by a single brain, in isolation. The "self" is created out of our collective definitions of what is significant. Maybe the idea of God that each of us has is an illusion generated by our collective needs.

But in the process of creating our selves, do we not create something real? Even if we can trace the neural patterns of "love" firing in the brain from cell to cell, isn't love more than chemical brain activity? In the process of creating or perceiving God, does not the same apply? Isn't our experience of the world as one of meaning as fundamental as our experience of it as material?

Why still talk about God at all? Because most of us feel there is something ultimately real or worthwhile. Religions are the different ways in which we emotionally, intellectually, physically relate to this feeling of reality. They are a kind of language we have spent a million years developing to help us talk in the broadest sense about the important things in life, the ones we can't explain or measure, the ones that aren't rational, but are still true – beauty, happiness, wrong, evil, love, transcendence. These are steps on the ladder of self-awareness, ascending from reptiles, through mammals, through human beings, to God. No one lives as if these intangible qualities didn't exist. Our understanding of them is imperfect, our attempts to describe them and pass them on (religion) worse. But each attempt is worth something, and better than not trying at all. The whole is more than the sum of its parts. The attempts make a road map of the different journeys we're on. They provide a quest to keep us stepping forward. Religion turns this quest into a story, called a myth.

A myth, like the Christian story of God, is our first best guess. It condenses truth down to essentials which legends then elaborate. No religion survives for 2,000 years if it hasn't got a story that helps us along. Equally, to say that one story alone is true, damages the whole idea of belief. When confronted with the infallible *Declaration Dominus Jesus* of 2000 that declares that the Roman Catholic Church is the "only instrument for the salvation of all humanity," you don't know whether to laugh or cry. Such claims, apart from being highly offensive to victims of the "religion of love," presuppose that 99% of belief down the ages has been a great mistake. If Christians then doubt the truth of their own 1%, they can be inclined to disbelieve everything, turning to ideologies of cruelty and despair. The twin bastard offspring of Christianity that have made the twentieth century a nightmare for so many – Communism and Fascism – are a product of this reaction against Christianity.

That's all by way of clearing some ground. Our experience of God is an individual one, albeit determined by the interaction of our culture, our background, right down to our genes. No one can disentangle this mess and look at it objectively. Maybe religion is just an evolutionary oddity, which compensates for the feeling of separation that came with self-awareness. Maybe it's like the tail at the end of our spine that we haven't quite got rid of. If so should we try and cut it off, or cherish it? Or is there something else? Is that sky God or Mother or Father or Great Spirit, or whatever it is we call it, actually out there somewhere?

18 BELIEVING IN AN AFTER-LIFE

*"Life is a surprise. I do not see why death should not be
an even greater one."*

VLADIMIR NABOKOV

Let's take one belief as a test case, to see if the lines of different
religions and science might ever converge. The most powerful religious belief over millennia has been the conviction that we don't
die, that our consciousness survives death. Today we still have this
lingering belief, or hope, that it's true, though teaching on heaven
and hell seems to have been dropped even in the churches. Many
though say its nonsense. This life is all we have, and all that counts.

Conviction and clarity about life after death varies in different
religions over time. At one end of the spectrum you have the
Egyptian civilization, the society that has invested most in the idea
of an after-life. The Egyptians believed in an immortal soul that
rose upwards to the sky and the sun. This was common in the early
farming civilizations along the Tigris and Euphrates Rivers, and in
Central America. The idea of judgement first comes in their Book
of the Dead from the second millennium BC. Preparing for the
after-life swallowed up a good proportion of the country's GNP.
Forget their palaces, it is their tombs that are simply extraordinary,
the greatest buildings on earth. The Great Pyramid of Gizah alone
used up more stone nearly 5,000 years ago than all the churches in
England ever built A single pharaoh invested more in his next
journey than 800 English generations in theirs. Millions of blocks
weighing two and a half tons each, were laid to a tolerance of one
hundredth of an inch, the walls being aligned by astronomical
observations for accuracy. We still struggle to work out how they
did it with the tools available. They may have been utterly mistak-
en about life after death, but they certainly knew how to take it
seriously.

Near the other end of the scale you have a tribe like the Hebrews. They didn't have much of a theology of life after death at all. They had a sense of heaven a few hundred feet up in the air, but it was not a place people went to as a reward for a good life, more part of a cosmology where the gods lived. There was no heaven or hell for people; they remained as shadows in the under-world, Sheol, where they were buried. It's a similar place to the Greek Hades or the Norse underworld ruled by the goddess Hel, from which we get our "hell" (the word that is used in some mod-ern translations for several different ideas in the Old Testament, blurring their meaning). In Ezekiel 31:14 all people are "delivered unto death, to the nether parts of the earth." "Let us eat and drink; for tomorrow we die," writes Isaiah (Isaiah 22:13). David says to his son Solomon, "I go the way of all the earth" (1 Kings 2:1-2).

A few outstanding individuals were treated specially, like Elijah who rode up in a chariot to join the gods in the sky. But even key biblical figures like Samuel are in Sheol. There's a spooky episode in 1 Samuel 28. Saul is facing a confrontation with the army of the Philistines, allied with the traitor David. When he can't get an answer from God "neither by dreams, nor by Urim, nor by prophets" he goes to the Witch of Endor and asks her to raise the dead Samuel from under the ground, which she does. Samuel complains about being disturbed but answers Saul's questions. The Old Testament world of life after death is one of grey and dispirit-ing shadows.

For the Hebrews, as we've already seen, there was no original sin, so no redemption from it was necessary. There was no judge-ment of the dead. There was nothing basically wrong with the world. All the rewards were in this life. Blessings for the Hebrew patriarchs are counted by the number of years you've lived, the number of goats and children and servants you've collected or stolen. It's also why two major themes of the psalms are unfairness and desertion by God. The psalmist demands and pleads for justice now. There is no sense of justice to come later, now is all there is. "For in death there is no remembrance of thee: in the grave [Sheol] who shall give thee thanks?" (Psalm 6:5). It's the world of the American evangelists today who count their success in the size of the audience or in dollars.

During the Exile in Babylon the Hebrews picked up Persian beliefs about the after-life, having apparently failed to absorb Egyptian ideas in the days of their slavery. But they never quite got the hang of it. At the time of Jesus the Jews were divided on whether or not there was an after-life. The Sadducees (the New Testament equivalent of the established Church) rejected it as a belief found only incidentally in the Book of Daniel, which lacked the authority of the Books of Moses. The New Testament writers as a whole are a bit confused. It's the traditional place of happiness and reward, but also of possible violence (Matthew 11:12), of different classes (Matthew 11:11) and it's temporary (Matthew 24:34-35). Paul talks about a different structure altogether, a series of heavens (2 Corinthians 12:2-4). In the first few centuries AD the early Christians extended and adapted this vague idea of heaven to make it revolve around the idea of salvation. The Muslims developed it further into a vision of a physical Paradise.

The Christian doctrine of heaven and hell that the Church developed is highly illogical. It was one of the reasons the Chinese rejected the Jesuit missions. In the seventeenth century Xu Dashou said of it: "The books of the Barbarians say: if you have done good throughout your life but have not made yourself agreeable to the Master of Heaven, all your goodness will have been in vain. If you have done evil all your life but for one single instant did make yourself agreeable to the Master of Heaven, all the evil you have done will immediately be absolved."

Xu hits it on the nail: if Hitler had repented in the last moments of his life, and then been shot by the approaching Russians, good Christians should believe that he went to heaven, and that the six million Jews he gassed went to hell. It's not only irrational, it's as immoral a doctrine as you can find in world religions. Of all of them only Christianity and its successor, Islam, condemn people to eternal damnation. And as Christians saw the majority as destined for hell (in the Middle Ages it was reckoned to be 999 out of 1,000, a proportion which hasn't changed much in fundamentalist thinking today) they created a cosmology of fear rather than wonder.

By the twenty-first century, most people in the UK have come round to Xu's way of thinking. A few fundamentalist Christians bang the drum on heaven and hell but are ignored. Liberals offer a more sensitive approach that doesn't have a strong enough sales pitch. We're back where the Jews were 2,000 years ago, uncertain as to whether there is any form of existence after this life.

This absence of an after-life doesn't affect us as much as it used to. Our medicines protect us from early death: the market economy from famine; our culture distances us from the process of dying. Death doesn't plague us as it did our ancestors. We don't fear hell as we used to, or look forward to heaven as an escape from a miserable life on earth. Life is good, mostly. Brilliant.

But is that it? No answer to our questions, no reunion with family, no final happiness, no eternal life with God? Some have invested heavily in the "NDE" (near death experience) phenomenon, which increasingly affects hospital patients as surgery improves the chances of last-minute rescue. Recent studies of NDE's suggest that the common experience of passing down a dark tunnel and encountering a being of light is not adequately explained by oxygen deprivation, as had once been thought. The suggestion is that some form of consciousness lives on. But there's nothing particularly Christian about this; people tend to have the experience that's appropriate to their tradition.

Are there any better ideas of the after-life around? The most powerful over history has been that of reincarnation. It's one of the most widespread and ancient of all religious beliefs, found in Taoism, Hinduism and Buddhism, with traces in the mystic teachings of Judaism and Christianity. Reincarnation is more moral in that the form in which you come back depends on how you've behaved in this life. It also makes more sense of the immortal soul. After all, eternity, by definition, doesn't oblige the individual by starting at the point of death. If we have eternal souls it stands to reason they've always been around and perhaps evolve through successive lifecycles into more advanced states.

But this has its problems as well. It was easier to understand in the past when the world's population was relatively static, but now it's increasing by a billion or so people every 15 years. Where do all these extra souls come from? Is the world getting more enlightened, with more bugs turning into dogs turning into people? But if people are more enlightened than dogs why are so many of them nastier? How does a dog, or a bug, make any kind of "choice" to do good or evil? Or a tiger show compassion? In Tibetan Buddhism the subtle consciousness that lies in all of us continues after death, carrying traces of our past lives into the next one. But in what way does a spider have the same kind of consciousness, however slender, as a self-aware human? A belief in the equal weighting of consciousness through all species leads to the view that all life is equally valuable; a human being is as sacred as a mosquito. But if we didn't kill them with pesticides and let nature take its course we'd have a global epidemic of malaria to rival the Black Death.

So if religion doesn't help us much here can we look to any other evidence that there is more to life after death than memories living on? Does science say anything about it?

19 DOES GOD TELL TIME?

"Life is not spoiled by its ending, and the mere absence of life is not an object to fear, nor distressing in itself."

EPICURUS

Science picks up no traces of consciousness after death. But it does suggest that the case is not as open and shut as it might seem to be.

Never mind the details of heaven, or the Nordic Valhalla, or Celtic Tir na n'Oc, or the Roman Island of the Blessed, or the Greek Elysian Fields, or the Buddhist Pure Land, or whatever. All these ideas have something in common. In all religions time is not a straight line, with our lives defined by a starting and ending point. It's more like a little box. In Christianity time is something that we've been put into to fulfill God's purpose. He rattles it occasionally. We're in the box for a brief period and then we're taken out again to fulfill our real eternal destiny. In Islam the future is already written. In Buddhism we keep getting reborn into this time until we manage to escape the earthly chains and arrive in Nirvana, maybe tens of thousands of generations away.

In religion generally it's not the passing moments that matter but how we spend them. One moment of salvation or enlightenment is worth a lifetime's trudge. In achieving these moments we are free of the box of time, and our true self escapes from the prison of the body. Time is not usually seen as an absolute but is shaped by choice. At a deep level, time does not matter and in moments of profound experience does not exist. Reality is eternity, "a great ring of pure and endless light," as Henry Vaughan puts it.

Is this any more than nice poetry? In the twentieth century our understanding of time was turned upside down. Time is now not a straight unbending line any more than the world is flat. It's a function of gravity. This idea is as strange to us today as the laws of gravity were to the eighteenth century. We now live in a world where time slows down as you go faster. If we were able to send astronauts to the nearest star and back again at a speed high enough for them to return in a couple of decades, they would come back to find their children older than themselves.

If the astronauts shot out into space far enough and fast enough they could swing back to earth and see themselves being born. Time doesn't even just go in one direction. If you go faster than the speed of light it travels backwards. The mathematics for this hasn't been worked out yet, but it has been for electro-magnetic radiation – for waves that instead of diverging from a point converge. The first type are called "retarded" because they arrive after they've been sent, the second "advanced" because they arrive before they've been sent.

Time doesn't move forward at all. It's a field, like space, through which we move. If you could surf a light wave created in the Big Bang you would see all of time simultaneously. In a real, physical sense the past moment has not disappeared and the future exists just as much as the present. If it were possible to step outside the dimensions that frame your conscious experience you could put your hand back in and pick out episodes from your life like an email from the ether. Eternity, in this sense, is indeed real, more so than passing time. Can we experience it? Think of a flat horizontal plane transecting a circle. The plane is time and space, across which we move. Maybe our sense of the spiritual is a vertical plane transecting the moment we're in. Occasionally we look up and step outside the moment, and see that everything we are and can be is present now. Now is all that matters. Now is all there is.

"*The disciples said to Jesus: 'Tell us how our end will be. Jesus said, 'Have you discovered then the beginning, that you look for the end? For where the beginning is, there will the end be. Blessed is he who will take his place in the beginning; he will know the end and will not experience death.'*"

GOSPEL OF THOMAS

So maybe we can change our experience of time? When "we" were single-celled creatures in the sea we had no consciousness of time at all. We moved on to evolve an awareness of passing time, three-dimensional vision, and the ability to interpret objects as images and images as ideas. Maybe we can go further and experience the world in four dimensions? Mathematically, we know that this fourth space-time dimension exists, but we can't experience it directly, we can only see its shadow in algebra. Could we develop a consciousness that is not subject to the illusions of the ticking clock? The odds of this happening must be at least 99% against. But when playing with your pet hamster, does this 1% seem less likely than the prospect of that rodent being able to write and read books in a few million years?

Perhaps our feeling of impermanence and our yearning for the state of eternity, which are at the heart of religious experience, are the beginning of this consciousness. And dying is a stage in a progression through experiences of deeper consciousness? Perhaps even if we are stuck in this box, our descendants a million generations in the future might not be? Are we then on the way to grasping the fruit of the second of the trees in the Garden of Eden, the tree of life? And if we do, are we then equal to God, as He feared? Genesis itself suggests this:

"And the Lord God said, Behold, the man is become as one of us, to know good and evil: and now, lest he put forth his hand, and take also of the tree of life, and eat, and live for ever: Therefore the Lord God sent him forth from the garden of Eden."

GENESIS 3:22, 23

20 WHAT ARE THE ODDS ON GOD?

"The Savior said to them: 'For some of them say about the world that it is directed by itself. Some, that Providence directs it. Some, that it is fate. Now, it is none of these. Again, of those opinions that I have just described, none is close to the truth, and they are from man. But I, who came from the boundless light, I am here.'"

THE SOPHIA OF JESUS CHRIST

We're maybe on a 1% possibility that consciousness is not trapped for ever in time, and fated to die with us. Or perhaps, if your "out of the body" experiences are stronger, you'd put this percentage higher. But this still seems a very slender basis for moving on to believing in God, or any spirit outside ourselves. After all, we have this impossibly vast universe, in which our planet, our solar system, and our galaxy, are the tiniest of invisible specks. It's taken 3.5 billion years for life on earth to slowly develop, through several mass extinctions, to produce human beings as one outcome of the trillions possible. We live in the wafer-thin atmosphere of the planet, crawling about on its surface like bacteria in cling-film around an apple. We have a brain designed to deceive us to help us survive. Surely there is no "God" that relates to us in all this.

Well, perhaps this is true. But we don't *feel* this way. I realize that this sounds stupid, but we believe that we can achieve love, find meaning, and indeed in doing so change ourselves, other people and the world. In every moment of life we are conscious of affecting things, albeit in a tiny way: we believe life is not subject to randomness. Our world seems small and friendly (some of the time), not vast, alien and incomprehensible. What counts is the purpose and effort we bring to things. If we can't believe this we tend to despair. This is not to say we despair without religion – humanists and atheists believe we can still create meaning. It can be even more valued because it is achieved in the face of a meaningless universe. But wouldn't it be great if the universe itself was meaningful? If in acting out of purpose we were going with the grain of creation rather than against it? Would we be kidding ourselves if we thought this?

There seems a greater readiness for cosmologists to believe in the possibility of God than biologists. It's a question of perspective. Think of life on earth over billions of years. We can know in principle pretty much all that has happened on the way, the how and when. For the biologist, everything is on the level of matter. It's only with the development of consciousness that we get uncertain. But in terms of how life on earth works, biology describes it well.

On the cosmological scale it's different. The sense of the earth being there to walk on, matter being there to experiment on, disappears. Our sense of control vanishes. When we add up all the matter there is in the universe we know we've only got 10%, the rest being called "dark matter" because we can't find it. It's not that it's too small or too far away for microscopes or telescopes to see it, it's in a form that we don't understand.

The biological world that we live in seems like everything there is. But it's more accurate to think of it as one slice in a million. What we see, hear, feel, is one wafer-thin aspect of "reality."

Our view of the universe has progressed from seeing the earth as a small flat table; as a sphere whizzing around the sun; and as an invisible dot in a galaxy which is itself an invisible dot in an ever-receding hall of mirrors. As we move through from the first to the third level, it gets harder to see any particular significance or role for humanity, any meaning or purpose. But there's maybe a fourth level where purpose is as integral to the universe as the pull of the sun is to the earth's orbit.

Beyond the smallest dimensions that physics can measure (about 0.01 of a meter with another 34 zeroes before the 1) there may be a "foamy" mass of wormholes, full of an infinity of virtual particles that can discharge extraordinary amounts of energy, enough to create and destroy universes. These virtual particles may have existed in up to ten dimensions, of which three exploded in a "Big Bang" to create the universe that we know. The others imploded to remain as "forces" such as gravity, electromagnetism, and various nuclear forces. We don't know what kicked it off. The probability is that it simply happened unpredictably. At this level there is no cause and effect. There is no need for an explanation, for a "Creator God."

But how do we get from this unimaginably colossal explosion to our fragile life on earth? It doesn't seem to make sense. You're right. Explosions make a mess. The second law of thermodynamics (the rule that order decays into disorder) would suggest that the Bang should have resulted in almost anything other than an ordered universe. If the explosion had been too strong the universe would have ended up as a massive soup with no structures like stars and galaxies, expanding infinitely without order. If it had been too weak the force of gravity would have caused it to collapse back into itself, to form one big black hole. The chance that the force of the explosion would have been at the level where it formed orderly galaxies is so remote as to be invisible. It's been calculated that if the Big Bang had differed in strength by only one part in ten to the power of sixty the universe as we know it could not have existed. That's the rough equivalent of firing a bullet from one end of the cosmos to the other and hitting a dime.

There's a raft of similar remote coincidences where, if variables had been fractionally different, life would not have been possible. The ratio at which hydrogen converts into helium is one example: a little slower and the universe would have been predominantly hydrogen, a little faster and it would have been mostly helium. Either way, stars, planets, people would not have formed. The same goes for the ratio of masses of electron and proton, the relative strength of nuclear forces, the gravitational force. And there are many other examples.

Similar astronomical odds accumulate with the emergence of the planet Earth and its life forms. There are dozens of these unlikely constants. For many scientists the inescapable conclusion is that there is an element of cosmic design. It's the old teleological argument for God, dressed up for today. Maybe the universe is "designed" for life, or is self-designing, in the same kind of way that the earth is, according to the Gaia theory. The earth "evolves" in the direction of life. Perhaps the universe does too.

If there is design in the universe, there must be an outcome for which it is designed. Is this us? The story of life on earth is less than halfway through. Our sun will shine for another 5 billion years or so before it expands and burns up. There's a further 10 billion years before most stars disappear. It's hard to believe in a God who waits for about 15 billion years for the purpose of the universe to begin with the creation of humankind. Who then intervenes sporadically for a couple of thousand years. Who is likely to come in judgement any time soon, bringing this short history to a close when there's 10 billion years still to run. But perhaps God is not particularly interested in us. Perhaps He has a purpose that He is seeing through to the end game. Perhaps if we can take religion in the sense of "belonging" and "sacred" seriously enough we'll still be around in 10 billion years to find out. If not, then the universe and its purpose will roll on without us.

21 THE MIND OF GOD

"God is the expression of the intelligent universe."

KAHLIL GIBRAN

We'll probably never know the answer to the question of purpose or randomness at the start of the universe, as we can't see to the other side of the Big Bang. Maybe our universe has just turned out to be extraordinarily lucky – the one in a trillion trillion of possible outcomes. That's just the way life is: one sperm in a few million makes it, the others don't. There's no more conscious planning in the universe than there is in a spider's web. The fact that we're here to see what has happened is just that, a fact. If it hadn't been us, it would have been someone or something else. There is no deeper meaning.

But we *are* here, so we're at liberty to wonder why. It seems so incredible that we are. Maybe we can now say there's a 25% possibility that purpose is not just what we create for ourselves but there already exists a purpose in the universe.

To follow this thought further let's go to the other end of the scale, to things that are smaller than us in the same proportion that the universe is larger. Here's where things get even more weird. We're into the area of mental injury. There's an increasingly widespread view among scientists that nothing "exists", in the way we take for granted. Maybe (and this is speculation) there is nothing real, except purpose itself.

Leucippus first proposed the idea of the atom as the smallest indivisible thing moving through empty space in the fifth century BC. We had to wait till the twentieth century to get much further, and find out that atoms are divisible, that they are little worlds of their own. Imagine an atom as the size of a cathedral. The nucleus at the center would be the size of a pea, with electrons the size of gnats, whizzing around the cathedral walls. There's so much empty space inside our bodies that if you took it all out from all the people alive today, the entire world's population could fit into a matchbox. This is the world of quantum physics.

The really odd thing though is that however powerful your microscope, you are never going to be able to see an individual atom. You can detect it by the photons of light it reflects, but light has momentum (a product of its mass and velocity) and the very process of observation, at this incredibly small scale, seems to cause the momentum to change. If you look for the light in one place, it's there, and if you look for it in another place, it's there too.

Electrons can appear either in "wave" form or "particle." One theory is that it's the act of observation that determines which form (wave or particle) the electron is going to take, and where it's going to appear. At this level reality cannot be separated from the point of view of the observer. Nobody really understands why this is. Like religion, it's expressed in metaphors and parables.

There are two further principles that relate to this. One is the Uncertainty Principle, which is about the "space-time" foam created by the smallest possible particles. They're not actually "things" at all, but random back and forth movements occurring at zero point energy. The Principle says that we can't know that these particles exist, and we'll never see them, but they are there, there is no nothing. One of the biggest puzzles in physics is what this stuff is. Maybe there's a kind of "superposition" which stops quantum objects crashing into each other and makes matter possible.

The other principle, called the Holograph Principle, moves on from this to suggest that physics is not after all a description of the world as it is, because there is no "it" to "be." Physics is simply about the information that flows from one part of the universe to another.

Atoms are not "things" but somehow "make a choice" whether to be or not to be, and appear where we look for them. To explain this some scientists are suggesting that there may be a form of "proto-consciousness" or "intelligent information" that's inherent in everything. It would be a fundamental property of matter like mass or spin. Complexity and chaos theory add weight to this, suggesting that there are patterns of information that we don't yet know about, beyond matter and energy. So perhaps mind and matter are just two sides of the same coin, an idea that the Church burnt Giordano Bruno at the stake for saying 400 years ago. Somehow consciousness may be crucial to the development of the universe – and we're not just restricting the argument to human consciousness. Our brains may be the most complex organisms we have yet found, but there's no more reason to suppose that we are key to the universe than our planet is at its center. It's whatever completed limit any consciousness anywhere in the universe may reach in the future.

There must be some kind of link between these two extremes: the impossible odds against the existence of the universe on such a grand scale, and the idea of "intelligent information" existing at the tiny quantum level. A unified theory which reconciles the theory of relativity (dealing with cosmological events that are bigger than us by a multiple of zeros) with quantum physics (similar numbers of zeros going in the opposite direction) has yet to be found.

There are many possibilities. One is that every time a particle seems to be in two places at once it is indeed just that, but in a separate universe. Every time we think or act we are materializing one possibility of many, while in concurrent universes the consequences of other choices are creating different worlds in an endless parallel series.

Another, more popular suggestion, is the "super string theory" which suggests that the universe is made of wave patterns of near infinite length. These waves are mathematical constructions rather than "things." The nature of the waves is such that they cancel out everywhere except in one tiny region, and it's there that you find the quantum entity. So everything is everywhere but manifests itself at one particular point, which is where you look for it. These seem to be the relatively simple theories. There are many more.

We're unlikely to know the answers in our lifetimes. But the range of possibilities on what "is" is vastly greater than most of us can imagine. In 1,000 years' time the ideas we now have about the universe will seem as shallow and crude as the idea of the earth as a flat table. Maybe the world of matter that we experience will be one tiny part of our new equation. The world of consciousness, choice and purpose will be vastly larger. We will have a different understanding of God. Perhaps belief will always be open-ended. But to make a huge speculation, maybe we will see the collective choices of all the atoms in the universe as making up His "mind." This mind has directed itself into being, creating the almost impossibly precise conditions that allow consciousness to form. Maybe our brains are evanescent vehicles with the stability and life-span of summer mist, fleetingly holding fragments of this consciousness, much as our bodies are temporary hosts for bacteria and genes. We have no idea how this might work, but then we have no idea how consciousness arises in our brains, or even how life started in the first place.

22 IS GOD THE UNIVERSE?

"Heaven knows what seeming nonsense may not be tomorrow demonstrated truth."

ALFRED NORTH WHITEHEAD

These chapters are getting increasingly speculative. The "science" might be there, in so far as the Newtonian view of the universe as totally explicable in terms of forces like gravity has changed over the last century to an indeterminate and subjective one, where consciousness may play a key role. The assumption though that this supports the idea of a God or any purposeful reality independent from what we create for ourselves is one that many scientists, perhaps most, would not agree with. But the idea that God "is" the universe in some way pulls together a number of threads. It means that the universe is not random, but has a purpose, and that purpose is an evolving one, supporting the growth of consciousness. In this sense it is a loving purpose, on "our side," creative rather than destructive. We belong. It means that all life is sacred, on the path to consciousness. Imagine traveling through empty space and seeing barren planets for millions of years. Then in some distant part of the galaxy you come across a plant growing out of a rock. Wouldn't it be an amazing moment? That's how we should feel about all life on earth, including our own. We see the beginning of religious "emotion."

Religions have been thinking about life this way for thousands of years. The idea of the conscious unity of everything fascinated the ancient Greeks. Anaxagoras, Plato, Seneca, the Stoics all spoke of the mind which "rules over all things." Philo, a contemporary of Jesus, a Jew living in Alexandria, created the first systematic theology in the West. Combining the best of Greek and Jewish ideas, he saw the *logos* as the "tiller by which the pilot of the universe steers all things." In the Christian New Testament it is most explicit in John's Gospel, which seeks to express the nature of the new faith in categories more akin to Greek than Jewish thought. "The mind of God became a man," wrote

John (see John 1:14).

Maybe these similarities between ancient religions and modern science are purely superficial. Maybe it's coincidence, or maybe, as we've only got one kind of brain, we can only read things in one way, whether through art, religion or science. Or maybe just as religion has to incorporate science, science will end up accepting that a different kind of truth is needed to help us look further than the laws that frame the universe we live in. This at least suggests the direction in which believers should be looking: to our common consciousness. To look for a deity who's interested in a few saved people is like looking for Him in a tree. Albert Einstein, perhaps the greatest scientist of all time, put it this way:

> *"You will hardly find one among the profounder sort of scientific minds without a peculiar religious feeling of his own. But it is different from the religion of the naive man. For the latter God is a being from whose care one hopes to benefit and whose punishment one fears: a sublimation of a feeling similar to that of a child for its father, a being to whom one stands to some extent in a personal relation, however deeply it may be tinged with awe.*
> *But the scientist is possessed by the sense of universal causation. The future, to him, is every whit as necessary and determined as the past. There is nothing divine about morality, it is a purely human affair. His religious feeling takes on the form of a rapturous amazement at the harmony of natural law, which reveals an intelligence of such superiority that, compared with it, all the systematic thinking and acting of human beings is an utterly insignificant reflection. This feeling is the guiding principle of his life and work, in so far as he succeeds in keeping himself from the shackles of selfish desire.*
> *It is beyond question closely akin to that which has possessed the religious geniuses of all ages."*

ALBERT EINSTEIN *THE WAY I SEE IT*

So how do we find this God, this universal consciousness that goes under many names? Is it possible?

Could God be pure intelligence, or thought, or love? Surely not in the way we understand these terms, because they are constructs of our own little brains. Maybe He is the original "point," splitting Himself into relationships. Since creation is not finished, maybe God is still developing. Maybe He's not an objective deity who created the universe and then left it largely to its own devices, occasionally chucking thunderbolts or interfering with nature, but eternally present in the universal bubble bath. He is the original energy from which matter bubbles out momentarily to give rise to life, to consciousness, and then returns to energy.

But if God is a process, how did the universe begin in the first place? If the form that reality takes has to await the participation of a conscious observer, how can anything exist before the observer is there to see it? The answer could lie in retrospective action because, remember, there is no straight line of time. Imagine an eye with a long stalk in the form of a loop, with the eyeball looking back at its own beginning. That, in the world of quantum physics, may be the most credible explanation of how the universe came to be. Perhaps consciousness is something created by its own workings that has already happened. So perhaps mind in some form is after all the reality, matter its creation. Religion is simply our attempt to realize where we are before we get there. It is the practice and growth of consciousness. Religion is not anti-evolution – it *is* evolution. Darwin is the Augustine of our time. God was not there at the beginning, but He is there at the end, and in the end is our beginning.

23 IS GOD US?

The senses, they say, are subtle;
More subtle than the senses is the mind;
Yet finer than the mind is intellect;
That which is beyond even the intellect
Is he.

BHAGAVAD GITA

If God exists as all relationships He is both "out there," and a
thought in our heads. And whether the thought comes from inside
or outside, it's certainly colored by the individual thinking process:
I don't see God in the same way as you because our brains are different. We all generate our own picture, dream our own dreams.

Religions have always been aware of this dichotomy – "inside
our heads" and "out there" – and two strands of faith have developed to reflect it. The first, called theism, externalizes God and
then prays and worships Him/Her/Them. The clearest example of
this today is Islam, which means "submission to the One God."
The second strand, called monism, believes that all reality is one,
and teaches that you find it within yourself. The main example is
Buddhism. Buddhists don't worship any god outside themselves,
but by means of meditation they seek the transcendence of the self
and its union with the larger reality.

The problem with theism is that it tends to push God out as a
remote, separate figure it's hard to believe in. Monism, seeing God
as everything, tends to make him indistinguishable from the world
around us. Christianity tries to get the best of both worlds by having a transcendent God who incarnates Himself into the physical
world in the form of Jesus.

In practice all the major religions embrace both theism and
monism. In the theistic tradition, you have the mystics for whom
everything – the dualities of inner and outer, good and evil –
resolves itself into God alone. So, for instance, Judaism has works

like that of Zohar in the thirteenth century that see the soul as an expression of God. In Islam the mystic tradition is represented most strongly by the Sufis. The leader of this tradition was Ibn al-'Arabi, also of the thirteenth century, who believed in the oneness of Being. The Christian mystic tradition has great writers like Meister Eckhart, Hildegarde of Bingen, Mechtild of Magdeburg, Julian of Norwich. More contemplative forms of Christianity – like the Quakers – stress the inner light rather than the external reality. The start of a new cycle in Christian circles can be seen in the current interest in spirituality, which seems to mean experiencing God without being too specific as to who He is.

Viewing religions this way helps us to see the similarities. Christian mysticism is often indistinguishable, felicities of style and approach apart, from Islamic Sufism. The mystics in both traditions are essentially saying that God is present in every human heart. Look into yourself and you will find him. The great Sufi leader Hallaj went further and was crucified for saying that everyone is God. Similarly there is little difference between Christian and Islamic fundamentalists, who insist most clearly on a God "out there." The words are changed, the Bible for the Koran, or Allah for God, but the sentiments are the same. The self-belief that their interpretation is right is the same. In both Muslim and Christian traditions the mystics who seek the inner light, outside the forms of the organized Church, have often been persecuted by the establishment. The Christian Church has preferred to make saints of legends, bureaucrats and charlatans rather than mystics.

Equally a monistic religion like Buddhism also has its theistic elements, particularly in the Amida and Theravada traditions, with prayer and worship of the Buddha. Hinduism is something of a halfway house in that the *Upanishads*, the sacred scriptures at the heart of the religion, are monistic, while in practice most Hindus behave like theists, offering sacrifices and praying to Shiva, Vishnu and other gods.

A general truth is that an intense focus on the religious "experience" often leads to an interior religion, where the "god without" becomes hard to distinguish from the "god within." After all, anything that's "out there" has to be processed in the head. There's the story of an English soldier who was hanged for heresy in the seventeenth century. A devout Christian, living in a time of extraordinary religious and social experiment when all the boundaries were suddenly fluid, he was asked at his trial why he claimed to be God. His answer went something like this: "One night I stayed up praying, and by the early morning I realized there was no one else there with me in the room. I was praying to myself. So I must be God." Or as the Sufi poet Rumi said in the thirteenth century:

> *"So what do I have to do to get you to admit who is speaking?*
> *Admit it and change everything!*
> *This is your own voice echoing off the walls of God."*

At the end of the day, God within and God without are surely the same. It's meaningless to draw a distinction between them. Our brains can't process these concepts without relevant sensory information which, in this case, by definition, doesn't exist, since God is not a "thing." And at the deepest level of reality we know, that of the quantum world, reality does not exist independently from the act of observing it. If we do not perceive God, He is not there. If we do, He is.

This is not to say any picture of God is of equal value. Or that one way of believing isn't better than another. But these pictures are personal. To claim them as uniquely and fundamentally true is meaningless. The disputes between different Protestant sects over who is saved and who is not are absurd. The differences between Protestants and Catholics are inconsequential. Those between Christians and humanists are questions of preference. The

differences between Christians and Buddhists are matters of interpretation. Perhaps we can simply learn from each other. For
instance, Christians say God is personal and to find salvation we
reconcile a personal self with a personal God. Buddhists say that
neither we nor God are personal. Neither exist. Reconciling nothing with nothing makes for enlightenment. Who's right? It makes
no difference. The nature of the experience is similar. The advice
on how to live is similar. Both exist as working possibilities, as
aspects of a larger whole, of something we have little idea about.
We're playing mind games. We'll never know if they're real or not.
Faith is acting as if they are.

In chapter 8 the suggestion was that there is no real distinction
between us and the chimps: we are all part of the continuum of
life. What is true of the material is also true of time, as outlined in
chapter 19. There is no dividing line between this moment and the
last, or the next. All exist in an equally real sense, now. And there is
no clear distinction between this world and the next, between us
and God. To ask, "Did God create man, or man create God?" is like
asking which came first, the grass or the grazing animals, the
chicken or the egg. They developed together. Life is a process. The
line may curve, swing around corners, it may zigzag. But it doesn't
stop and start again. Reality is not sliced like salami. In the bigger
picture there is no time. There is no space. There is no matter.
There is only light. Reality is "one," which is why the experience
of "oneness" is at the heart of religion. You are not alone.

24 OUT OF THE BOX

"The purpose of words is to carry ideas. When the ideas are grasped, the words are forgotten. Where can I find a man who has forgotten words? He is the one I would like to talk to."

CHUANG TZU

But what kind of a stake do we have in this universal consciousness that is called God?

Here's the problem. We live in a universe that in some way seems to be dependent for its existence on consciousness. We are conscious. Consciousness has developed on this planet over millions, hundreds of millions of years. It may have flowered in the human brain in the last million years through the medium of language. But that is extremely recent. We haven't created the universe. Our minds lack the power even to bend spoons (disputed). If it's our future consciousness that has created the universe retrospectively, it relates to our current consciousness as ours does to that of a worm. If our consciousness is equivalent to our body warmth, "full consciousness" would be the equivalent of trillions of suns. How can we possibly relate to it without being instantly frazzled?

Perhaps it's simply that we're on a line of consciousness that stretches way into the future. There's no reason to suppose that consciousness has stopped developing. Indeed, it develops in all of us. At birth our brains are relatively unwired, prioritized to keep the heart and lungs going. The next few years are a dialogue between brain and surroundings, with the child taking on board the culture of parents and others. The frontal part of the brain, where we reason and choose, is not fully wired up till the teens or even twenties. Which is why the Jesuits and all Churches try to get teaching in early.

But in a more general sense consciousness is developing in life as a whole. If you take the ratio of brain to body of an earthworm as 1, the most intelligent dinosaurs had a ratio of 20, and human beings have a ratio of 350. But this increase is not unique to humans. All furry animals are vastly more intelligent than scaly ones. And the kind of consciousness we've been talking about – "self-awareness" – is only the tip of the iceberg. Most consciousness is of the collective kind, the sort that enables termites to build nests like cathedrals, and birds to migrate thousands of miles to roosts they've never seen. In becoming aware of the self, we may have lost, or buried, our own collective consciousness. Much of twentieth-century psychology explores areas of the brain's beliefs that we've suppressed. Jung studied hundreds of his patients' dreams and found similarities across time and cultures. This discovery led him to develop his idea of a "collective unconscious," in which recurrent dream images and situations are related to inherited "archetypes."

Maybe we should turn things around and instead of thinking of ourselves as the end product of evolution, the center of the universal purpose, think of ourselves as close to the beginning. After separating from the evolutionary line of Common chimps it took us a few million years to get the hang of language. That led to an increase in brain size of 50% or so, after which nothing much happened for another million years. Then 50,000 or 100,000 or 250,000 years ago (the dates will continue to be debated) something triggered imagination. We started to produce art, to improve tools, to work skins, and about 10,000 years ago, to grow crops. And then to write. The rate of change is escalating. The Stone Age, 1 million years; Bronze/Iron Age 4,000 years; Industrial Age, 200 years; Information Age, 100 years, and next? The forthcoming Genetic Age is likely to bring more change than the previous 1 million years. And we've got a long way to go. The humble hedgehog has been around 15 times longer than we have.

In the natural world an increase of complexity to the power of 10 often heralds a new evolutionary development. A dog, for instance, has 10 to the power of 9 neurons in the brain. Self-awareness seems to develop at our level of neuron complexity: around 10 to the power of 10, or 100 billion, the number of stars in our galaxy. Maybe in another million or so years, natural or artificial evolution could raise the number of neurons in our brain to 10 to the power of 11? Why not? If not in a million years, then 10 million? 100 million? We've got several billion years to go before the sun burns out. If we're still around, we will either have reverted to the caves or we'll be expanding across the galaxy. In the latter case we have no idea what we will be like, or how we will think, or whether, indeed, thinking will be the highest level of mental activity. How can a dog know what its owner's brain is like? And why shouldn't complexity continue to develop further? How far from dog to God? 10 to the power of 12 neurons? 20? We're all on the same line of relationship. Maybe it will be a different species that goes along the path toward God. Or maybe, if it is *Homo sapiens*, we will just be a lot more neurotic than we are now. Maybe such life forms may exist on many of the trillions of other planets that we have yet to discover.

In the meantime, religion tries to describe and deepen the link between the individual and the universal consciousness. Theistic and monistic traditions each say that we can heighten our awareness through prayer, meditation, and ritual. The monistic Hindu way, described in the *Upanishads*, sees the ego as a deception which separates the "I" from the Ultimate Reality. This was developed further in Buddhism, which believes that the "I" is the cause of attachment and suffering. There is no real self/object duality at all. Through meditation we gradually reduce the sense of self, clearing the mind of conscious thought. We can arrive at the source, the creative intelligence that gives rise to all thought, the "O."

This cannot be easy to achieve. But that doesn't mean it doesn't happen. Imagine the struggle a chimp would have if it tried to think of itself as "me." Now try imagining yourself as not being "you." Try thinking for a moment of your name, the letters, but holding them in your mind with no connection to yourself. Your name is just a label someone else has given you, and has no real meaning in terms of who you are. Imagine applying the same exercise to what you think of as your "self." It's a label your emotions have given you in order to control you. You can find your "inner" self by going deeper. It's an insight that all religions try to achieve. Most people never manage it but have a glimpse that it might be there. It's not impossible in theory. We know that religious rituals do have an effect on the brain. Practices like *raja* yoga or *vipassana* meditation (the "insight meditation" developed and taught by Buddha) have been shown to lower blood pressure, slow metabolism and produce increasingly coherent brain-wave patterns.

We also know that we use only a tiny fraction of the mind's potential power. The term "savants" describes some rare individuals who have prodigious, superhuman skills but also suffer from autism, which disables them in other ways. With no previous experience a young man can play a piano concerto from memory after hearing it once, or a girl will produce the most beautiful and elaborate drawings from memory, or calculate huge numbers as fast as a computer. The flip side of this skill is that a savant cannot select or analyze and is often unable to speak or count. The "survival skills" of the brain are in abeyance. Experiments have suggested that we all have this potential, but that parts of the brain have been "shut off" to free up other areas. The idea that we may scale up consciousness to a level inconceivable to us today is beginning to take shape.

The theistic Christian and Muslim path is different from the monistic. These religions see Buddhism as regressive, losing individuality in the mass. The monotheistic religions keep a stronger sense of the self, and of "God without." The purpose of life for them is to develop the individual consciousness rather than merge it, to become aware of possessing the knowledge that the unconscious already holds. They affirm that we find God by going deeper into ourselves, not by losing ourselves, meeting God at the point where our unconscious borders the conscious. We then need to act out of this for the good of humankind. Our purpose in life is to become a further expression of God.

But is there any sense in which the brain can possibly be said to operate in either way, whether freeing itself from the conscious self and disappearing into Nirvana, or finding within itself the consciousness of God? In the future we're going to know more about how the brain works and how it relates to quantum mechanics. What we do know is that it's more complex than anything else we have yet come across in the universe (not so far having found any life forms outside our planet). Of the trillion or so cells in the brain about 100 billion are neurons, the ones that create brain activity. Each of these neurons ends in a little bunch of feelers like coral polyps. The gaps between these feelers are called synapses. Chemicals called neurotransmitters transmit nervous impulses across them.

The number of possible pathways between the synapses of the brain exceeds the number of atoms in the universe – around 10 to the power of 72 . The gap between them, about a millionth of a centimeter, approaches the atomic scale, where quantum uncertainty comes into play. In other words, our brain operates at the level of quantum particles where reality is "created" by the observer. Is it then so inconceivable that we are ourselves part of the process of creation? Or that perhaps, at some level, we can "link up" with a universal mind?

The idea that in some way we don't understand we are part of an ongoing creation of the world around us is not science fiction. The laws of physics that seem absolute at the moment will be superseded in years to come, much as relativity superseded gravity. Perhaps we'll come to see the speed of light as a threshold rather than a limit. On the side of our physical existence, where we live, is the world of particles, the atoms that make us up; on the other side, the cognitive part of our being, we find the world of waves. There our collective choices add a little to the mind of God.

So maybe we have a mind – or we could call it a soul – which doesn't exist in space or time. It arises from the brain, but is more than it in the same way that life is more than matter. We can't describe it adequately yet, any more than we can describe "life." We can surmise, though, that "soul" is outside space because at the quantum level of description there is no such thing as space. It is outside time, because, ultimately, time is not a process – it's just a passing measurement like position on a painting. But how does a soul outside space and time act in the everyday world we live in? How do choices happen?

The past is in some sense inevitable. Maybe the future is different. It is not there waiting to happen, we collectively bring it about. Maybe at the quantum level choice determines time as much as position. Perhaps there is ultimately no clear distinction between random events, choice and the acts of God. They're all part of the description of the picture. Accepting this is a process common to many religions. We make sense of the circumstances that seem to dictate our lives through assimilating them. In the sense that we have responded to events we have chosen who we are. When we can say "yes" to our existence, and don't regret a single moment of it, good or bad, past or future, and can see it as "one," we have reached enlightenment.

In this strange, new world of no-time and no-place maybe extraordinary events – near death experiences, clairvoyance, synchronicity, psychokinesis, coincidences, telepathy, precognition, miracles – can happen, with consciousness making little jumps along the line. Millions of people have had the experience of the effect of healing hands, or of seeing an angel, or a dead relative, or other forms of the paranormal. Maybe they're projecting these, creating them in their heads, making these phenomena real for themselves alone. Or maybe, if there is a "spirit" that is separate from mind, it can move between different choices, different worlds, different times, and sometimes our physical brains may capture traces of its passing. Maybe they exist at the level of light or information much as rocks exist at the level of matter.

Maybe it's just a rush of oxygen to the brain that produces these experiences, sometimes accidental, sometimes willed. Or maybe the universe is weirder than we imagine. Maybe the "real" universe is one of light, from which matter is created, and the thousands of accounts of individuals seeing a being of light or becoming aware of the effects of light catch something of the process of creation. Maybe the God that we call the universal mind occasionally influences and creates from outside the space/time dimension in the way that wormholes in space twist and bend the laws of known physics. Scientists are already experimenting with the creation of wormholes on a tiny scale in the laboratory. Maybe in a thousand or million years we'll look back at the twenty-first century and see it as still in the early stages of scientific understanding, and the time when we reached a new level of truth. A real "New Age" to which the present one bears as much relevance as ancient medicine does to modern, as Christianity does to true religion.

So maybe we live as fragments of this universal mind. In our fields of time and space we experience the choices that are bringing our particular universe into existence, out of the infinite number of possibilities. When we die our borrowed bodily forms return to the recycling machine of nature, turning the chemicals from which we are made into further people or cars or whatever. Our fragments of consciousness return to the background energy-state of the universe – a state that we describe as Nirvana, God, Tao, Brahmin, Reality or simply a sea of "things that might be." This is the only thing that is "One," that doesn't change, that cannot change because it includes all possible changes: "I am that I am" (Exodus 3:14). There may even be a further choice for us to make, a choice between merging into the Godhead and being re-incarnated on earth, or hanging around in another form in some kind of celestial waiting-room.

We don't have a language yet for exploring this level of con-sciousness, if indeed it exists at all. We're still stuck with the scientific categories that were developed in the eighteenth centu-ry, that allow no room for it. Different writers try to express it as best they can, as in the words of the *Bhagavad-Gita* chapter 2:20:

"He is never born, nor does he ever die;
nor once having been, does he cease to
be. Unborn, eternal, everlasting,
ancient, he is not slain when the body
is slain."

Or of Jesus:

"While ye have light, believe in the light, that ye may be the
children of light."

JOHN 12:36

PART 4

THE HISTORY
OF GOD

25 CHANGING PERCEPTIONS

"Truth seems to come with the final word; and the final word gives birth to its next."

RABINDRANATH TAGORE

There are a lot of loose ends and unanswered questions in the last few chapters, and an awful lot of "maybes." Perhaps any idea of "Spirit" in the world, or outside it, in any form, is simple fantasy. After all, the million dollar prize on offer for proving any aspect of the paranormal remains uncollected year after year. But there are enough scientists around who say that a materialist or reductionist point of view is not the only one, or even the right one, to make a more religious perspective seem credible. Maybe we've got to 50/50 odds on God existing. Maybe that's good enough as a jumping off point.

This is where faith comes in. That the universe is one of love and meaning rather than random noise, with ourselves as isolated beacons of consciousness. This God may be just another God of the gaps. Or He may be a possibility. As we're the ones making the judgements there's no way we can arrive at a fully "objective" understanding. We'll never see God "straight and true" because we change what we see by looking.

A credible faith today might suggest that we're not, as atheists or humanists would say, the highest known form of consciousness, so everything beyond that is our projection. We've only just started on the road to a self-awareness that already exists. We're one tiny strand of a line of consciousness that cumulatively ends up as the creative force behind the universe. It's not that there is a void beyond our horizon of self-awareness, but this is a journey without a horizon. We just happen to be aware of the point we're on – as we're aware of our point in time – and can occasionally see a little way forward. Believers and non-believers can agree on where we are, the question is whether we're going anywhere.

Scientists accept that a fuller understanding of each of their theories will come in the future. Science may turn out to be the friend of God rather than the enemy, if we're prepared to accept that any understanding of God keeps developing. But it doesn't tell us anything about Him. And theology, as the great Sufi Ghazali taught, is at the end of the day useless. What matters, is expressing what we believe in a compassionate life. "Beliefs" can hinder this rather than help. What we're left with is developing our own approach to life.

To most Christians these chapters will seem more akin to "Christian atheism," a stance fashionable in the 1960s, and they won't see a God they recognize in this book: He is not unchanging, separate, personal, eternal, omniscient. They will see this as jumping off into the unknown, not into belief. The point about Christianity for them is that it is a revealed religion. In the Bible, or through the Church, statements have been made about God which stand as ultimate truth.

And in a way they're right. A theoretical belief in God is of no practical use. What counts is our experience of Him, and for this we need bodies, minds, language. We need services, goals, icons, words, and sacraments. For most everyday purposes Newton's law of gravity is more use to us than Einstein's law of relativity. The latter operates on a scale beyond our immediate experience.

But we can live in the framework of Newton's laws while still accepting those of Einstein as representing a deeper truth. Perhaps "Christian atheism" is no more "atheistic" than the early Christians – who were called atheists by the Romans. The Romans couldn't understand these Christians – what were gods if you couldn't represent them in images? Meaningless. How can you worship words? Perhaps orthodox Christians are demonstrating the same approach when they insist on the necessity for Capital Letter Doctrines. The doctrines are no more than the old carved images, equally crude approximations of truth. We can go beyond them.

But if humankind is not fallen from Eden in the way Christianity describes, if God is not personal, and Jesus is not His only Son, what is there to hang on to in this religion?

Perhaps it's not so much a question of hanging on, more of shedding an old skin. With the same delight the Romans felt when many of them abandoned their worship of household gods for the invisible, almighty, only God. Think of the new picture of God as a similar step on the journey. As larger than the first-century Christian picture of Him as their picture was larger than the statue of Zeus. But, to phrase it in the old ways, four things matter. One is simply that we still think in ways molded by Christianity, and can't understand ourselves without understanding where we're coming from. Secondly, even if God is as different from the Christian God as the Christian God was from the Roman deities, we still need ways to describe Him and relate to Him, much as the first Christians still continued to use icons, writings, rituals, and sacred buildings for their new invisible God. Thirdly, the collective experience of many Christians down the ages gives insight into the best ways of living, though there seems no good reason not to benefit from the insights of other faiths as well. The last reason, the main one, is that Jesus models the best way we have of relating to the world and God.

Maybe, whatever image we have of God, what Jesus says about living is equally relevant. Maybe it's the best way of relating to the world even if God doesn't exist. After all you don't need the Church to be a Christian, that came later. So did the Bible. The huge majority of Christians got through 1,500 years without having the Bible to hand. Maybe you don't need God either.

It's difficult to think about Christianity without God. Orthodox Christianity today is rooted in history rather than philosophy, in contrast, say, to Buddhism. It embraced and was shaped by Greek philosophy in the early centuries AD, but its driving force was the Hebrew belief that God intervenes in the world through history in particular ways, as revealed in the Bible. What we need to do now is understand a little more about the Christian God; who He is, how we came to understand Him, how our understanding has changed. The fact that our understanding has changed seems undeniable.

After all "God" is simply a relatively modern English word (with Germanic roots) that means "good" as opposed to "evil." Whereas the Semitic words for God in the first millennium BC, "*Elat*," "*Elohim*," "*Alaha*," "*Allah*" (Old Canaanite, Hebrew, Aramaic, Arabic respectively), stem from roots more correctly translated as "One," the "All," that embrace evil as well as good. Perhaps our word for "God" has now become too stale with use, too broad in its application, and we need to think of a new word. How about "GD," missing out the vowels as the Hebrews did. Perhaps we shouldn't use personal pronouns. Or perhaps we should just accept that the meaning of the word will continue to evolve, and try and influence its direction. Find a new definition that works for us.

These next seven chapters are for those readers interested in history, in the changing perception of God through the Old Testament. If you want to move on to suggestions for how Christians should believe today, go straight to the chapters on Jesus, starting with chapter 33.

26 SACRED WORDS

"It is fear that first brought gods into the world."

PETRONIUS

Where did we get the idea of "revealed religion"?

It came with writing. Prior to the invention of writing religion was revealed in many ways – dreams, trances, divination, signs, channeling, singing and others. Perhaps most of all by telling stories. In telling stories about how we came to be we realized who we are. It's like not knowing what you think till you hear what you say, or see what you write. Now we only see something as really sacred, "revealed," if it's "written;" if it's the "Word of God."

Which is not surprising. Writing is the second most important thing that's ever happened on the planet. The first was about 3.5 billion years ago when cells learnt the trick of storing information and finding it again, with DNA. Around 10,000 years ago (the date is very uncertain) we invented a system of putting thoughts into squiggles that did the same. A third key event may have occurred in the past year, with the decoding of the human genome. This opens up the prospect of putting DNA and writing together: in the future we may be able to manipulate DNA and store information in new forms of life, writing it as easily as we now write books.

A few thousand years ago the words describing our experience of God were shaped into pictures and then letters pressed into damp clay tablets which were baked in the sun to make the writing permanent. These tablets were read by successive generations, changing the way they thought. Learning does actually alter the brain, creating new neural networks. And writing must have seemed magical. It had to be true. How could writing contradict itself?

It would have seemed natural to early civilizations that some of these clay tablets should have come from gods or God, much as dreams, prophecies and ritual did. All literate societies have sacred writings, and there are lots of them. Think of a study lined with shelves, floor to ceiling. The Holy Bible is one book. The death of Buddha alone generated the equivalent of 50 Bibles. The Bible is also a fairly recent addition. Much of the world's sacred scripture was written before the Hebrews learnt to write. By far the oldest extant religious texts are the great Hindu writings, the *Vedas*, which may have been started in the fourth millennium BC, with the canon being fixed after 1000 BC. They are seen as more than sacred: they are part of the fabric of the universe, existing before time itself. In the book of *Prasna Upanishad*, the *Vedas* recreate the universe at the beginning of each cycle of existence. There's a reflection of this idea from the *Vedas* in John's Gospel chapter 1: "In the beginning was the Word...."

Much later than the *Vedas* in the Hindu tradition came the most revered of their classics, the *Bhagavad Gita* ("Song of the Beloved"), written around the fifth century BC. It's the earliest literary attempt to arrive at a comprehensive view of existence. The setting is a battlefield that symbolizes life itself. As the dialogue ripples out into deeper subjects a whole philosophy of life unfolds. It's a work of deep wisdom and tolerance. As Krishna says, "Whoever with true devotion worships any deity, in him I deepen that devotion; and through it he fulfils his desire" (7:21).

Other religions also have a high view of their sacred scripture. In the Koran, for example, the very words are sacred, even their shape. The words themselves represent the "incarnation" of God on earth. If they're translated the meaning is altered, so to worship Allah correctly you should use Arabic. It's easier to think of the Koran than the Bible, as "revelation," written as it was by one individual over a twenty-year period, in a white hot heat, in the most extraordinarily beautiful Arabic.

Christians don't see the Bible in quite the same way. The words are inspired, yes, but not divine in their own right. After all, they were written down in different languages over a period of about 1,000 years by many different authors living up to 1,000 miles apart. There's nothing special about much of the language. Much of it is not particularly "religious" in the way the *Bhagavad Gita* is. Half of it, the Old Testament, is even "borrowed" from another religion, Judaism. Nor is it coherent. The Old Testament itself is a miscellany of history, poetry, genealogy, and laws. Some of it has itself been borrowed and adapted from other traditions. Some of the psalms and parts of Proverbs are taken from Egyptian writings, praising very different gods. Ecclesiastes seems inspired more by the skeptical philosophy of the Greeks than the Hebrew idea of God. The Song of Solomon is a sexually explicit love poem included because the compilers mistakenly thought it was by Solomon. By the time the books of the Old Testament get included in the "Christian Bible" the inspiration has followed a long and devious route, crossing many religions, regions, cultures and languages.

Many Orthodox Jews, though, believe that God dictated the first five books of the Old Testament directly to Moses, in Hebrew. Many Christians come close to believing the same thing about the Old and New Testaments. They hold that the Bible "as originally written" is "infallible," or "inerrant" (which means pretty much the same: the Bible doesn't say everything that is right, but it doesn't say anything wrong either). It's hard to get your head around this idea today – it sounds like automatic writing, or New Age "channeling." Books written in the belief that the words have come from "outside" can obviously sell in huge quantities, as in fact the Bible still does. A recent example is the best-selling *Conversations With God* by Neale Donald Walsch. We publish one ourselves, a more orthodox Christian book (*God Calling*) that has sold over six million copies.

Most people in the world are happy to accept the idea of inspiration, but the idea that this one book (or collection of books) in the sacred library is inspired in a way that no other book is seems like the literary equivalent of the flat earth theory. It's an example of the exclusive/ignorance ratio: the less individuals know about other sacred scriptures the easier it is to believe theirs is the only true one. If you find the Bible inspiring try paying the same kind of attention to other sacred scriptures. If you find it boring or irrelevant, just turn it around in your head. Think of it as maybe 10% revelation, 90% description and error. We can read it to learn how the Hebrews got God wrong, not right, and how they learnt along the way from their mistakes.

27 THE TWO GODS

"Man makes religion; religion does not make man. Religion is indeed man's self-consciousness and self-awareness so long as he has not found himself or lost himself again."

KARL MARX

How literally can we take what the Old Testament says about God and His dealings with humankind? Scholars line up at different points on a spectrum on the question of historical value. At one end there are those who say there's no historical basis to any of the Old Testament books. It's all myth and legend. Noah and the Flood are no more historical than Atlantis. The great heroes of the Old Testament – Moses, David, Solomon, Samson, Samuel – are fictional figures.

In the middle, and largely in the Christian camp, you have academics who say there is some historical basis, but with an overlay of myth, mistakes, and anachronisms caused by later compilers and editors. For example, there was a significant regional flood in Mesopotamia, and the many ancient flood stories in the Middle East reflect this. Maybe, for instance, it was the time when the Mediterranean broke through the Bosphorus and created the Black Sea. Or maybe it's just that in the wide open river valleys of the Tigris and Euphrates floods were a regular occurrence, leading to many different survival stories. There would certainly have been folk memories of climbing into boats with animals and belongings, and surviving until the waters subsided. But there's no reason to suppose there was just one individual Noah. As the Old Testament progresses, though, we get more historical fact. After all there was a kingdom of Israel, there was a Temple, so there's no reason to suppose that David and Solomon didn't exist, and that what is said about them is broadly true.

At the other end, a minority of scholars, working largely in

Church-related institutions, affirm that everything that the Old Testament says happened did actually happen, though not necessarily in the way it says. For instance, not only do they believe there was a flood (regional, not worldwide, which would be a physical impossibility, and would have affected the very orbit of the earth in ways we could measure today) but there was an individual called Noah, though clearly he didn't have two of every species in the world in the ark (or seven, there are two versions of the story in the Old Testament). How could he collect sloths from South America, or the tens of millions of other species that the Hebrews hadn't heard of, and that wouldn't have survived the journey or the Mesopotamian climate? But maybe he had two each of the "useful" animals, the domestic ones. By the time we get to David and Solomon we can take the Bible stories as factual. Not only did they establish a "Greater Israel" but the stories about them are true. David really did fight Goliath, love Jonathan, and send Uriah the Hittite to be murdered in battle so he could have sex with Uriah's wife.

There are no reputable scholars who say it all happened exactly as the Old Testament says. The "bones of Adam recovered in a garden," or "ark found on Mount Ararat" stories are like the "battleship found on the moon" headlines of the sensationalist press. Fodder for the Flat Earth brigade.

This is put very crudely. But what few scholars would dispute is that the Old Testament books didn't exist in their present form until about the eighth century BC, around 500 years after the Hebrews entered Canaan, or even centuries later. They represent different traditions, and were edited and compiled over a long period. The idea of the "Bible" is later still. The Old Testament heroes didn't have a "scripture-based" faith in the way we think of it.

Let's start at the beginning, taking a few snapshots. The following survey would attract a fair consensus of scholarly opinion.

In one of the most wide-ranging of recent histories of the world, the 600-page *Civilizations* by Felipe Fernandez-Armesto, neither Hebrews nor Jews are mentioned. That is a useful counter to the Christian assumption that the stories in the Bible are central to world history of the time. We have to read the Bible stories today in the context of two of the first great civilizations in the world: the Mesopotamian civilizations (successively the Sumerians, Babylonians, Assyrians, Persians) based on the Rivers Tigris and Euphrates, and the Egyptian, based on the River Nile.

These civilizations were sophisticated. The Egyptians had started to build the pyramids (in 3400 BC). Phoenicians were importing tin from a land that would be known as England in 3,000 years' time. In Greece the Olympic Games had been running for generations. To the east the first legal code of Hammurabi had been inscribed on a black basalt stele, all 282 laws. This happened several dozen generations before Moses brought the Ten Commandments down from the mountain – and unlike the clay tablets handed to Moses, the Hammurabi slabs actually exist and are displayed in the Louvre Museum in Paris.

For thousands of years these civilizations had been telling stories and had begun to write them down as well. Writing was known in Babylon around 3500 BC, maybe much earlier. Temple hymns in Sumeria in about 2350 BC credit the first known author: a woman named Enheduana. By 2500 BC the Egyptians had libraries, with stories, poetry, prayers, religious plays, and books on medicine, mathematics, census lists and tax registers. There are hundreds of thousands of partially preserved clay tablets from the Egyptian and Babylonian periods and similar numbers of archaeological sites, half a million along the Tigris and Euphrates rivers alone. Yet the first scrap of evidence, written or archaeological, that we have that the Hebrews or their God might ever have existed, doesn't appear until the eighth century BC.

The oldest surviving story in the world is the Babylonian epic of Gilgamesh, in which the hero is robbed of physical immortality when he gains knowledge through the deceptions of a snake. It also includes the Noah story of the ark and a great flood. There are similar Egyptian stories of a snake's ancestors being cursed when the world was young so that it lost its legs and was forced to crawl.

There's little doubt that the writers of the Old Testament would have been familiar with Gilgamesh. Its origins are probably earlier than 3000 BC, and it was told all over the known world in the second millennium BC. It was first written down around 2000 BC, about 1,500 years before elements of it were collated into what became the Old Testament. There are versions of Gilgamesh in a number of ancient languages: Semitic Akkadian, Indo-European, Hittite, and Hurrian, to name a few. Fragments of this epic myth have been found in several places along the eastern Mediterranean coast where the Hebrews are known to have traveled. Wherever the Bible has traditions in common with those of neighboring societies the Bible stories tend to be of a later date.

The symbolism of the serpent, the tree and the land of immortality in the Garden of Eden story in Genesis go back thousands of years before the Bible was written. They go further back than Gilgamesh, to the Old Sumerian cylinder seals, and to the rituals and art of ancient people around the world. The serpent himself is a character out of an older, larger tradition. In ancient art he is often seen as a god in his own right and he appears in many religions, being associated with healing, wisdom and immortality. He is still the emblem of medicine. Even today, many religions retain a fascination with snakes, as do some Christian sects, like the snake-handling churches of the Ozarks in the USA.

So far, all this is a matter of historical record, and there's little disagreement among scholars. But here's a bit of speculation. The Jewish God Yahweh may have developed from a serpent God, or at least one with snake-like qualities. Traces of the divine serpent appear throughout the Old Testament. Moses plants a serpent rod in the wilderness so the Hebrews can look on it and be healed (Numbers 21:4-9). The rod is given a name, Nehushtan, and is worshiped for several hundred years before King Hezekiah breaks it in the eighth century BC (2 Kings 18:4).

But how did the Old Testament writers think of God? Genesis itself contains two creation stories, introducing us to two images of Him. The first account opens with the words, "In the beginning God created the heaven and the earth ..." and leads on through the six days of creation. This God is a disembodied "spirit" (*ruach*), an impersonal force, sweeping over the waters. It's a depiction of God that doesn't occur again anywhere else in the Hebrew Bible, but is common in Persian literature. God acts, speaks, and creates the world, in a continuous narrative from the first verse of Genesis through to the end of the seventh day in chapter 2:2. The verses describing the creation of humankind are: "And God said, Let us make man in our image, after our likeness... So God created man in his own image, in the image of God created he him; male and female created he them." God gives the appearance of being omnipotent, omniscient, acting through his word to make things happen rather than getting physically involved. This is the beginning of the tradition that sees divinity as being within human beings. There is no mention of sin and disobedience, garden or serpent. Male and female are equal. Everything is "very good," and is blessed.

Then there's a surprise because in Genesis 2:4 the story starts again with: "These are the generations of the heavens and of the earth." The construction of the earth is different, and man comes before the trees, birds and animals rather than later. God is physical rather than a spirit. He walks, speaks and creates like a man. This second God is a lesser being than the exalted God of the first story, and the details of His creation are correspondingly downgraded. He doesn't create man in His image, but out of earth and then plants a garden for the man to live in and look after. When God realizes that Adam will be lonely, He puts him to sleep and creates a woman from one of his ribs (the story doesn't explain why we still have pairs of ribs), rather than creating the man and woman together as in the first story.

This God says to the couple that they will die if they eat the fruit of the tree of knowledge of good and evil. The serpent urges them to go ahead and eat, telling them that that they will not die. He adds, "Your eyes shall be opened, and ye shall be as gods [plural], knowing good and evil." The serpent is right. Adam eats the fruit but lives till he's 930. He and Eve realize they are naked and hide from the Lord God who is "walking in the garden in the cool of the day," evidently finding the noonday sun as uncomfortable as we would in the Middle East. God interrogates them, curses the snake, tells the man that his work will become hard labor, and the woman that child-bearing will be painful, and condemns them both to return to dust (no mention of heaven or hell here).

This second God, as skilled a tailor as he is a surgeon, makes clothing for the two out of animal skins. He feels threatened because the man and woman have upgraded their status to equal His own and drives them away, before they can taste the fruit from the tree of life, putting guards with flaming swords at the entrance in the east wall. This time He's not pleased with what He created (Genesis 6:5-6).

Jewish and Christian scholars have been through all kinds of mental hoops to explain why there are two different stories here. In the early eighteenth century a German minister suggested the obvious reason: they were written by two different people at different times. We now know that the second came first, in about the eighth century BC. The first was later, written in the sixth century BC when the Jews were in exile, and uses a more sophisticated idea of God borrowed from the Persians. A third writer combined the two stories some time before 400 BC. Perhaps both were too well known for either to be dropped. This is generally agreed by scholars. Why many Christian teachers persist in saying there is no contradiction in the Bible is hard to understand. There are hundreds. Genesis is not unusual.

Both Gods are still present in Christian tradition today. There's the Almighty who created the world and saw it as good, but has remained largely absent since, leaving it to its own devices. There's also the more human personal God who intervenes, taking sides and answering petitions, judging and condemning. It's hard to believe in both at the same time.

28 THE NOMAD'S GOD

"We pick out a text here and there to make it serve our turn, whereas if
we take it altogether, and consider what went before and what followed
after we should find it meant no such thing."

JOHN SELDEN

The story of the Hebrews, though, starts way before the creation
stories were written down. What image of God did the first
Hebrews have? To look at that we need to go further back in
history, to the second millennium BC.

Linking the two great civilizations of Mesopotamia and Egypt
was the Fertile Crescent – a band of habitable land that stretched
in a great arc up to what is now south Turkey and down the coast
to Egypt, skirting the Arabian desert. In those days, as its name
suggests, this land was full of fertile valleys and wooded hills,
though as early as the second millennium BC over-irrigation was
reducing yields in the river valleys of Persia. Further deforestation
and overgrazing by goats has turned it into the barren landscape it
has largely become today.

Between these two civilizations nomadic tribes wandered with
their flocks as the seasons and grazing dictated, along trails that had
been followed for tens of millennia. Some were called *Habiru*, from
which we get the word Hebrew. There was no suggestion that they
were a defined race, the term has connotations of "mercenary,"
"vagabond." One of these characters may have been called
Abraham. He was a shepherd who left Ur in Mesopotamia roughly around 1400 BC (there are no dates in the Bible). The
uncertainty over whether he existed as an individual is reflected in
the range of dates put forward different scholars: anything over a
1,000-year period. An equivalent time frame would range from the
Norman Conquest of England to the present day.

The Jews start their history from the time of Abraham, their
"father." Or at least the tribes of the later Southern Kingdom of

Judah saw him as father, the Northern Kingdom looked to Jacob, whose name was changed to Israel. The first 1,000 years of the Bible story are based around the theme of journeys back and forth around this arc. Some of the journeys are in the nature of tribal wanderings, following the good grazing. Some are motivated by greed for plunder, others are forced on to the Hebrews by defeat. You may find it helpful to look at the timeline at the back of the book to keep track of where we are.

The Book of Genesis doesn't really explain what Abraham believed in, or in what way his faith was different from the beliefs of his parents or neighbors. Whatever it was, there is no record of a new revelation of a single, all-knowing, all-powerful God bursting on to the scene. Abraham's God was one of many local gods: a nomad's god, a "house deity," carried around with the household goods, of the kind that Rachel could steal from Laban (Genesis 31:17-35). This God is described as El, also the name of the highest god of the Canaanites, and a common god in other tribes. He's also referred to in the plural: Elohim. As one of many local gods El is not special to Abraham's family. He speaks in dreams to kings as well as to Abraham and Jacob. He is recognized as a god by the pagan priest Melchizedek (Genesis 14:18-24) whose own god Abraham also recognizes. He is not all-powerful: in Genesis 19:22 He says to Lot, "I cannot do any thing till thou be come hither."

If you want to take Abraham literally he is not an attractive figure. He makes his fortune by prostituting his beautiful wife (though apparently she's over ninety) "in every place, wherever we go" (Genesis 12:11-20; 20:1-18), much to the disgust of his hosts when they find out. This doesn't seem to worry God, who backs him up by sending plagues and threatening death to those he has deceived. Abraham is in the old tradition of the trickster who fools everyone, even twisting fate and God to his advantage.

Abraham prospers through his pimping, and begins to see this God as special to himself. He is a God who can be persuaded,

(Genesis 18:22-33). Sometimes He appears in human form, for example, as one or more men (Genesis 18:1-8), who need feeding like any other guest. He advises Abraham on domestic issues, family relationships, grazing for the flocks, and which direction to wander in. He can be called to account. He's a God Abraham can "deal" with. He and God bind themselves together in a covenant, in much the same way as people do in a legal document (Genesis 17:1-14). It's repeated several times, as if it's not quite certain.

Up to this point Abraham has been making reasonable arrangements with his neighbors, like taking his herds in a different direction to Lot's to avoid conflict over grazing. But now this new personal God promises Abraham and his descendants the land of Canaan. Unfortunately God doesn't ask the people in Canaan to leave the land first, so setting the scene for thousands of years of trouble, trouble which still makes the news today. Abraham becomes the shepherd's nightmare, the guy who won't co-operate, who wants it all for himself. He worships a God that reflects his own interests rather than the powers of nature that affect everyone alike. God is the God of Abraham and no one else, a tribal God who even divides families down the middle: "Yet I loved Jacob, and I hated Esau" (Malachi 1:2-3). A God of individual greed rather than collective responsibility.

Not many people read the Abraham story this way. Many Jews take it literally: the story is what it says it is. God gave Abraham this land, they are his descendants, so the land is theirs, by divine decree. Some Christians agree with this and encourage the US government in its $3 billion a year subsidy to the Israeli army. Some Christians look for other meanings, interpreting the story to fit their own times and circumstances. The Dutch Boers, for instance, trekking into the African interior, saw it as a story for them: God was giving them the land they saw before them. From this and other Bible passages the Dutch Reformed Church developed the doctrine of apartheid. More mainstream Christians look for other interpretations. For instance, Abraham wasn't a bad guy. And God wasn't really going to let him cut his son's throat, because He wasn't one of those nasty deities, common at the time, that people were expected to sacrifice children to. That particular story is about Abraham's faith. God challenges him and he rises to the occasion. It's a story about God confounding our human expectations of Him and leading us on to a greater understanding.

All read their own idea of God back into the text. You have to read these stories for yourself.

With Abraham's descendants the scene shifts from Canaan to Egypt for the great story of the Exodus.

29 THE WARRIOR GOD

"1. And they sought for a Better Sign from Arnold Bros (est.1905), and there was a Sign.

11. And some spake up saying, Well, all right, but it is really nothing but a Co incidence:

111. But others said, Even a Co incidence can be a Sign."

FROM THE *BOOK OF NOME, SIGNS*, 2:1-111, TERRY PRATCHETT

Abraham's descendants move to Egypt to escape from famine in Canaan (according to the biblical story, though the Ishmaelite camels Joseph was supposed to ride on probably didn't arrive in the area for another six centuries). The Egyptians had created a remarkable civilization – the longest-lasting in human history to date – of at least 3,000 years. Only China comes close. Our own modern Western civilization, if you date its birth from the Renaissance, 500 years ago, has barely started to register on the Egyptian timescale. Their religion was tolerant, albeit under the absolute authority of the Pharaoh. To be regarded as an Egyptian citizen, it was simply necessary to accept their beliefs and practices – to become "civilized." It is one of the ironies of history that the Egyptian religion has virtually disappeared (only a few hundred thousand people still practice it) whilst that of the early Hebrews has survived.

After a number of generations the Hebrews feel oppressed in Egypt, and want to leave. It's difficult to know how to take the story. There's not a scrap of evidence outside the Bible for the Hebrews having ever been in Egypt, which is surprising, given the sheer volume of Egyptian records. Apparently the Hebrew population has now swelled to over 600,000 men (Numbers 1:46), though they all managed to leave Egypt in one night and the women were serviced by two midwives. The number must be massively exaggerated, it would have made them a good proportion of the whole Egyptian population. It's not an isolated mistake, as the figure is also implied in Exodus 38:26 and Numbers 1:46. But it was pointed out as early as the eighteenth century that 600,000 men with families, carts, cattle, sheep and goats would have created a column so long that when the front entered the Promised Land the back wouldn't have left Egypt, even allowing for circling the Sinai peninsula.

This is not to say that no Hebrews ever lived in Egypt; some scholars say it's possible, and why invent such an extensive story? The Exodus is probably based on fact to the extent that the movement of a subject people did occur, and many scholars identify the Pharaoh with Rameses II (1304-1237 BC). But there's no evidence for the story on the scale described in the Bible, or for the more dramatic details. Some experts have linked the Exodus with the volcanic explosion of Thera in 1628 BC which destroyed the Cretan civilization and could account for the darkness falling on the land, the cliffs of water crashing on armies, and the plagues – but the dates don't fit.

It's also very unlikely that large numbers of Hebrews spent many years wandering in Sinai. This desert country was virtually unpopulated then, as it is now. Traces of Bedouin encampments and tiny settlements survive from up to 5,000 years ago – well before the Exodus period – but there's no sign of a large group of people moving through.

But whether or not the Exodus happened, the story is interesting for what it says about the kind of God that the Hebrews now believed in. We'll go into the story in a little more detail, because the way it seems to read in the Bible is very different from the image we have of a gracious God saving his grateful people and leading them safely through the desert to a promised land.

Like the cunning and commanding Aeneas in the *Aeneid*, the equivalent Exodus story for the Romans, Moses dominates the Hebrew Exodus. The God of Moses is very different from

Abraham's God. But He is not yet the Almighty we are familiar with today. Some of the miracles that God does through Moses the pharaoh's magicians can also do. It's a question of degree, not nature.

The new, more-powerful tribal God comes to be called YHVH or Yahweh ("Jehovah" is a mistaken translation). Where did the idea of Yahweh come from? Remember that Abraham had believed in one of many local gods. His great-grandsons and their descendants probably lived in Egypt some time between 1400 and 1200 BC. During this period the Egyptians had developed the idea of one all-powerful Sun God to reflect the glory of the pharaoh. The Sun God, called Aton, was worshiped as the only God by Amenhotep IV around the year 1360 BC. After the Exodus the Hebrews seem to have picked up this idea of a single all-powerful God. Coincidence? Or is the Judaeo-Christian God really Egyptian? Some scholars say it's possible.

Other scholars say it's more likely that Moses adopted Him in some form from the religion of the Midianites during his stay with their high priest, whose daughter he married (Exodus 2:16-3:16). Alternatively, some Christian scholars accept that God simply called to Moses from a burning bush and introduced Himself (Exodus 3:1-14).

Whichever is true, Moses was one of those extraordinary characters like Napoleon or Hitler who can change the self-image of a nation. When God talked to Abraham it was like a chat between neighbors. But when God talks to Moses He speaks out of fire and storm and the very ground is holy. Jacob had seen God face to face (Genesis 32:30), but now looking at His face would kill you (Exodus 33:20). Moses, though, is allowed a glimpse of God's backside (Exodus 33:18-23), and the glory is reflected on to Moses' face so that it shines. Even looking at Moses after he has looked at God can kill the Hebrews, so he has to wear a veil. The nomadic God of Abraham, who was carried around with the luggage, has taken on the majesty of the higher gods – the ones like Zeus who the Greeks believed would burn you into ashes if you saw his true form.

On Mount Sinai, the covenant God had made with Abraham is now renewed and put into writing. He gives detailed laws on how the Hebrews are to conduct themselves, mirroring an earlier story of laws given by the sun-god to King Hammurabi around 1,000 years before. God now provides an answer to the question of what to do with the people already in Canaan: He will "blot them out." He's not just a terminator but also a military strategist: "I will not drive them out from before thee in one year; lest the land become desolate, and the beast of the field multiply against thee. By little and little I will drive them out from before thee, until thou be increased, and inherit the land" (Exodus 23:29-30). This marks the early stages of the "holy war" ideology, later to become institutionalized in Islam as one aspect of *Jihad,* and to find expression in Christianity through the Crusades. Some detailed instructions on how to wage such a war are given in the Old Testament, including ritual cleansing before battle (Joshua 3:5); abstinence from sex (2 Samuel 11:11); rules of engagement (Deuteronomy 20). There was probably more in *The Book of the Wars of Yahweh*, referred to in Numbers 21:14, but this has been lost.

By the time Moses comes back down from the mountain with the Ten Commandments the people have returned to the bull worship of Jacob (translated into English in Genesis 49:24 as "the mighty God of Jacob"). They are quite ready to believe that this was the god that brought them out of Egypt. Bull worship continues through the centuries in the Northern Kingdom of Israel (1 Kings 12:28). It's a common feature of ancient religions, traces of which can still be seen today in the bullrings of Spain. Moses, however, seems to have a different view of God from most of his fellows. He and God are now angry. God wants to consume the people, sparing Moses to continue the line and the dynastic plans for a great nation (Exodus 32:9-10), but Moses persuades Him to change His mind on the grounds that it would encourage their joint enemies, the Egyptians. God repents of His evil thoughts (Exodus 32:14) but Moses still considers punishment necessary. He calls on his elite guard, the loyal sons of Levi, to "slay every man his brother, and every man his companion, and every man his neighbor" (Exodus 32:27), which they do, killing 3,000. In his rage Moses has smashed the tablets on which the commandments had been written so he goes up the mountain again for a second set.

The Book of Leviticus follows Exodus as an extensive interlude, largely about what foods are "clean" to eat, and what are "unclean." These rules do not follow any modern dietary or health logic. The Hindu law codes, the *Laws of Manu*, belonging to the first century BC, or the first century AD, reveal an even greater concern with the right performance of everyday life. The only significant difference here is that the Hindus were many and the Israelites few. The Hindus could separate their people up into castes and enable the priests and aristocrats to keep control that way; the Israelites only managed one or two "castes" of "priests" and set themselves up against their neighbors.

The Book of Numbers picks up the thread of the story. After a year at Mount Sinai, the Hebrews set out again with their new "ark," in which God is now living, having left His mountain home. The people soon complain about the catering that Moses and God provide, but are answered with plagues; dissent is silenced with leprosy. They get to Canaan but spies sent out to survey the land come back disheartened because of the military strength of the people living there. God wants to destroy the people for their lack of faith and fighting spirit, but Moses reminds Him about how jubilant their enemies would, be so God sends another plague instead.

Two of the Levites, along with 250 other leaders, complain to Moses that they want some democracy. Nomadic tribes, after all, tend to govern themselves through consultation and kinship ties. Moses is turning himself into king/high priest/leader all rolled into one, a complete tyrant. "Ye take too much upon you, seeing all the congregation are holy, every one of them, and the LORD is among them: wherefore then lift ye up yourselves [Moses and his brother Aaron] above the congregation of the LORD?" (Numbers 16:3). There is a stand-off the following morning, before the earth opens and swallows the leaders with their women and children, taking them all down into Sheol, after which God sends a fire to consume their followers. The morning after that, the people again rebel, accusing Moses of murder. After all, how many of them has he killed by now? The Lord smites them all with the plague until Aaron manages to stop the carnage with a sacrifice. This time the dead number 14,700. Further rebellion and plagues follow: 24,000 are killed when some of the men start having sex with the local Moabite women (Numbers 25:1-15). The deaths only stop when an offending couple are caught in the act and speared through. The ringleaders are rounded up and hanged in the sun. The climax of Numbers comes in chapter 31 with the battle against the Midianites. The Israelites slay all the males, but Moses is angry with them for sparing the women, so they get the plague again. Moses commands them to slay all the women except the virgins, who they can keep for rape.

These chapters are so rarely read that we forget what a brutal and bloodthirsty God this is. Is He mad, bad and dangerous to know, or is this just the God of Moses' imagination alone? How are we to separate the two? Who knows what really happened to Moses on the top of Mount Sinai? Time and again God wants to go over the top and slaughter. Even when a man is found gathering sticks on the Sabbath, and the people aren't sure what to do with him, God commands that he be stoned to death (Numbers 15:32-36). The continual complaint from God and Moses is that the people aren't brutal enough in their treatment of their enemies. It's not as if this was inevitably the culture of the period. The drama of poetry like the *Iliad* (written at roughly the same time) lies in the sympathy with which the Greek poet treats the Trojans, particularly the hero Hector whose death is the tragic centerpiece of the poem. Similarly Aeschylus imagines the Greek defeat of the Persians through the eyes of the Persian women left at home. Throughout this period you can find better morality in the writings and gods of "pagan" cultures than in the pages of the Old Testament. The strength and weakness of the writers in the Bible, and perhaps also the Jewish people as a whole, is their narrow concern with the tribe, at the expense of seeing the viewpoint of others.

After circling the Sinai desert for a couple of generations the Hebrews make their assault on Canaan. Again, there's no other evidence for this invasion. The Canaanites appear to have been already pushed out by tribes coming from the north, the same movement of peoples that gave rise to the tales of Homer describing the same period: the *Iliad* and the *Odyssey*. The usurpers were the Phoenicians, with their god Baal.

But whether the stories are legend or fact, God has lost none of His appetite for bloodshed. Having slaughtered tens of thousands of their own people, He and Moses' successors aren't going to treat their opponents lightly. Joshua is instructed to kill the 12,000 inhabitants of Ai; and in the battle against an alliance of five southern kings God keeps the sun suspended in the sky so there's enough daylight to finish off the enemy. The change in tone from the time of Abraham can be summed up in a comparison between the fate of Abraham's son and Jepthah's daughter. God lets Abraham off the sacrifice of Isaac, but Jepthah has to burn his daughter alive, (Judges 11).

30 A GOD AMONG MANY

"Every time in history that man has tried to turn crucified truth into coercive truth he has betrayed the fundamental principle of Christianity."

DOSTOEVSKY

Whether any of the biblical story so far really happened, we'll never know. The Hebrews simply didn't leave a large enough historical footprint for us to say. But we learn enough about the Hebrew God to know that at this stage He was no more or less barbaric than thousands of similar tribal deities scattered around the planet.

As we approach the first millennium BC the historical framework becomes a little more solid. Most scholars agree that over the twelfth to tenth centuries BC it does seem likely that the Hebrews, increasingly referred to in retrospect as the tribes of Israel, gradually began to forge a common identity, occupying the hilltops in central Palestine and raiding the more prosperous Phoenician cities in the plains. Their success was limited as the Phoenicians had already entered the Iron Age (Judges 1:19), and Goliath, for example, has an iron sword when he faces David. It's not until the reign of David that the Israelites manage to occupy Jerusalem (around 1000 BC).

Under David and Solomon the nation of Israel (more like a federation of tribes) reaches its peak. After that it splits into two: northern and southern. There's still a degree of speculation here because so far there's no evidence outside the Bible that any of these Israelites kings existed, though it's increasingly likely that they did. There's no good reason to dispute the outlines.

The first non-biblical historical reference to the Hebrews or Israelites is an Assyrian notation of a defeat inflicted on them by King Ahab in alliance with the kings of Damascus at Qarqar in 853 BC. Ahab is the only Israelite king credited by a non-biblical source with inflicting a significant defeat on his enemies.

The first historical event to be mentioned both in the Bible itself (2 Kings 17:1-6) and elsewhere takes place in 722 BC when Assyrian records tell of the conquest of the Northern Kingdom of Israel. The Assyrians were brutal conquerors, putting the early Israelites in the shade. They would intimidate the inhabitants of a city they were besieging by bringing forward captives from the last campaign, impaling them on spears around the walls, or skinning them alive, or sticking hooks into the flesh and dragging them to death behind chariots. The Israelites may not have fared this badly – their God was irrelevant to the Assyrians, but apparently they were valued as skillful musicians and chariot drivers. Ten of the twelve tribes were carried into captivity; the southern tribes of Benjamin and Judah were left to carry on the nation.

During the following century the Babylonian Empire replaced the Assyrian. In 586 BC Nebuchadnezzar, the Babylonian monarch, destroyed Jerusalem and carried the Israelites of the Southern Kingdom off to captivity in Babylon. With the Babylonian captivity they are back in the land which Abraham had been called to leave 1,000 years earlier. Over half the history of civilization on this planet has now been covered, and Jesus is still half a millennium away in the future.

The interesting question, though, is what kind of God did the Israelites believe in during this period? Christians (and Jews) tend to read the Old Testament as a record of faithful worship punctuated by disobedience and backsliding for which the Israelites were punished by defeat in battle. The reality was probably very different.

The fury of the warrior God of Moses seems to have diminished. After settling down in Canaan the Israelites seem to forget about Him and return to beliefs and behavior virtually indistinguishable from the tribes around them, particularly those of the more powerful Phoenicians who had settled the prosperous coastal regions. Warrior desert gods are not necessarily good at making the crops grow.

This is made clear in the Bible when in 621 BC, centuries after the arrival of the Hebrews in Canaan, King Josiah sends his secretary to the Temple to collect taxes. The high priest Hilkiah gives him an old book he's just found buried in the Temple somewhere among the cast-offs. This turns out to be all or part of the "Book of Moses" and Josiah realizes that for centuries Israel has been worshipping the wrong gods and has forgotten about the God of the Exodus. He tells the people to celebrate a Passover feast and the writer of Kings adds: "Surely there was not holden such a passover from the days of the judges that judged Israel, nor in all the days of the kings of Israel, nor of the kings of Judah" (2 Kings 23:22).

Josiah starts a campaign to cleanse the kingdom. He destroys all the pagan altars and throws out the foreign statues and idolatrous clutter from the Temple, gets rid of the cult prostitutes and slaughters the priests. From here on the worship of Yahweh seems to predominate among the Israelites, though the next four kings "did what was evil in the sight of the Lord."

So when did the idea of there being only one God (monotheism) rather than one god amongst many (henotheism) really take root among the Israelites? It's much debated. Doesn't the first commandment that Moses brought down from the mountain proclaim the one and only God who alone is to be worshipped? "Thou shalt have no other gods before me." Not necessarily. The translation is argued over. It could just mean, "I'll be your first God." The dating is no more certain: it's generally reckoned to be between the eighth and ninth centuries, hundreds of years after Moses, possibly as late as the sixth century.

It's a complicated picture. One thread, for instance, that persists through the Old Testament is that God was not necessarily the God of the Israelites only. He hedges His bets, supporting other peoples as well:

"Are ye not as children of the Ethiopians unto me, O children of
Israel?" saith the Lord. Have I not brought up Israel out of the land
of Egypt? and the Philistines from Caphtor, and the Syrians from
Kir?"

AMOS 9:7

You have to look carefully in the Bible to find the balance.
There's a dual narrative running through Judges, Samuel, Kings and
Chronicles. On the one hand the later scribes record the doings of
the men of God. On the other hand there's the almost buried but
frequent acknowledgment that "the high places [the foreign altars]
were not taken away" (2 Chronicles 15:17). The oldest Hebrew
inscription that exists, the Moabite stone, makes reference to the god
Chemosh. Saul names one of his sons after the Phoenician god Baal,
as does his son Jonathan. And much of the book of Hosea is about
changing allegiances: "For I will take away the names of Baalim out
of her mouth, and they shall no more be remembered by their
name" (Hosea 2:17). In Psalm 82 it's clear that God Himself doesn't
have everything His own way, and could do with some help:

"God presides in the great assembly;
he gives judgment among the 'gods':
How long will you defend the unjust
and show partiality to the wicked?"

PSALM 82:1-2 NIV

Most scholars would agree that monotheism is not established in
Israel until well into the first millennium. Some even say it doesn't
appear in Israel until the sixth century BC. The old stories, in which
God is one of many, with many names, went through their final
compilation and editing as late as the fourth century BC. The writers retrospectively ascribed the grand deeds of their semi-legendary
ancestors to their worship of the one God, Yahweh.

31 HOW THE STORY OF GOD WAS WRITTEN

"Human beings are perhaps never more frightening than when they are convinced beyond doubt that they are right."

LAURENS VAN DER POST

Christians tend to think of God, the teaching in the Old Testament about Him, and the Old Testament itself, as something unchanged, everlasting, as though one book after another was slotted into the planned frame like pouring concrete into a mold. But it would be better to compare the Bible with the mud or stone houses and towns of ancient times. Every generation extends, develops, and rebuilds its houses. After millennia you get tells – the mounds rising from the plain – which indicate different layers of occupation, one on top of the other. In the view of modern scholars the image of God in the Old Testament is built up in the same way.

We've now arrived at the Babylonian captivity – the Exile – which took place in the sixth century BC. The Israelites have by now been living in Canaan for around 600 years. Their religion focused on the land, to which they had a sacred right because God gave it to Abraham. From the time of Solomon, God had physically lived in the Temple and all the festivals and sacrificial rituals were bound up with it. Whether this God was the monotheistic Yahweh, whether he had been the main God for centuries or just a few generations, is uncertain but what is certain is that the people couldn't continue with this religion of "place" in Babylon.

When Assyria had carried off the ten Israelite tribes of the Northern Kingdom into captivity, in the previous century, they had disappeared from history. The amazing thing is that the remaining two tribes of the Southern Kingdom, Benjamin and Judah, managed to survive when they were deported. The Israelites were now one of many minor races shuttled around within the Babylonian Empire. The all-conquering Hebrew war God obviously didn't fit into this scenario. Whether it was because the people had broken the covenant, or because Yahweh had not been strong enough to keep His side of it, the religion changes, transformed into a religion whose purpose is to preserve national identity through ritual and law. It is now imperative to preserve the stories of the race before they are forgotten. They had to be collected into a book, fast, and that's the origin of the Old Testament. It was in these years of exile that the Israelites forged the religion of survival that later enabled them to keep going despite the destruction of Jerusalem by the Romans and two thousand years of wandering, down to the last century.

Parts of the Bible were already in written form when the compilers in Babylon set to work. Parts may simply have been lost in the forced evacuation. Panic rather than planning was probably the order of the day. The Old Testament itself refers to 18 books which have since disappeared: *The Songs of the Wars of Yahweh, The Book of Jashar, The Chronicles of the Kings of Israel (referred to 18 times), The Chronicles of the Kings of Judah (15 mentions), The Records of Gad the Seer, The Visions of Iddo the Seer, The Annals of Jehu Son of Hanani*, and so on.

Then there's a body of writing which was at times taken as authoritative but didn't make it into the later canon – *The Book of Jubilees, The Book of Noah, The Genesis Apocrypha, The Testament of Levi, The Sayings of Moses, The Book of Giants/Enoch*. The latter is quoted in the New Testament Book of Jude (13-16).

The compilers (who were probably priests) began to collect the different oral stories and traditions (which may well have varied from tribe to tribe) and put them, together with the existing written material, into one body of sacred writings. We end up with a diverse mix – everything from erotic poetry to boring genealogy. Large tracts are only of specialist or historical value, and indeed weren't read on a regular basis by the Israelites themselves. One of the flourishing areas of biblical studies today involves the attempt to trace the origin of different sections of the Old Testament and to work out when they were put together, and by whom. All scholars accept that the process of revision and re-interpretation of the existing material was continuous and lengthy. The gaps and joins still show, as we have seen in Genesis. Different writers describe events in different ways, reflecting changing beliefs and agendas. For instance, David's decision to take a census in 2 Samuel 24:1-2 is said to be due to God's anger with his people. But in 1 Chronicles 21:1, written after the Exile in Babylon, the inspiration comes from Satan.

The Israelites were exiled in Babylon for about seven generations. It's a crucial period. The writers couldn't help but be influenced by the society in which they lived, much as early nineteenth-century immigrants to the USA are now part of that culture. In summary, as we have seen, the religion of the Hebrew shepherds had been relatively primitive, with little theology and no sense of individual salvation. During the Egyptian years some aspects of monotheism may have been taken on board. As the nomads settled down in the conquered areas of Canaan they merged their beliefs and practices with the more settled agricultural gods and rituals of the Phoenicians. They created the Temple culture, similar to that of many other societies, which they had lost now they were in exile. The Persians, who in 539 conquered the Babylonians to create a vast empire stretching from Libya to the border of India, followed the ancient Persian religion of Zoroastrianism, inherited from the Medes. They already had their own sacred books, the *Zend Avesta,* now mostly lost. They had been studying the stars for thousands of years – the world's first observatory, the Temple of Belus, is believed to have been established in 2350 BC. The Wise Men who came from the East to the birthplace of Jesus were most probably Magi, the Persian priests.

The Persians asked the kinds of questions we ask today: Why should good people suffer and innocent babies die? Zoroaster had answered that time moves forward to its appointed end when those who have done good in this life will be rewarded. He taught that the world was created by a wholly good God, Ahura Mazda. His evil brother Ahriman fights against him, and rules for 7,000 years. In due time the world Savior will be born of the seed of a prophet and a virgin mother. All men and women must choose between good and evil. There will be a cataclysmic final battle between the forces of both in which the good will triumph. The bodies of those who died earlier will be resurrected and the Last Judgement will take place.

The facts of this aren't in dispute, just the interpretation. Some Christian scholars say: Okay, there are similarities between Persian beliefs and the later Israelite religion. The Israelite religion is inspired, with the Holy Spirit revealing the truth to humankind, whilst the Persian religion is not.

But most scholars would say that this is putting the cart before the horse. The Persian religion came first and was overwhelmingly more important in the first two millennia BC. It influenced the beliefs of the Israelites, who adopted many Persian ideas during their exile. The Hebrew idea of a tribal, warrior God who could do both good and evil, change his mind twice a day and help them in battle slowly changes until God is seen as a holy, just God.

Evil came to be embodied separately in Satan and along with God and Satan came the hierarchy of angels and demons, life after death, heaven and hell, resurrection, the judgement of the dead and the spirit of God working through humankind. Many of these ideas still had centuries of development to go and are still developing. Today we think of them as Christian, though they also fed into Islam, and even influenced Hinduism and Buddhism.

During the Exile the change was more than religious. The Israelites also largely dropped their own Hebrew language and took up the Persian language of Aramaic as their first tongue – the language that Jesus and the disciples later spoke.

Nebuchadnezzar's successor eased the hardships of the captivity and many of the exiles were assimilated into Babylonian culture, as we can see from the book of Daniel, but others longed for home. The last Babylonian ruler, Nabonidus, was overthrown by the Persian emperor Cyrus, who allowed those who wished to return to Jerusalem. They made a start on rebuilding the Temple but were opposed by the locals (Ezra 3:3), mostly people from other nations who had been resettled in the land by the Babylonians. These people, who followed a syncretistic religion, later became known as the Samaritans. They created a rival temple on Mount Gerizim and followed their own version of the five Books of Moses. They still sacrifice there in the same way today, and may be closer to the religion of Abraham than the Jews, not being so contaminated by the Persian influence.

A determined effort to rebuild the walls of Jerusalem was made a hundred years later under the reign of Artaxerxes I. By this time many of those of Israelite descent in Babylon and other centers of the Empire were enjoying lives of some comfort and prosperity. Nehemiah, a trusted royal servant, was even given an escort of army officers and cavalry (Nehemiah 2:9) to take a group back to Jerusalem.

Here for the first time the Bible joins the mainstream history of the region, maybe 1,000 years after the time of Abraham, about 445 BC. We're still only talking about tiny fragments of information, but their historicity is confirmed by non-biblical writings. Nehemiah had the resources and authority to rebuild, and Ezra, described as priest, scribe, and descendant of Aaron (Ezra 7:1-6) had the spiritual authority to teach. He took with him, and may well have had a hand in composing, a large part of the Old Testament that we have today. Ezra assembled the "men, women, and all who were able to understand" in front of the Water Gate in Jerusalem and read to them "the Book of the Law of Moses which the Lord [Yahweh] had commanded for Israel" (Nehemiah 8:1-3 NIV). A fortnight later, they celebrated the Feast of the Tabernacles in memory of the 40 years spent wandering in the wilderness after the escape from Egypt. The Hebrews began to draw together in weekly meetings to read the scriptures. They became the first "people of the book."

Many date this occasion as the moment when the Jewish religion really came into being, and it's from now that most historians talk of the "Jews" as an identifiable body of people.

32 WHY THE STORY STOPPED

"Man's last and highest parting occurs when, for God's sake, he takes leave of God."

ECKHART

The Jews still write sacred scripture after the return from Exile, but it doesn't have the same kind of authority as the Books of Moses. Still to come are the Books of Daniel, Esther, Ezra, large parts of Isaiah, and Nehemiah, among others. The image of God here is different from that in the earlier books. One or two miracles happen, notably when Daniel's friends are thrown into the fiery furnace, but this is mysterious; the fourth figure seen in the fire is not identified. In Esther, where the Jews are saved from being massacred by a woman who is the wife of the Persian king Ahasuerus, God is not mentioned at all. The story is about the power of the Persian rulers over the Jews, not the power of God over the enemies of the Jews. (Ahasuerus, incidentally, is better known in history as Xerxes, whose defeat by the Greeks was one of history's great turning-points.) We are a long way from the Exodus. The transition is so marked that it has been called "the disappearance of God."

Obedience to the warrior God hadn't saved the Israelites from being slaughtered and exiled first by the Assyrians and then the Babylonians. And as the centuries after the Exile moved on it became apparent that being faithful to the Law didn't work either. Israel was still oppressed by its enemies, and never regained its independence, despite huge efforts, particularly during the time of the Maccabees. A new thread of writing – the apocalyptic literature – reflected this problem. The Jews felt that the problem couldn't just be with them and developed the theory that the earth as a whole had grown so wicked that it was past saving. God would therefore destroy it, letting only a faithful few survive.

The process of God removing Himself from the earth and projecting Himself into the future had already begun before the Exile.

In the centuries after the conquest of Canaan there is little theology, just skirmishing as the balance of power and pillage swings back and forth between the various tribes. Yahweh no longer "comes down" as on Sinai; He intervenes less and less. Of the 41 kings of Israel he speaks only to the second and third. Much of the power of the psalms is in their reflection on why He does this, and on how human beings are to survive without His presence. With 1,000 years of the Old Testament story still to be told, He doesn't appear again. God "hides his face," a phrase used 30 times in the Hebrew Bible, increasingly in the prophets.

Prophets were groups of people akin to the later dervishes of Islam. The trances and ecstasies of the dervishes led people to believe that they were divinely possessed, able to pronounce oracles, and so forth (you can still see them today). But the prophets do not call up the kinds of miracles that Moses achieved. Instead of grand events like the ten plagues of Egypt, or the parting of the Red Sea, we have Elijah refilling a jar of oil that never empties, or Elisha ordering two bears to tear up 42 small boys because they teased him about his baldness (2 Kings 2:23-24). A level of gratuitous violence surpassing our worst mass murderers today. There's little pretense of national interest here, no protection against tribal enemies – and no hint of criticism in the text.

The simplest, most obvious explanation of why God disengages Himself from direct involvement is that it is a function of distance. The further away something is in time or space the easier it is to believe. It happens in our own history. In the UK, when we look back over a similar period of more than a millennium we have our stories of Arthur and Excalibur, Merlin and his magic powers. Once in the area of reliable records less is left to the imagination. When the Jews (maybe Ezra) compiled and wrote down the old tales they incorporated the magical, but as they got closer to their own time, they wrote what they knew had happened. That translates, as it always does, into mundane politics. They were adjusting their faith to reflect the reality of the times.

So revelation slows, and ends. By the time we get to Jesus the Jews had no doubt that there were inspired scriptures, but which were they exactly? The "Old Testament" had come to exist as an entity in the past couple of centuries. Jewish national consciousness had come to the fore with the rebellion of the Maccabees against the rule of the Greek Hasmonean dynasty, successors to the Alexandrian Empire, which had toppled the Persians. It found expression in a sacred history. But the "book" had fuzzy edges. Some Jews thought the writings of Moses were the only authoritative scriptures; others, all the books in the Greek Septuagint translation; yet others only the books originally written in Hebrew and Aramaic. So when Jesus refers to scripture it is not necessarily scripture that is now the Old Testament. In John 7:38, for instance, we read that Jesus says, "He that believeth on me, as the scripture hath said, out of his belly shall flow rivers of living water" – there is no such verse in the Old Testament as we know it.

The Old Testament wasn't given its current form until a generation or two after the death of Jesus, when the destruction of Jerusalem in AD 70 scattered the Jews (and the Jewish Christians). The response of the Jews was similar to that during the Exile. Having again lost their Temple and their homeland they turned to the holy writings to keep their faith and identity. In AD 90, the surviving scholars came together at the Academy of Jamnia, near Jaffa in modern Israel, under Rabbi Johanen ben Zakkai, and decided which books would go into the Hebrew Bible. However, the text itself was not finally agreed till the seventh and eighth centuries AD.

Between the time of Ezra and the destruction of Jerusalem in AD 70 there arose a substantial body of Jewish writing. Some of this writing was included in the Septuagint but was not accepted as canonical at Jamnia, and so does not appear in the Hebrew Bible. The Roman Catholic Church, following the Septuagint, includes in its Old Testament canon twelve books which are not in the Hebrew or Protestant Bibles. Called "deuterocanonical" by Roman Catholics and "Old Testament Apocrypha" by Protestants, these twelve books are: *Ecclesiasticus, Tobit, Susanna,* a *Letter of Jeremiah, Judith, Baruch, The Song of the Three Children, Bel and the Dragon, 1 and 2 Maccabees*, additions to *Esther* and *The Wisdom of Solomon*.

So what's the relevance of the Old Testament for non-Jews? These chapters have probably given a very lopsided view of the Old Testament. We can take from it other, more sympathetic ideas of God. There's the compassionate God of the prophets: "The Lord ... though he cause grief, yet will he have compassion according to the multitude of his mercies. For he doth not afflict willingly nor grieve the children of men" (Lamentations 3:31-33). There's the idea of God as the embodiment of moral holiness. This is stronger in the latter part of the Old Testament (and in the Gospels) than in any other religious literature. After the Exile the Jews are very aware of the precariousness of their nation's position in the world and the injustice that smaller peoples suffered at the hands of stronger enemies. Indeed God becomes defined as the embodiment of the way we should behave. He's not an almighty ego in the sky demanding worship and sacrifice like the neighboring idols. He's a principle of justice, as in the dramatic words of Amos:

> *"I hate, I despise your feast days, and I will not smell in your solemn*
> *assemblies. Though ye offer me burnt offerings and your meat offer-*
> *ings, I will not accept them: neither will I regard the peace offerings*
> *of your fat beasts. Take thou away from me the noise of thy songs;*
> *for I will not hear the melody of thy viols. But let judgment run*
> *down as waters, and righteousness as a mighty stream."*
>
> AMOS 5:21-24

In many ways the Judaism that had developed by the first century AD was more attractive than the Christianity which grew out of it. It was concerned with how we lead our lives, how we treat each other, with social fairness, with the environmental heritage we leave our children. It was a religion of community and forgiveness, of personal relationships. Jesus did not drop out of the sky with a new message, he was a product of the times, a credit to Judaism.

The point of the last few chapters is that through the course of the first millennium BC the Hebrew and Jewish idea of God evolved. Some Christian writers explain this by saying that He only reveals Himself to people in so far as they can understand Him. The understanding develops through the Old Testament and into the New, and we move from a God of anger and violence to a God of love and justice. This misses the point that the God of the Revelation to John at the end of the Bible behaves much like the God of Noah and of Moses, slaughtering humanity wholesale. But in any case why not take this thought further? We can continue to change our idea of Him.

Most Christians still retain the Jewish idea of God as a Spirit separate from us who (in the Christian view) incarnated Himself into an individual on earth. Rather than seeing God as slowly edging out of sight in the Old Testament He explodes back into the world in the New, appearing as a baby rather than locking Himself in a box or Temple. But maybe if there is this God of all relationships in the universe who truly loves humanity, He would indeed disappear. The disappearing God of the Old Testament suggests that as we grow up we find that God's choice is our choice, His love is our love. There's a developing strand of this thought in the Old Testament itself. It's summed up in Jeremiah 31:31, 33:

> "Behold, the days are coming, saith the LORD, that I will make a new covenant with the house of Israel . . . After those days, saith the LORD, I will put my law in their inward parts, and write it in their hearts; and will be their God, and they shall be my people."
> (See also Jeremiah 31:34; Joel 2:28.)

This new covenant would replace the one made with Abraham and his descendants that kicks off the Hebrew story. The promise of land to Abraham is not relevant to us today. Nor are Moses' stone tablets, or Solomon's Temple. In the new covenant God ceases to be an objective deity, and is distributed around, entering the inner life of each believer. We move from the gods of stone and wood, through the written descriptions and images of God, to God-consciousness. The people of the land, who became the people of the Book, are to become the people of Spirit. The people of Spirit no more need the Capital Letter Doctrines than the believers in those days needed the Ark of the Covenant. A Christian interpretation of the Old Testament for today takes this new covenant as its starting point. Jesus fulfills the Old Testament in that he symbolizes God becoming embodied as humankind. Maybe we can take it further and say that in crucifying Jesus we killed the old understanding of God. We can take the words of Jesus on the cross: "My God, my God, why hast thou forsaken me?" (Matthew 27:46) as a metaphor for own experience of God. In so far as we kill others, we kill Him. If we don't realize Him in our lives, He's not there.

PART 5

GOD AND JESUS

33 WHO WAS JESUS?

"If God were able to slide from the truth I would fain cling to the truth and let God go."

ECKHART

The Old Testament stories reflect back to us the worst and best that we can achieve, the hatred of people who are different from us, the ideal of justice for everyone. They talk of our fears and desires, our horror of emptiness and isolation, our need for communion, love and worship. They explain how we came to be as we are, a still-tribal people scratching food from the ground, while building our towers of Babel to the skies. But it is distant history, if history at all.

When we come to the New Testament we've reached home ground, a mere 80 or so generations ago. It's not quite newspaper reporting, but we begin to expect real-time events. So what can we say about Jesus? He's one of the handful of people – Mohammed, Buddha, Confucius, St Paul being among the others – who have been the most influential in history, but about whom we know virtually nothing with any certainty. Was he really God? Did he have any kind of special relationship with God? Did he exist at all? Does it matter?

The amount of research carried out in an effort to determine whether Jesus is a historical figure, and if so, what he really said and did, is equal to the research that has gone into areas of science like the atom bomb and space travel. But the average Christian is unaware of it. Most still assume the stories the Church tells are true in a way the similar stories of other religions are not. Ministers and priests don't want to engage with the questions for fear of upsetting faithful Christian believers. They carry on speaking words and formulas that haven't changed for centuries. But people sense that this way of looking at things has increasingly less relevance, so numbers and influence seep away from the Church. We can't live in the twenty-first century as if we were still in the nineteenth, or the first. After the bomb and space travel the world is not the same. Nor is religion.

What's the consensus on who Jesus was? How should the Church honestly describe him? Think of scholarly opinions of Jesus as stretching along a line. On the left you have a few who say he never existed. Everything in the Gospels is *midrash*, interpretation, a story built up around a mythical figure who is no more historical than, say, King Arthur.

The larger number along the line would agree that Jesus was born around 6 to 4 BC, came from Galilee, was baptized by John the Baptist (whose apprentice he probably was), and, accompanied by a group of followers, exercised an itinerant healing and preaching ministry within the borders of Palestine. He got involved in a dispute over the Temple in Jerusalem and was crucified by the Roman authorities. That's fairly certain. Many, including a number of Christian scholars, would say that some (say ten) of the healing stories are based on fact. The other miracles, including all the nature miracles, are not. He most likely said maybe a fifth of what he is recorded as saying. Another fifth is probable. That's about it. The overwhelming likelihood is that he didn't think of himself as divine. He was a charismatic religious preacher, healer and leader who wanted to bring people closer to God. He was scandalized by the wealth of the Temple authorities and the injustices in his society, and came to believe that in some way he represented the true Israel, that he could bring about a spiritual kingdom on earth. He may have felt that his death would help bring this about. He failed.

Further along the line to the right are many theologians and scholars in Christian establishments who claim more than this. They say that the proportion of what we can take as factual is higher. They agree that there is some contradiction in the Gospels, that the writers added interpretation to events and that some things didn't happen in the way they're described. But they add that in comparing the Gospels, reading underneath the surface text, and looking at the intentions of the writers, the basic story is seen to be credible. Jesus did believe himself to have a special relationship with God, he did perform miracles, he did rise from the dead.

There are no serious scholars working in reputable institutions who say that every word in the Gospels can be taken literally and everything happened exactly as they say. There are thousands of "Bible teachers" who do say this. They tend to work out of the colleges of the American Bible Belt, and they have their equivalents in the seminaries of Iran, or the monasteries of Tibet. They have little idea of the larger picture. It's like insisting that earth was created a few thousand years ago while ignoring the geology underneath your feet, the evidence in the libraries, the ruins of older cities, fossils, the cosmology of the solar system, pretty much everything we know about life. They argue, for example, that the evidence for the historicity of Jesus is greater than that for any other historical figure, for Alexander the Great, for instance, or for Julius Caesar. Yes, there are 5,000 or so manuscripts of the early New Testament books compared to, say, a dozen of Caesar's *Gallic Wars*, and these manuscripts do go back to within a couple of centuries of the originals rather than 1,000 years. Even this, incidentally, means that the Greek manuscripts of the New Testament on which all our translations are based are more than a century older than the first Greek versions, themselves translations of Aramaic source material, verbal or written. What happened in between the original versions and the later copies is unknown. The work of reconstructing the original New Testament text began about 300 years ago when scholars noticed the differences between the Greek, Syriac, Latin, Armenian, Ethiopic and other language versions which it had been translated into in the early centuries. The standard edition of the Greek text ("Received

Text") was seen to have tens of thousands of errors and question-able readings.

But all this is rather beside the point. Alexander the Great wasn't trying to start a religion. After his death he didn't have thousands of followers treating his words as sacred scripture, copy-ing them and handing them down. There is huge circumstantial evidence for his life and conquests. In comparison, Jesus was a nonentity. There is no reason to suppose that at the time of his death he was more important historically than the two criminals crucified on either side of him. There are no references to him in contemporary secular writings, with the exception of two disput-ed references in Josephus. Which is no big deal. Josephus lived in Rome. He may have been following unreliable information. After Jesus' death, it's 50 years or so before we read about him in non-Christian sources. All this makes it possible to argue that he never really existed. But the fact that Jesus did live is not in dispute for most people. What's in doubt is whether he was really God, or the Son of God, or performed miracles: statements of a different kind. We believe Alexander achieved what he did, as a historical figure, but we don't accept that he was divine simply because he and his Empire believed him to be so.

We're on fairly sure ground when we say that Jesus lived, and that a proportion of what he said and did in the Gospels happened to some degree or other. But the Church asks us to make this mental jump from seeing Jesus as a fairly nondescript criminal or rebel who was tortured to death like thousands of his contempo-raries, to believing he is the Son of God. What's going on? By the way "nondescript" is meant literally, not insultingly. There are no descriptions of Jesus in the Bible, and he was probably indistin-guishable from those around him. Judas had to point him out to the soldiers in the Garden of Gethsemane. There's scarcely any personal background. Was he married, for instance? With children? Most probably, virtually all Jewish males were married. The

Gospels don't mention them, but then they barely mention the families of his disciples either.

The question is really this: "How reliably do the Gospels reflect what happened?" We have to take evidence as we find it. The Gospels may coincide with history at times, but the Jews had little more concept of history than of science. "History" was developed by Greeks like Thucydides and Herodotus in the fifth century BC. They had an idea of objectivity. Before that time in the epics of Homer, for example, events were driven by the fickle gods. Herodotus traveled around the eastern Mediterranean sifting facts, looking critically at legends, rejecting the improbable, the contradictory, putting forward different points of view. The gods are largely absent. In Thucydides there's no reliance on divine events at all. A couple of the later Bible authors who wrote in the Greek style – the author of 1 Maccabees and the Gospel according to Luke, for example – were influenced by this approach, but as a whole the world-view of the Jews was different. The Gospels are today known as "foundation documents," written for the instruction of a community. Similar in their aims to the *Rule of the Community* and the *Covenant of Damascus* written for the guidance of the Essene Dead Sea community.

In the Gospels there's no distinction between the probable and improbable, no extra explanation for what today we start by discounting. Angels appear to Mary, Joseph, Zechariah, and the devil confronts Jesus, but how do the writers know this? Private thoughts, dreams, conversations are described with no reference to sources. How about Jesus in the Garden of Gethsemane? Only he knew that he prayed with intense agony, sweating blood: the disciples were asleep.

There's no explanation of how any information came to be in the Gospels. They're not written along the lines of: "This is how we know." The approach is more: "Have you heard this one?" The result is that there is more doubt about what Jesus really taught than about the teaching of most founders of religion. He's the only one of whom we don't even have a record of his words in the language in which they were spoken. To take a comparison with Buddhism, soon after Buddha's death the first Buddhist council was called to corroborate his teaching (the *sutras*) and check the wording. His words were recited by a close companion, Ananda, to a group of 500 disciples who made their corrections and gave their approval. The words were handed down orally under supervision for nearly 200 years till the third council wrote them down. We can be reasonably sure that there is a close correspondence to what he said. There's no comparable assurance with the Gospels (for more on this see chapter 52).

Perhaps the main problem of all is the fact that Jesus himself seems relatively uninterested in having his teaching handed down to posterity. He doesn't seem to have written anything down himself, and as far as we know, didn't ask anyone else to. In so far as the Gospels are biography at all, they are unauthorized. They are written with hindsight, by later generations, at a time when early Christians were trying to make theological sense of what had happened, adding interpretation to story. Perhaps Jesus would have been as surprised by their contents as we are.

34 CHANGING THE MESSAGE

"You have to go past the imagined image of Jesus. Such an image of God becomes the final obstacle, one's ultimate barrier. You hold on to your own ideology, and when a larger experience of God approaches, an experience greater than you are prepared to receive, you take flight from it by clinging to the image in your mind. This is known as preserving your faith."

JOSEPH CAMPBELL

Nevertheless it's the religion credited to Jesus that generated the framework of ideas and morals that a third of the world's population believe and practice. So what are the ideas that he handed on?

Orthodox Christianity today says that God sent His Son, Jesus, to earth, born of the Virgin Mary (the incarnation). He was condemned to die on the cross (crucifixion) to redeem our sins (redemption), but after three days rose from the dead (resurrection), descended into hell, appeared to his friends, and later ascended into heaven. This provides our hope of salvation. By believing in him Christians are forgiven their sin (justification) and can join him in eternal life (after a period in purgatory, according to Catholics).

Well, that seems a long stretch from what we have in the Gospels, which are some distance from Jesus. Jesus himself doesn't seem to have any doctrine. The closest he comes to a creed is the Lord's Prayer.

Let's try for the moment to forget about what Christianity has become, and start at square one. Did the idea of starting a new religion even cross Jesus' mind? It seems unlikely. He insists that he wants to fulfil the law, not replace it ("Think not that I am come to destroy the law or the prophets: I am not come to destroy, but to fulfil." Matthew 5:17). He's clear in the Gospels that his message is to the Jews only ("I am not sent but unto the lost sheep of the house of Israel" Matthew 15:24; see also Matthew 10:5-7). There are verses that seem to say the opposite ("Go ye therefore, and teach all nations." Matthew 28:19), but faced with this contradiction, it makes sense to say that the latter were added later when the faith was already spreading amongst Gentiles, having been rejected by most Jews.

Jesus simply doesn't talk in terms of founding a new religion. Nazareth, Jesus' hometown, was a morning's walk from Tiberias. This was a large, bustling cosmopolitan city on the shores of Lake Galilee which Herod Antipas had built and which he made his capital. Jesus must have been aware of the multiplicity of beliefs that jostled for space in every corner of the Roman Empire in the first century AD. He doesn't mention one of them. He never says to the worshipers of Zeus, Osiris, Mithras, Ra, Mercury, Diana, Isis, Adonis, Attis, the apostates, agnostics, Epicureans, "You're going the wrong way. You believe in the wrong God. I've come to put you right." The "cursing" passages in the Gospels, of which there are many, are invariably directed toward the Jews themselves, not for their belief, or lack of it, but for their hypocrisy. It's his co-religionists who are destined for hell, the ones who think of themselves as spiritually right, those who say they love but show no compassion.

Jesus always assumes that he and his listeners know the same God. He never describes God, except in relation to himself. He never tries to convert anyone to the God he believes in. As an evangelist he doesn't impress. The fact that the Roman centurion and the Syro-Phoenician woman whose daughter he heals, believe differently from him is not an issue. It's how you act that counts, where your heart is. Love and faith are the bottom line, not faith in one god or another.

Neither does Jesus act as though he's founding a new religion. Paul – he was different. He went everywhere he could, talked to whoever he could, preferably the top guy. He traveled thousands of miles, walking for the most part, setting up churches along the way; it was a tremendous effort. Jesus was the opposite. Today, you could drive along the route of Jesus' longest journey in a couple of hours, depending on the traffic.

Jesus' message was for his contemporaries, his peers, for the people he met. He shows little awareness of being the vehicle for an urgent message from God to all humankind. In that respect he doesn't try hard, and nor did God. Obviously if there is a God who sent his Son Jesus to earth, He could have presented us with a clearer picture if He'd wanted to. At least clear enough for Christians to adopt consistent beliefs. He needn't have sent Jesus to a far corner of a remote province of the Empire. He could have waited 2,000 years till we had television or radio. He could at least have seen to it that we had original copies of the Gospels. He could have produced His own text and engraved it on non-destructible materials so there was no doubt for succeeding generations. He could have written it in lights in the sky around the planet.

And this, of course, is how the Israelites in the Old Testament believed God did act. God made Himself so apparent that it was impossible not to believe. He appeared in pillars of fire, parted sea and river, sent lightning strikes and earthquakes on demand to consume enemies, dropped food from the sky, wrote commands on stone. He appeared on earth Himself, or sent angels with instructions. He has no difficulty in providing the equivalent of detailed architect's drawings and interior design specifications for the Tabernacle, the Ark, and the Temple. He issues laws that cover every aspect of behavior. But as we've seen, these instructions dry up the nearer the writers get to their own time. Jesus even has a mountaintop meeting with God (the transfiguration) that parallels Moses' encounter on Mount Sinai. This would have been an ideal occasion for him to come back with a scroll that spelt out the new covenant. But it doesn't happen. His followers have to remember, and recreate an image in their heads.

Perhaps the followers didn't remember everything right. And in the process of being handed down orally through the generations the message changed. People brought their own hopes and expectations to it. And over the centuries the interpretation of the story of Jesus by the early Christian writers developed into the creeds that the Churches follow today. Maybe today's Churches have been left stranded with the wrong notions about the Bible, Jesus and God. Perhaps some of the ideas they rejected a couple of millennia ago are closer to the truth, and it's time to pick them up again. For example, if you read or talk to mainstream biblical scholars today they are virtually unanimous in saying that at the heart of Jesus' message in the Gospels is his teaching on the kingdom of God. They're not so much in agreement about what that is, but there's no doubt it's a difficult, self-sacrificing, uncompromising message that involves changing yourself and society. It appeals to the heart rather than the head. It deals with the things that matter to us – truth, peace, freedom and justice – the great ideals that we still aspire to model in our imperfect world. It never played well to the establishment, however, and the Church soon abandoned it, losing the plot very early on, a fact which every Christian sect since has implicitly recognized. The word "kingdom" is mentioned often in the earlier Gospels, over 50 times, for instance, in Matthew. But John, probably a generation or two later, though incorporating some early tradition, doesn't mention it at all. Rejected by the Jews, kingdom teaching was even less likely to appeal to the ruling Romans. And the Church has rarely discussed it since. Both Catholic and Protestant branches have consistently persecuted people down the centuries who tried to take this teaching seriously.

The Church talks instead about individual salvation. But Jesus says nothing directly about going to the cross to save people from their sin. Most scholars see the few verses that obliquely point to this as later additions. Nor does he talk of setting up a Church and sacraments through which people can be forgiven their sin. The doctrines of the Trinity, the divinity of the Holy Spirit, the dual nature of Christ are not mentioned in the Bible. Capital Letter Doctrines are later interpretations by the Church formulated to define and control access to God. They are not words that relate to the way we all live. Indeed, they take away the responsibility for change from the individual and give it to God. These matters of sin and salvation have a role to play in the psychology of faith, but a secondary one. They're tools for improvement, not descriptions of the problem or the solution.

That's why the Church hasn't made a difference for the better in the last two millennia. On the spiritual insight and guidance that Jesus offered it re-imposed the old, old religious role of propitiating the divine through sacrifice. If you've ever seen an evangelical preacher whipping a congregation into frenzy over the "power of the blood" you can see the ancient practice of blood sacrifice still exerting its pull. The unique angle that the Church took was to turn the idea of sacrifice around and see it as a once-for-all event. In a bold step, it made Jesus into the Son of God so that God was sacrificing Himself for humankind rather than man cutting and burning chickens and children to keep disaster, death and demons at bay.

35 THE SON OF GOD?

*"If your faith is opposed to experience, to human learning and investiga-
tion, it is not worth the breath used in giving it expression."*

EDGAR HOWE

But isn't the whole point about Jesus the fact that he claims to be
the Son of God?

There's a joke about a priest and a Rabbi talking about job promotion prospects.

"I've got a chance next year of being made bishop," says the
priest.

"And what after that?" asks the rabbi.

"Well, I couldn't expect anything more, but who knows, maybe
a cardinal?"

"What's after that?"

"Well, there's only the Pope. I couldn't hope for that."

"There must be something else."

"There's nothing after that. Only God comes above the Pope."

"Well, why not? One of our boys made it."

In the Book of Job God lives in heaven with his family and
friends, an eagle's flight from earth. In the first century AD most
people in the Roman Empire still believed god/God to be physically close, living on mountaintops, chucking thunderbolts,
kidnapping the prettiest girls for sex. Zeus fathered hundreds of
children by women, mostly virgins. His son Hercules is the best
known today, thanks to Walt Disney. Alexander the Great, Plato,
Augustus, were all believed to be born of virgins. Today the idea
that God has a "son" is hard to take seriously, unless you've been
brought up to think that way. It's a return to the old Hebrew, pre-
monotheistic way of thinking, like seeing God as a serpent. By the
time of Jesus the Jews thought of God more in terms of spirit than
as a sky God, and most scholars say it's improbable that the first

disciples thought of Jesus as a literal "son" of God, as divine. They would probably have thought it blasphemous. It was the way pagans thought of gods. But the Gospel writers refer to Jesus as both Son of God and son of man. Son of man is the expression Jesus uses most and seems most comfortable with. What do the words mean?

They're slippery terms, no more easily defined than "spirit" or "mind." You can't get into this without talking about language. Over a few hundred years words can change their meaning many times, even without the complications of shifting populations and changing languages. "Gay" is the obvious example in the last generation. The Hebrew or Aramaic term which is generally translated as "son of man" is the same sort of term as "mankind" in English, for example in Psalm 8:4: "What is man [son of man], that thou art mindful of him?" It can also mean the original man, Adam. It can refer to Israel (Exodus 4:22; Hosea 11:1), or to the king of Israel (2 Samuel 7:14; Psalm 2:7). It's likely that when Jesus refers to himself as the son of man at his trial in front of the Sanhedrin he sees himself as the true Israel, personifying God's holy people, which seems to be the meaning of Daniel (Daniel 7:13-14, 18, 22).

The meaning of "son of man" overlaps with "Son of God." Adam in Luke's Gospel is said to be the son of God, the man who comes from God (Luke 3:38). Both terms can also have further ranges of meaning. Angels are referred to as sons of God (Job 1:6), as were other prophets around the time of Jesus. Jesus calls peacemakers sons of God (Matthew 5:9). In general "son of God" denotes a particularly close relationship with God, like that of a child with a parent. In Jewish scriptures it doesn't mean "of divine origin."

Jesus is also described as fulfilling the Jewish tradition of the Messiah (Hebrew for "anointed one," the Greek term being "Christ"). The Messiah would be a great leader and obey the Law perfectly, but he is nowhere described as God, or the Son of God.

"Messiah" meant someone through whom God worked in history in a striking way. The Persian emperor Cyrus is called *mashiah* in Isaiah 45:1, because through his actions in returning the Jews to Judah he was fulfilling the will of God, even though he may never have heard of Him.

In the first century AD Jews believed that whatever form the Messiah took he was definitely going to make a difference. At the very least the Romans would be driven out, the exiles would return and a reign of peace would begin. At best the dead would be resurrected, God would rule the world and judge humankind. Life on earth would be transformed. None of these things happened when Jesus came. Few outside Palestine knew for generations that Jesus had lived on earth at all. For these reasons Jesus' own people do not accept him as Messiah, and still regard "Son of God" as an essentially pagan idea.

As to whether the first Christians saw Jesus as divine, there's evidence on both sides. The first proclamation of the gospel by Peter opens with the words, "Jesus of Nazareth, a man approved of God among you by miracles and wonders" (Acts 2:22). Jesus is specially favored by God, he is God's servant, his is the one name by which men can be saved. But he is "the Son of man standing on the right hand of God" (Acts 7:56), not identifiable with God. Paul refers to him as "Lord" more than 200 times, which is ambiguous. "Lord" (Greek *Kyrios*) can mean "God" or "Sir," or pretty well anything in between. Paul never comes straight out and says Jesus is divine. There are one or two verses that suggest it, like Philippians 2:6 ("being in the form of God"), but the balance is on the other side. The translation of Romans 9:5 is disputed. In some translations Christ is God: "Christ, who is God over all, for ever praised" (NIV), whilst others do not link Christ and God. There's no certainty.

Moreover, many verses in the Gospels suggest that Jesus defined himself as "man" in the ordinary sense of humankind – as "son of

God" rather than the unique "Son of God." He frequently distinguishes between God and himself, saying, for example, to the rich young ruler, "Why callest thou me good? None is good save one, that is, God" (Luke 18:19). In Gethsemane he prayed, "Not my will, but thine, be done" (Luke 22:42). He told his disciples that only the Father knows when the son of man will return (Mark 13:32). The synoptic Gospels (Matthew, Mark and Luke) lean in this direction.

John, however, suggests a higher view, with Peter's proclamation: "We believe and are sure that thou art that Christ, the Son of the living God" (John 6:69). The higher claims bring him to the brink of being killed by stoning (John 8:59). In John, though, Jesus raises the disciples to the same level as himself: "I ascend unto my Father, and your Father; and to my God, and your God" (John 20:17). John, too, puts words in the mouth of Jesus that suggest a distinction: "My Father is greater than I" (John 14:28). John's Gospel, incidentally, stands at some distance from the others. The Greek style is better, the chronology and selection of events different, the theology more developed. Jesus doesn't talk in parables but long monologues, with carefully constructed literary images of himself (the true vine, the shepherd and so on). Most scholars would say that the words spoken by Jesus in John's Gospel are less likely to be his than the ones in the synoptic Gospels.

For most scholars the evidence in the New Testament is that Jesus did not think of himself as divine. He certainly doesn't make it clear, or the disciples wouldn't be so confused. Their misunderstanding is a constant theme. He keeps teasing and puzzling people about who he is, where his authority comes from, why he is doing what he's doing. If he had openly claimed to be God his ministry would probably have been over in days rather than months or years.

The idea that Jesus was in some way a unique Son of God was developed by the early Christians as the faith spread amongst the non-Jews who thought of God as a being able to have sons. Even so, it wasn't till the fourth century that the phrase "Son of God" was promoted to mean "God the Son." Most scholars, even those who are Christians, would agree on that. Very few, if any, serious scholars say that Jesus saw himself as the later Church saw him, with two natures, one human, and the other divine. There are some who say that never mind what Jesus thought about himself, if the Church says he was divine, he was. Some theologians try and retain some uniqueness for him by saying that though he wasn't literally the Son of God he lived in such harmony with God that he became identified with Him, and this is what the first Christians thought. In some way, he was perfect. Which is a nice idea, but how would we know? Are we to imagine he never had the tantrums of a two-year-old?

Of course it's possible that Jesus thought of himself as divine. Even well-adjusted people can still be psychotic in some respects. And many in Palestine were not rational. There was a frenzy of expectation around. Josephus reports several individuals claiming to be the Messiah. Hypnogogic hallucinations are common, even probable after 40 days and nights in a desert with little food and sleep. Having visions and hearing voices doesn't require you to be divine or mad. Just under too much stress. And Jesus was clearly pushing himself.

And he's not the only one. Thousands of people have suffered from the delusion that they have a closer relation to the divine than anyone else. It's common in epileptics. Even in our little business today there's a manuscript in every week or so from someone who believes they are the Son of God, or the mother of God, or a descendant of Jesus, or they've discovered the secret of God revealed to them alone, or whatever.

If you do want to believe that Jesus was the Son of God, per-haps you'll also credit the many other "Sons of God" around today. Millions believe in the divinity of certain individuals. Hindus believe that God manifests himself in avatars, divine beings taking on human form to aid humankind in its spiritual evolution. They can materialize holy ash, or jewelry and watches, heal illness, even raise people from the dead. The largest Hindu temple in England is dedicated to Swami Narayan, who died in 1820 and whose followers believe he was the last divine manifestation. There's Meher Baba, who kept a voluntary silence for 44 years till his death in 1969. Or there's Shiva Mahavatar Babaji, who reportedly disappeared in a ball of light in 1922. The miracles of Sai Baba, still alive today, are as well chronicled as anything in the New Testament. There's a line of holy Mothers, the most famous of whom is Mother Meera, living in Germany.

Are all these individuals and their followers deceiving themselves, or are there many routes to the divine? It's hard to credit these stories of divine beings on earth today if you've never met them. Perhaps if you did you'd put the miracles down to trickery, or self-delusion. Equally it's hard to disbelieve sincere and intelligent individuals who are absolutely certain they have seen astonishing things. Maybe some individuals can perform the impossible, as savants can. Perhaps it's wisest to be equally gullible or disbelieving in every direction. The experiences of followers of Jesus or Sai Baba are real for both groups. Maybe these are experiences they're imagining, but there are no real grounds for saying that one is true and all others false.

36 LOOKING AT MIRACLES

"So little trouble do men take in the search for truth: so suddenly do they accept whatever comes first to hand."

THUCYDIDES

But what about the miracles reported in the New Testament? If we can believe in time stopping, atoms making choices, the universe having a mind, why can't we be more sympathetic to a literal understanding of what the Bible says about Jesus?

The next five chapters are written to persuade you that Jesus was not the Son of God, didn't have a virgin birth and didn't rise from the dead. So if you don't believe this anyway you can just skip this section.

It's not that modern scholars start from a position of atheism. Most have a high respect for the Bible and what it means to our culture today. Otherwise they wouldn't bother to enter what is an overcrowded field. Doubt about how literally you can take the Bible is kick-started by the logic of the texts themselves. For instance, the evidence within the texts that Matthew and Luke drew on Mark as a source is overwhelmingly accepted. So where there are differences between Matthew's and Luke's accounts of the same incident or saying as that of Mark they are generally taken as later revisions. In this way the scholars work back from the differences to deduce what the original sources, oral and written, may have said. The occasional scholar will treat the sources as going back to separate, independent sources and so equally valid, and treat stories as credible that only have one source. But then where do you stop? There are as many stories and sayings again outside the New Testament which could then equally be included.

Sometimes you simply can't decide on which version to choose. For instance, throwing out the money-changers from the Temple is a key public event in the life of Jesus, the one that got him into trouble with the authorities. The synoptic Gospels put it at the end of the ministry, at the start of Passion Week (Matthew 21:10-17; Mark 11:15-19; Luke 19:45-48). John has it at the beginning (John 2:13-17). When was it? To say, as conservative commentators do, that this is because it happened twice, is simply shutting your mind to the sense of the Bible text. You may as well say that Jesus ascended to heaven twice, at different times: first on the same day as the resurrection (Luke 24:50-51, from Bethany) and again 40 days later (Acts 1:1-12, from the Mount of Olives).

So how far can we take the Gospels literally? How far do we take them as an expression of the faith of the time? Was God really drawing a line across history 2,000 years ago, marking a turning-point from certain punishment to the opportunity for redemption?

We can't go through the whole of Jesus' life. But let's take perhaps the two central miracles, the virgin birth and the resurrection. God incarnates Himself on earth in the human form of Jesus. He dies and is then resurrected to heaven, triumphing over death and sin and evil, and by believing in this we can follow Jesus there. Did it happen this way? Does it matter to Christian faith if it didn't?

Let's start with applying common sense to the virgin birth. Imagine yourself into the situation. We find ourselves straightaway in a common human problem. You discover your teenage fiancée is pregnant. She hasn't told you, but the evidence is there to see. (Joseph "found" Mary to be pregnant; Mary didn't tell him till it was too obvious to conceal, or didn't tell him at all.) You haven't had sex with her yourself, and believed her to be a virgin. You ask her how it happened, and she says as a result of a dream. You might think she is lying, or mentally disturbed. You certainly don't believe her. What really happened?

Here's one possibility. Perhaps Mary really believed God had impregnated her. Perhaps she had sex and didn't know what was happening, translating this experience into a divine event. Perhaps she was the village idiot. Then here's a second possibility. Perhaps she was raped, scared out of her wits, and invented the story out of fear. And a third: maybe she just had enjoyable sex with someone else and lied about it. The penalty for having sex outside marriage was death by stoning, so there was a strong personal reason for finding an alternative explanation for an unwelcome bump in the tummy when it was too large to conceal. Girls are still murdered by their families today in remote hilltop and desert communities in Pakistan, and in British towns, for having sex outside marriage, willing or not.

Or here's a fourth possibility, the strongest. Maybe it didn't happen this way at all. Maybe it was an ordinary marriage, an ordinary legitimate birth, and the story was added later.

But let's suppose for the moment that the two New Testament writers who record the virgin birth report the story accurately, in so far as both Mary and Joseph believed Jesus was born by divine assistance. How are we to be convinced? Imagine the kind of evidence we would want to see – medical examinations, scientific reports – to prove that of all the ten billion or so births in human history this one alone was uniquely conceived. Some desperately extreme arguments are put forward to suggest that a virgin birth is a physical possibility – it occurs naturally in about one in a thousand species – perhaps this was a one off occurrence. But as far as we know, a virgin birth for humans is impossible. A woman can't produce a male child without the Y chromosome that is contributed from the male.

So could it have been a miracle? Yes, it could. But the difficulty in accepting miracles lies in getting to the point where that seems the most likely (or only) explanation. When a woman today says, "I was raped by aliens from a flying saucer," we don't take it too seriously. It wouldn't change our view of the world. But this has the supportive evidence of 3.7 million Americans who claim to have been abducted by UFOs. As many as 25 million claim to have flown through the air without mechanical assistance (Roper poll 1992). The majority are perfectly sane, intelligent people. Most of the memories are "recalled" later, sometimes under hypnosis. The psychological word for this is "confabulation," the unconscious mixing of fantasy with reality to the extent that the individual cannot distinguish between them.

So if we don't believe the evidence of millions of Americans today who can be interviewed, why should we believe the reported words of a village girl in the ancient Middle East 2,000 years ago who we can't talk to? There are no witnesses and no first-hand evidence. Mary doesn't speak to us directly in the Bible, nor does Joseph. We don't know how many people the report went through before it was written down. What we do know is that the people of that time believed differently from us: gods coming to earth and mating with women or raping them, virgin births, these were part of the mental landscape. It wasn't just a common belief among Romans. The same stories were told of Greek gods, or Arabian djinni, Greek satyrs, Celtic dusii, Hindu bhuts, Samoan hotua poro, various demons good and bad, "powers of the air." It's a universal belief. Why should we credit this one and not the others?

Put this report of a virgin birth into perspective. Imagine a present-day Luke writing, in English, in London, about a story his grandmother has told him of a village girl in a remote part of troubled Kashmir in Pakistan, around the time of the second world war or earlier, who gave birth while still a virgin. That's the kind of timeframe we're talking about. His grandmother heard it from a friend who lived in the village as a child and later migrated to England. Other than this second-hand reporting there is no evidence of any kind. The modern Luke may even travel to the village to check it out. He asks the elders about the story, through an interpreter – they know the family, the oldest of them can remember the child concerned, but cannot remember anything remarkable about the birth or any gossip about it ("Is not this Jesus, the son of Joseph, whose father and mother we know?" John 6:42. "Is not this Joseph's son?" Luke 4:22).

What about the circumstantial evidence pointing to an unusual birth? Outside the Gospels there's no mention of the birth of Jesus, or of anything out of the ordinary happening at the time. If Herod had really ordered the massacre of all children under two years old it would have been remembered and recorded. Josephus, the great Jewish chronicler of the time, was anxious to write every bad thing about Herod that he could find, but he doesn't mention it.

The story doesn't even figure much in the New Testament. You would surely think that the miracle at the heart of the incarnation, one of the major doctrines, would have had a central place there. But not so. The first of the New Testament writers was Paul, who in many ways laid the foundation of Christian teaching. He doesn't mention the virgin birth – indeed, quite the opposite. In Galatians 4:4 he describes Jesus as "made of a woman," not "made of a virgin."

The first of the canonical Gospels to be written was Mark, approximately 30 years after Jesus' death. He doesn't mention it either. There is nothing in Mark's Gospel to suggest that Jesus had anything other than an ordinary birth. Mark refers to Jesus' brothers and sisters and speaks so naturally of Joseph as the father of Jesus that it is difficult not to believe him. And Jesus himself doesn't refer to his birth. If his business in life was to explain himself as the Son of God on a mission to humankind, wouldn't the fact that he came from God via a virgin birth be significant?

So we start with an impossible event, for which there's no direct evidence. Both the circumstantial evidence of the times and the paucity of evidence within the Bible itself suggest it never happened. If God tried to bring a paternity suit he wouldn't stand the remotest chance of success. Still convinced it's true?

37 WRITING DOWN MIRACLES

"To assert that the earth revolves around the sun is as erroneous as to claim that Jesus was not born of a Virgin."

CARDINAL ROBERT BELLARMINE, AT THE TRIAL OF GALILEO

Okay, you want to be persuaded further. Let's look at the two reports of the virgin birth we have, in Luke and Matthew, most likely written in the seventh or eighth decades after the birth.

The first thing to notice about these stories is that they have different plots, and a very different style. In Luke, Joseph and Mary travel from Nazareth to Bethlehem because of a census. With its manger and shepherds, the story is domestic in tone. In contrast, Matthew doesn't appear to have heard of the census, and Joseph and Mary don't live in Nazareth till long after the birth. He doesn't record the visit of the shepherds, but starts with wise men from the East, who Luke doesn't mention. In Matthew, Herod hears from the wise men of the newborn King and sends his troops to kill all the baby boys in Bethlehem, a few miles down the road from his palace. Mary and Joseph flee to Egypt. Compared to the Christmas-card sweetness of Luke's story, that of Matthew involves messages from angels, a miraculous moving star, a jealous king frightened for his throne, wise men paying homage with expensive presents, massacres, night flight, escape across borders.

We have these two different stories because we have two writers phrasing a story for different audiences. Matthew and Luke are propagandists for their faith. As a Jew, Matthew was concerned to find the place of the gospel in the divine scheme of things, to understand the Christian faith by tying it in with that of his ancestors, to interpret events in the light of Jewish beliefs. Bible writers were working from stories that had been handed down for one, two, three generations, by teachers who felt free to add the perspective of their groups. This is the midrashic tradition of passing on sacred stories, more akin to the tales you read about Robin Hood, which revolve around the same plots and characters, than academic history. The arrival of the wise men echoes Isaiah 60 as well as the visit of the Queen of Sheba to Solomon (1 Kings 10). The star recalls a prophecy in Numbers 24:17. The character of Joseph is shaped by the Joseph of Genesis 37-50. The stories get mixed up with explanation, the events with elaboration.

Matthew shapes his story primarily for Jews who had begun to be hostile to the Christian sect that had infiltrated their worship. The Pharisees were throwing Christians out of the synagogues and Christianity was fighting for survival as a strand of Judaism. The main issue between the communities was whether Jesus fulfilled the scriptures or not, whether he was the promised Messiah. By the second century this was not such an issue, Christianity had spread to the Roman world and was seen as a new religion; the Jews were being written out of Christianity. But Matthew's Gospel, with its 60 or so references to the Old Testament, is dominated by this debate. He begins with a pedigree in which he traces the 42 generations from Abraham to Joseph through the kings of Judah, to emphasize his theme of Jesus being king of the Jews. He scarcely writes a verse about the birth without mentioning it as a fulfillment of prophecy: "that it might be fulfilled by the prophet" (1:22-23); "for thus it is written by the prophet" (2:5); "Then was fulfilled that which was spoken by Jeremiah the prophet" (2:17); "that it might be fulfilled which was spoken by the prophets" (2:23).

The birth story is written around these prophecies. Jesus is born in Bethlehem to fulfill one, the family flee to Egypt and back again to fulfill another, the children in Bethlehem are massacred to fulfill a third, the family move to Nazareth to fulfill a fourth. Conservatives will say these are examples of prophecies coming true and deny that the author was searching the Old Testament for material that could be spin-doctored to persuade the Jews, but today we can work out exactly what Matthew was doing. The key prophecy he picks up on is a line from Isaiah 7:14: "Behold, a virgin shall be with child, and shall bring forth a son, and they shall call his name Emmanuel . . ." which Matthew introduces with the words: "Now all this was done, that it might be fulfilled which was spoken of the Lord by the prophet" (1:22-23).

But Isaiah didn't actually say this. It's often pointed out that the original words were written in Hebrew about 300 years earlier, when the Hebrew *almah* means simply "young woman." Isaiah is saying to King Ahab: "Before the son of that young woman grows up your enemies will be defeated." So how did Matthew come to use the word "virgin"? The original Hebrew words had been translated into the Persian language, Aramaic, after the Exile. They were then translated again into Greek in the third century BC, in a version called the Septuagint (to which I've already referred). This was a translation made for the benefit of the Jews overseas (primarily Alexandria) who no longer spoke Hebrew or Aramaic. Matthew, writing his Gospel in Greek, quotes from the Septuagint which translates *almah* by *parthenos*. Greek has more shades of meaning than Aramaic (and English; Greek, for example, has four words for our one word "love"), and by the time Matthew was writing *parthenos* meant *virgin* – one particular type of young woman. You could have no clearer example of prophecy being written into the story after the event rather than the event fulfilling prophecy.

Luke came to the story from a very different background, with different aims, which explains why the accounts are so dissimilar – indeed, at times, contradictory. He was writing for the non-Jews, the Gentiles, to persuade them that here was a faith they could follow. And he framed his story in a way that would make sense to them. So there's no prophecy at all in Luke.

Because he's writing for the Gentiles, Luke gives a different chart of ancestors. In contrast to the wholly Jewish pedigree provided by Matthew, Luke traces Jesus' line of descent back to Adam, father of all. This paves the way for his later emphasis on the spread of the gospel to the Gentiles. Luke mentions that Mary was the kinswoman of Elizabeth, who was, "of the daughters of Aaron" (Luke 1:5), which means Jesus was of Aaronic and not Davidic descent, so wasn't the son of David as Matthew says. Luke has absorbed the sacred language of the Roman world, and uses terms that echo those applied to the emperors. He speaks of "good news," and of the Savior or Son of God who brings peace and justice to the world. He's also more specific. The angel gets a name, Gabriel, and has more to say. He appears in person, not in a dream.

Luke's story conflicts with the outside evidence that we have: the fact that he's not as concerned as Matthew with fulfilling prophecy does not necessarily make him more reliable. Luke says that Mary and Joseph lived in Nazareth "in the days of Herod, the king of Judaea" and traveled to Bethlehem for a census decreed by the Emperor Augustus "while Quirinius was governor of Syria" (Luke 2:2 NIV). This is a mistake: the dates of Quirinius are known from sound extra-biblical sources, and they do not coincide with the known dates of Herod. There was a local census in AD 6-9 (not Empire-wide as Luke maintains), and Quirinius became governor of Syria in AD 6, but Herod died a few years earlier, in 4 BC. Luke may be referring to an earlier census of 8-5 BC, in the reign of Herod, when the governors of Syria were Saturninus and Varus, but not Quirinius.

The idea that Joseph needed to travel to Bethlehem is probably a mechanism for getting Bethlehem into the picture. There's a record in an Egyptian papyrus of a census in 104 AD when everyone had to return to their ancestral home, but it's very unlikely that this was normal practice, with people travelling all over the Empire to their ancestral homes of centuries earlier. Imagine trying to do it today. It's more likely that standard procedure was to register in the towns where they were living. But even if Joseph had to go to Bethlehem, Mary would not have had to register with him. Luke is stitching together possibilities long after the event and making mistakes. It's like our third generation immigrant in London giving an account of how the taxation system worked in his great-grandfather's day back in Karachi.

These arguments over details though are rather beside the point. If every inconsistency were explained, if the story were fixed exactly in time and space and every circumstantial detail agreed and pinpointed, if there were only one Gospel, there would still be no hard "evidence" for a virgin birth. What we can do is understand why inconsistencies and improbabilities such as the virgin birth are there. Why was this particular story important to Luke? It's unlikely he invented it, but it was one of the many in circulation that he obviously felt should be included. Why?

Romans and Greeks believed in a classification of beings described by Hesiod way back in the eighth or ninth centuries BC. They included angels, heroes, human beings down to animals. But they all interacted. The divine and human realms were intertwined. An emperor must be divine almost by definition. A great athlete must have something of divinity about him.

Examples of this belief of the interweaving of men and gods are found in the New Testament itself. In Acts 14:8-13 Paul heals a cripple and as a result he and Barnabus are hard put to prevent the townspeople from thinking they are the gods Jupiter and Mercury. In Acts 28:6 Paul is declared a god because he has survived both drowning and snakebite. It was the way people thought. It didn't take much to be a god in the Roman world, or to believe yourself divine.

So it would have been natural for the early Gentile Christians to assume that Jesus, their leader who commanded the waves, the heavens, life and death itself, was born of god and woman rather than man and woman. It would be stranger to believe there was nothing divine about him. Luke wasn't deliberately, cynically, inventing a story here (at least we hope not); like Matthew he took a hint and expanded it, putting the best gloss on the story for his readers, just as Paul, Augustine, Aquinas, Luther and every theologian and spin doctor has done since.

Why don't the other New Testament writers mention the virgin birth? There's probably a simple answer to that as well. It's a story that needs a certain distance from the source to be credible. Paul and Mark (or whoever was the writer of Mark's Gospel) were too close in time to the life of Jesus, and the story simply wasn't around, or wasn't believed. Matthew and Luke are writing when there's no one left alive to refute the story, and they put it in, one of many legends about Jesus current at the time. John (or the writer of the Gospel of John) is writing later still, with a more developed theology of the incarnation of the Word, and has no need of the more fanciful elements. He simply ignores it, along with many other tall tales of Jesus' early life that haven't made this collection of Gospels.

38 HOW MYTHS ARE BUILT

"This doctrine was revealed by God and therefore is to be firmly and steadfastly believed by all the faithful."

PIUS IX, BULL INEFFABILIS DEUS 1854 (IMMACULATE CONCEPTION)

Religion never stops reinventing itself. The story of the virgin birth didn't finish with the two Gospel writers: it turned into Christmas. Christmas hasn't always been important to the Church, perhaps because until the advent of hospitals and medicine the idea of birth was associated more with death than life. In the Middle Ages the story developed in art, adding elements we now tend to take as part of the original scene. On the principle that every passage of the Bible illuminates every other, new elements were taken from other verses. The ox and ass were added to the manger scene on the basis of Isaiah 1:3. The wise men of Matthew become kings because of Isaiah 60:1, 3, 6. The story continued to grow through to the modern period, with tree, decorations, Christmas cards and presents added in Victorian England.

Along the way the status of Mary the mother of Jesus improved as well. Making Jesus into God was not enough. After all if Jesus' father was divine, why not his mother also? Many of the early Church Fathers regarded the virgin birth as an unhelpful superstition and Mary as irrelevant, but the idea grew in importance as the years went by. In this Mary was probably fulfilling the needs that the male-dominated monotheistic religions often fail to satisfy. The worship of the mother of Jesus took over from the old mother goddesses and fertility goddesses. In AD 431, at the Council of Ephesus (a few miles down the coast from Nicea), she was given the title "God-bearer," so that Ephesus, the city of the virgin huntress Diana, became the city of the Virgin Mother/Goddess, Mary the mother of God.

In the twelfth century Mary began to be seen as miraculously conceived herself, by her mother Anne, who became the center of another cult. Mary becomes the Queen of Mercy, with Jesus matching her as the King of Justice. The Church was effectively creating a Greek-like family of gods and goddesses. The idea of Mary having sex, though, was so horrible for the Church that bizarre traditions arose, like the theory that she conceived through the ear rather than the vagina. Sex, symbolism, relics all combine in the Middle Ages to produce beliefs and behavior that we now think of as utterly weird, as in the story that Catherine of Sienna had the foreskin of Jesus as her wedding ring. As we begin to move into the modern age the mood changes. In the sixteenth century we see a switch from the holy family as extended kinship (embracing a good many gospel characters, particularly disciples and various Marys) to the nuclear family of Joseph, Mary and child.

The creation of myth in the Church continues to the present day. In 1835 Pope Pius IX made it an article of faith for all Catholics to believe in the Immaculate Conception: the idea that Mary didn't sin from the moment she was conceived till the day she died. The present pope has now made him a saint, one of the 279 he has made so far. Pius was an arrogant, anti-democratic, anti-Semitic individual, who enclosed Jews into a locked ghetto in Rome, and kidnapped a Jewish child whom he brought up in his own home as a Christian. He was so deeply unpopular that when he died the people of Rome tried to throw his coffin into the River Tiber. Which is not to say that he wasn't right in his saintly pronouncements, but it doesn't encourage us in that direction.

In 1950 Pius XII pushed the myth surrounding Mary further with the claim that she had been bodily transported to heaven after her death (the assumption). The present pope promotes the cult of Mary at every opportunity. In 1987 he wrote in "Redemptoris Mater" that Mary "preserved her virginity intact." Not only is she too pure to have had sex with her husband but the process of birth itself is defiling, so Candelmas celebrates her purification from that. It may seem extraordinary that in the twentieth century the Church should still be inventing even more ridiculous things to believe, but there you have it.

That Mary and Joseph had normal sexual relations after the birth of Jesus is, incidentally, quite explicit in the Gospels. Jesus had at least five brothers and several sisters (Matthew 1:25, Mark 6:3). Some try to interpret these as cousins (or stepchildren, Mary having married an elderly widower) but there are no real grounds for these suggestions, other than a wish to detach him from the messy business of being human.

There's no direct evidence for the virgin birth; the circumstantial evidence suggests it didn't happen; the two stories that do give it conflict in all the details; the writers' motives in creating the story are clear, the methods they used can be analyzed. We can trace its development since New Testament times.

In the Roman world powerful individuals were often half divine and born of virgins. Today we know that Jesus was born like the rest of us. He wasn't God, or half God, or some other strange being. There was no incarnation as described in Matthew and Luke: that was a story for the times. It's part of the process of turning Jesus the man into Jesus the God, and losing his message along the way.

39 DID JESUS RISE FROM THE DEAD?

*"And the Son of God died, which is immediately credible because
it is absurd. And buried he rose again, which is certain because
it is impossible."*

TERTULLIAN

There's not one serious scholar in ten today who would say that
the virgin birth definitely happened as the two Gospel accounts
describe it. Some conservative ones take the approach that you can
believe it if you want to. They will take issue with certain points in
this argument, they'll admit that it's hard to reconcile the two
accounts, but after all God is in the business of miracles. He could
have done it. Believing in it literally isn't essential to faith, though
it doesn't hurt either.

There are even fewer scholars who would say that a miracle like
the ascension literally happened. The idea of Jesus physically rising
through the air is clearly linked to the idea of heaven existing as a
place a few hundred feet above our heads. The Gospel writers simply believed that if Jesus went to heaven that's how it must have
happened. It's harder to believe in this today because no one thinks
that heaven is still up there in the clouds as a physical place. Even
as a miracle it doesn't make sense. In fact churchmen may say that
believing in the ascension doesn't help faith at all, it's more likely
to undermine it.

When we get to the resurrection it's different. It's like Custer's
Last Stand. If this isn't true then nothing is. If Jesus didn't rise from
the dead he's not the Son of God, and the Christian faith is meaningless. Even many liberal scholars who accept the virgin birth and
ascension as mythical draw the line at applying the same reasoning
to the resurrection. But is the evidence for the one of a different
quality from the other? Or is this the last of the Emperor's clothes,
which the Church can't bring itself to remove because then it

would need to find another reason for existing?

At first sight the resurrection may read differently from the virgin birth. It has less of a mythical flavor, more named witnesses. But mythical-type elements are still there, in the darkness, earthquake, dead walking the streets, and there are no eyewitnesses to the resurrection itself. No one claims to have seen Jesus rise from the dead. The story is that the body of Jesus was put in a tomb which two or three days later (unclear which) was found to be empty. Various men or angels (unclear which) said to various disciples (unclear who) that Jesus had risen. Later he (or his ghost, unclear again) appeared to his disciples (or some of them). Given that that's impossible (though others also are raised from the dead in the Bible, so it's not unique) we need a lot of persuading. Is the story a starter?

There are dozens of books examining the evidence for and against the resurrection. But "evidence" is not really the right word. If there was a "trial for the truth" in a court today there's no evidence in favor of the resurrection that would be allowed to stand. To be allowed, evidence needs the confirmation of forensics or some means of investigation. The legal definition of what we have in the Gospels is "hearsay." The most we can do is speculate on degrees of probability.

The idea that you can be a Christian without believing in the resurrection may seem outrageous. A key verse of Paul is often quoted: "If Christ be not risen, then is our preaching vain, and your faith is also vain" (1 Corinthians 15:14).

But Paul, the first New Testament writer, isn't talking about a literal bodily resurrection here. In this passage he is referring to the resurrection of Jesus as part of a general resurrection (which as we know hasn't happened yet), of which Jesus is the "firstfruits" (1 Corinthians 15:20-23). Indeed, "If the dead rise not, then is not Christ raised" (verse 16). Paul believed that the end of the world was not only at hand, it had already begun – the dead were rising from the graves – and it was this that drove him on. Apocalypse was now. The idea of the resurrection as a one-off historical event referring only to Jesus doesn't appear in Paul's letters. With the exception of the Lord's Supper (1 Corinthians 11:23-26) he never mentions any details of the Passion narrative. When he talks about the appearance of Jesus to Peter, then James and all the disciples, then the five hundred, and finally himself, he mixes up these supposedly factual sightings with his own visionary experience. To Paul there is little difference between "visionary" and "real." It's the same for most Christians today. They feel their experience of the living Jesus proves he is alive.

If you take the New Testament references in the chronological order (much disputed, but this is a rough consensus) in which they were written you can trace the development of the story, and see how it grows as time passes.

Paul, 1 Corinthians 15:4-8, probably 55 AD: "He rose again the third day according to the scriptures: and that he was seen of Cephas, then of the twelve . . . last of all he was seen of me also, as of one born out of due time." Here there is no distinction between a physical appearance and the visionary. There's no mention of the empty tomb, or Mary Magdalene or the other women, or any details of the resurrection. To put it more crudely than Paul would have wanted, any individual's vision of Jesus is as good as anyone else's.

Mark 16, 70 AD: Mary Magdalene, Mary the mother of James and Salome go to the tomb and see that the stone has been rolled away. They enter and see a young man sitting there in a white garment (apart from the unusual circumstances he seems pretty ordinary, not an angel, but there's no indication of who else he might be). He tells them that Jesus has risen, and says that they must go and tell the disciples that he has gone before them to Galilee. The three women flee, and are too frightened to tell anyone. No appearances of Jesus are reported. (The remaining verses of Mark's Gospel, 16:9-20, do not appear in the most reliable early manuscripts and are not written in Mark's style. Almost all scholars agree they were added later.)

Matthew 18, 75 AD: Mary Magdalene and "the other Mary" go alone to the tomb; when they reach it there is a great earthquake. An angel of the Lord ("his countenance was like lightning") descends from heaven and strikes fear into the guards so that they become like dead men. He rolls back the stone and sits on it. He tells the women that Jesus is not there but risen, and is going ahead of them to Galilee. They depart in fear and joy and run to tell the disciples, but on the way they meet Jesus, who tells them not to be afraid but to tell the disciples to go to Galilee. In Galilee the eleven disciples meet Jesus on the mountain to which he had directed them. They worship him, but some doubt.

A further new element in Matthew is the story that the priests bribe the soldiers guarding the tomb to say that they had fallen asleep, and his disciples had stolen the body. Unlikely, given that the penalty for falling asleep on duty was death.

Luke 24, 80 AD: Mary Magdalene, Joanna, Mary the mother of James, and "other women" find the stone rolled away and on this occasion go inside, where they find two men in shining garments, (and these are probably angels). The men tell them Jesus is not there but risen. The women then tell the other disciples who do not believe them. Jesus appears to two followers on the road from Jerusalem to Emmaus, and later that evening to them all in the upper room at Jerusalem. There are no appearances in Galilee.

John 20-21, 100 AD: Mary Magdalene goes by herself, finds the stone moved and the body gone, and rushes to fetch Peter and John, who come running. They enter the tomb, but don't see two angels. Peter and John go away, leaving Mary outside the tomb. Bending down she looks in, sees the two angels and has a brief conversation. Standing up again and turning round, she sees the gardener. They speak, but only when Jesus calls her by name does she recognize him. There then follow a series of detailed appearances both in Jerusalem and Galilee.

The story continues to be expanded in other gospels not included in the New Testament. In the *Gospel of Peter* (50-100 AD) the soldiers on guard at the tomb see two gigantic angels who come down to bring Jesus out with his cross.

Other non-canonical gospels take a more "spiritual" line. In the *Gospel of Mary*, Mary sees Jesus in a vision, not in reality. Peter is suspicious of the vision but Mary is vindicated and joins the apostles as they go out to preach. As far as tradition rather than text goes there's a further variety of interpretations. One early tradition says that James was the first witness; another says Peter, rather than Mary, giving him more authority.

What happened in the three days (or two, different time scales are given) between the death and the empty tomb? Was Jesus in hell, as Acts 2:31 implies, and the later creeds affirm? Or was he in the "heart of the earth" (Matthew 12:40), or in paradise (Luke 23:43)? We don't know. Then there are problems about the post-resurrection appearances, which lend themselves to different interpretations. The disciples clearly experienced Jesus' presence in a new form, but of what kind? The Greek word *ophthe*, "appeared," is used more for inner spiritual vision than physical sighting. Sometimes he's more of a ghost than a body. When Jesus speaks Mary's name she recognizes him, but is ordered not to touch him. In John 20:19, 26 he appears twice through a wall, and in verse 17 again tells his disciples not to touch him: "Touch me not; for I am not yet ascended to my Father." On the other hand, there's the eating of fish, and his invitation to Thomas to touch him. At other times he appears to be human, but unrecognizable. The whole episodic nature of the post-resurrection appearances is as confusing as anything in the Gospels. Weeks apparently go by without an appearance. What was he doing the rest of the time? And then there are the further appearances after the ascension: to Stephen

(Acts 7:55), Ananias (Acts 9:10-16), to Paul (Acts 9:3-7; 18:9-10; 23:11). And what should we think about the later appearances to saints? To people today? Visions of Jesus are not uncommon, to put it mildly.

Perhaps the most instructive episode is the walk to Emmaus. Cleopas and another (unnamed) disciple, possibly his wife, are walking home, and they meet a stranger who explains the recent events. They don't recognize him as Jesus until they invite him to stay the night and they sit down for a meal. When he blesses the bread and breaks it, "their eyes were opened." Then he vanishes. In retrospect it's: "Did not our heart burn within us, while he talked with us by the way?" They see, with hindsight, what they want to see.

The fact that accounts of the resurrection contradict each other in every detail doesn't necessarily make it untrue – it suggests it might be. We have to judge. Many arguments have been put forward to show that Jesus *must* have risen, and the Gospel accounts *can* be reconciled. For instance, there was no one else to move the stone away: the soldiers wouldn't have done it, the women weren't up to it, and the disciples weren't there. If the authorities had wanted to quash the story they could have produced the body easily enough, except they couldn't because Jesus had risen. If the disciples had wanted to invent a story they wouldn't have used women as witnesses, as women were considered unreliable and their word didn't count in a court of law. Apologists even say that the very fact that the accounts contradict each other proves, or indicates, that they are true. It's like witnesses today giving an account of a robbery seen in the street – the details can be wildly different, sometimes they don't seem to be describing the same event.

But anything can be reconciled if you work at it hard enough. The question is whether it's convincing, given what we know of the times, the way the stories were written, and the nature of life and death. There are crucial differences between witnesses of a street crime and witnesses to the resurrection. Detectives and barristers can cross-examine witnesses today, have them up on the witness stand or in the interviewing room for as long as it takes, get forensic evidence, psychiatric reports. Where the resurrection is concerned, many questions immediately come to mind. Are we sure the body was in the tomb? Why don't we hear again from Nicodemus if he was the one who put it there? Were the guards there or not? Was there an earthquake? Was the angel already there or not? Was it one angel or two, or any? Who actually went to the tomb? How do we know they found the right one? Which of them gave accounts afterwards? Did the women tell the disciples or not? Which people did Jesus first appear to? Why was he so hard to recognize? Had his voice changed? What was he wearing, if anything? We'll never know.

Scholars are broadly agreed on the fact of the crucifixion. In Roman society crucifixions were for criminals or people who were a danger to the state. It wouldn't look good on a curriculum vitae, and it's very unlikely that the Gospel writers would have invented it. The crucifixion also explains the sudden disappearance of Jesus from the scene. There could have been a trial, but on balance probably not. Peasants like Jesus were beneath the protection of the law. And as the disciples had run away, where were the witnesses to provide the details? It was against the law to hold a trial at night, and unlikely that the Sanhedrin would have convened on the evening or night of the Passover.

There was no practice of releasing a prisoner for the crowd. As for the special effects that took place at the time of Jesus' death – the Temple curtain splitting in two, the earthquake, and the darkness over the land – these are things that would have been mentioned in sources outside the Gospels if they had taken place. The population of Jerusalem increased to around 250,000 at the time of the Passover, and if these events had really happened someone like Josephus would have referred to them.

Today, we can work out that there was no eclipse over Palestine at that time. And we can trace the development of the story. Again, the special effects increase the further in time we get from the event. Mark mentions only the darkness over the land. Luke adds the curtain of the Temple being torn in two. Matthew an earthquake and tombs opening. John, though, doesn't mention any of it. As with the virgin birth, he may simply have considered these divine interventions too crude to be taken seriously. They are in any case rather mouse-sized effects to accompany the death of the Son of the Ruler of a universe of several hundred billion galaxies. You would at least expect them to be felt around the Roman Empire - even around the planet. If no contemporaries on the spot noticed anything out of the ordinary happening, why bother with any effects?

Many alternative explanations for the disappearance of the body of Jesus have been given. Muslims believe that Jesus didn't die on the cross in the first place. Many early Christians believed the same – how could anyone crucify "God?" The idea was blasphemous. New Agers today variously believe that Jesus didn't die, that he survived and moved to India, or Glastonbury, or Kashmir, or wherever. There's no evidence for this either, but it has more credibility than the argument that he went up to heaven. After all, there were no twentieth-century doctors and medical equipment around the place to confirm death, and the soldiers were surprised that he seemed to have died so quickly. Mistaken diagnoses of death were common enough for there to be a Jewish tradition of going to check the tomb on the third day just in case (*Tractate of Mourning*). Josephus reports one individual surviving crucifixion.

There's a very simple reading of the resurrection. It's not necessary to invoke conspiracy theories or the supernatural; nor is it necessary to accuse either the disciples or the authorities of deceit. We don't have to make a choice between "true" or "hoax." That's too simplistic. The times were fraught and dangerous. Jesus' followers were beside themselves with hysteria and fright. People at the time were quite prepared to believe in angels descending, darkness covering the land, reports of decomposed dead walking the streets and saying "Hi" to their friends. They lived in a world where everyone believed that these things happened. The Emperor Nero was seen for 20 years after his death. And things haven't changed that much. Many people in the last century believe they saw Elvis Presley after he died.

The probability is that there was no tomb in the first place. Crucified people weren't generally given burials. Their bodies were left as warnings to would-be offenders and were scavenged by dogs and crows, rather like the corpses of people hanged on gibbets in England in recent centuries. To be denied a proper burial was part of the horror of the death. This is why of all the tens of thousands of people crucified in Palestine in the century around Jesus' death only one skeleton has ever been found, preserved in a casket.

Why didn't the authorities squash the disciples' story by bringing the body out and showing it to the crowd? Simple, because they didn't have it, the dogs did. Or simpler still, perhaps there wasn't even a story around to squash, which is why Paul scarcely mentions it. It may have been thirty years before the story was sufficiently well known for the first Gospel writer, Mark, to include it. We have no idea whether Mark interviewed Mary or any of the witnesses himself, or whether, given average lifespans of the time, they were still alive. They were probably not.

But let's assume for the sake of argument that the body of Jesus was laid in a tomb. The only fact that all four Gospels agree on was that Mary Magdalene went to the tomb. Of all the excitable and hysterical of Jesus' followers she was the most disturbed – he had healed her of seven devils. Most or all of the disciples had scattered in fright, probably back to their homes in Galilee. Mary was the most committed, the bravest, or the maddest, and stayed on. Perhaps it's significant that in John's Gospel the disciples don't see the angels in the tomb but she does, a moment later. Perhaps she hallucinated under the stress of the times – even today 10% to 25% of ordinary, functioning people repeatedly say in surveys that at least once in their lives they have experienced a vivid hallucination. Perhaps she was an epileptic, prone to visions and imaginary experiences. Perhaps she believed she spoke with Jesus but was simply mistaken. Perhaps the gardener was just a gardener. Perhaps she simply went to the wrong tomb. Perhaps she imagined it all much later, having stories drawn out of her by excited grandchildren. Perhaps she lied. In any case, whatever the motive, she started a hare running. Then as the story gained ground some (but not all) of Jesus' followers believed it. Other women wanted to be part of it, and added experiences of seeing Jesus, or an angel. Some of the disciples started to add their bits. A generation later, two generations later, third-, fourth-hand accounts turned into the collection of different stories we have now.

That's a lot of ifs and maybes, but that's the point. There are so many possible scenarios. Many Christian books present an argument that says: "If it didn't happen, explain this . . ." Believers in UFOs argue in the same way. But the burden is not on skeptics to explain a physically impossible event they don't believe occurred in the first place. It's up to Christians who believe in the resurrection to provide evidence of an acceptable kind. There is none. The evidence for the resurrection is as close to zero as makes no odds. We'll never know what really happened.

40 READ IT FOR YOURSELF

"Our final experience, like our first, is conjectural. We move between two darknesses."

E. M. FORSTER

Conservatives and fundamentalists will say, "Read it for yourself. Look at all the detail. It must have happened. Okay, the ascension certainly has to be treated metaphorically, and maybe the virgin birth, but the passion narrative and the resurrection are different. They're at the core of the Christian experience. When Peter denies Jesus three times and the rooster crows, it crows for all of us. We all know that we're weak, we all betray the good when we're afraid, and it's Christ alone, raised from the dead, who can save us."

Indeed it's hard to read Matthew's account of the passion – the most detailed of the four – and not feel moved by it. Many people have been converted to the Christian faith and their lives have been changed as a result of being persuaded by the power of the writing that Jesus died on the cross and rose again. But this is a credit to Matthew the writer rather than Matthew the historian. Most scholars (taking them across all traditions, Jewish, as well as secular and Christian) see the passion story as a theological construct rather than fact. The story is carefully built up, with the details added for a particular effect. "Three," for example, is one of the "power" numbers, like seven, twelve, and forty. If something is said three times it's likely to be true. If a man swears three times it is binding. So Jesus returns three times in Gethsemane to find his disciples sleeping (though who was there to see and report it?). Peter denies three times that he is a follower of Jesus (again, none of the other disciples were there). Jesus is mocked three times as he hangs on the cross, in a group of three crosses. He rises on the third day (why not the second, or as soon as he dies?). Most of all, though, the impact of this story is a credit to the power of the

universal and ancient myth that the man who is God can overcome death and live again.

Matthew is writing to impress Jews with the way Jesus fulfills
the Old Testament, and since they know much of the Old
Testament by heart, the story would have even more resonance for
them than it has for us. He constructs the episodes to echo
prophecy and builds it up from scripture references just as he did
with the virgin birth. The ride on a donkey into Jerusalem parallels
Zechariah 9:9. Indeed because Zechariah confusingly mentions an
ass and her foal Matthew seems to say that Jesus rode both at the
same time (Matthew 21:7). The Gethsemane experience on the
Mount of Olives brings to mind David in tears and prayers
(2 Samuel 19). Pilate washing his hands parallels the Jewish legal
custom of washing hands as a statement of innocence when a
murder has been committed (Deuteronomy 21:6). The suffering
on the cross refers back to Isaiah 53:3-12. The two thieves on
either side of Jesus have echoes of the evildoers encircling the
psalmist in Psalm 22. Jewish readers would recognize other links:
the wine and the gall given Jesus on the cross (Psalm 69:21); the
words, "My God, my God, why hast thou forsaken me" (Psalm
22:1); dividing the clothes of Jesus (Psalm 22:18); 30 pieces of silver (Zechariah 11:12); Judas hanging himself (David's betrayal by
Ahithophel in 2 Samuel 17:23). The writers lived and breathed
scripture every day. Things didn't just "happen" because they
"happened." They were part of God's unfolding purpose. Every
act, every moment, had spiritual meaning.

Similarly Christians today "know" the resurrected Jesus as
Savior. They talk with him, experience him. He lives for them as a
"presence." Perhaps they are framing their experience in the terms
of the story, much as they regard believers of other faiths as doing.
Jesus isn't actually "out there" in a physical sense, speaking to them.
We shape these experiences in terms that make sense to us, we
have to provide some kind of coat hook. Break the thin ice and

our minds are full of shadows, images, fears, the good and bad. Psychology explains some – life hasn't been the same since Freud described the battle between our id and our ego, our subconscious and our reason. Perhaps as Jung said we collectively create archetypes that can be more real to us than our individual selves.

Or maybe we're getting this wrong. Maybe we should be more open to the Spirit. Maybe the boundaries of time and space are peppered with holes, and miracles do happen. Maybe they happen for you – or will, if you believe them. Maybe we all live in slightly different universes, shading from one to another. Maybe Jesus had a virgin birth, walked on water, rose from the dead. And Peter walked on water, too, and an angel led him out of a locked and guarded prison. Maybe this is what faith is about.

But what goes for one religion must go for another. If you want to believe this there are no grounds for denying that Buddha equally had a form of virgin birth, with his mother dreaming that the baby-to-be took the form of a white elephant and entered her womb. Or that he walked on water and through walls, and flew through the air cross-legged. And that his monks did the same. After all, Buddhists have a more developed theology of miracles than Christians. They rank them in levels of difficulty through which a bodhisavatta ascends on the path to full enlightenment. All of Jesus' miracles can be categorized in this way, including the resurrection.

Religions model a relationship between ourselves and the world. They picture a reality that answers our needs. Miracles are incidental to this, not the major plank. The idea of the man who becomes God or the God who becomes man is one of the ideas we've developed to link our consciousness with a possible universal one. We choose the model we want. The virtue of the choice lies in the extent to which it develops us as individuals, growing in awareness and practicing love. Not in the miracles that grow up around the model, obscuring the meaning.

41 THE MESSAGE

"Happiness is the only good; the time to be happy is now, the place to be happy is here, the way to be happy is to make others so."

ROBERT INGERSOLL

But if you take away Jesus as God, don't you take away the point of Christianity? If he wasn't God on earth performing miracles and rising from the dead, what's left?

Many Christians feel they need to take the Bible stories literally to make sense of their faith. That's one option. Others are more prepared to accept them as stories that represent a greater truth. This is not to slide away from the truth. It may have been the way the Gospel writers thought, though I'm more inclined to think they took them literally. But there was certainly a strand of that way of thinking in their mental make-up. It's the way Hindus think today. Whether a star literally appeared to mark the birth of Krishna isn't significant to them. The story has a truth of its own, which is that one of the three high gods, Vishnu, was prepared to incarnate himself in human form as a divine child. To investigate whether there was such a star in the sky at the time is irrelevant at best, sacrilegious at worst.

For many Christians it's their personal experience of the Jesus who lives for them that's important, not his teaching on this or that issue. For over 20 centuries he's been made into a kind of Hamlet of the spirit world, focusing our anxieties about the life to come, our ambivalence about "self" and "other," body and soul, ourselves and God. He's filled a multitude of roles, from revolutionary to judge, ruler to servant, lover to friend. He is strong, but aware of weakness. Self-sufficient, but lonely. Judgmental but loving. He is meek but angry. He reconciles but divides. Following his teaching is easy but all consuming. Out of all these contradictions devotional writers create the character they want. Many Christians journey from one image to another, interpreting him differently according to their own changing experience of life.

If we met Jesus today, would we like him? Admire him? There's no way of knowing. Perhaps he was a religious crank, a wild-eyed, scary-looking guy. It's unlikely he came out of the desert looking like a film star after six weeks of no food, no washing, confrontations with devils. Even making allowances for later additions to the text, we have to accept he was a fanatic. Many of his followers left him when he talked about them eating his flesh and drinking his blood (John 6:52-66). Some thought he was crackers: "Many of them said, He hath a devil, and is mad; why hear ye him?" (John 10:20). Some thought he was too disreputable to be a Jew, and must be a Samaritan (John 8:48). At one point, his own family said he was mad and tried to take him away (Mark 3:21-35). Maybe his leaving Nazareth hadn't been a happy parting, maybe they encouraged him to leave, we don't know. His own brothers didn't believe in him (John 7:5).

The many verses where Jesus seems to attack our (and the Jewish) idea of family values are accepted as authentic by the vast majority of scholars. Why would his followers choose to invent such ugly words? "For I am come to set a man at variance against his father, and the daughter against her mother, and the daughter in law against her mother in law. And a man's foes shall be they of his own household" (Matthew 10:35-36; see also, Matthew 23:9; Mark 3:31-35; 6:4; Luke 9:59-62; 14:26; John 2:4, etc.) There are too many curses in the Gospels for us to be able to argue that they bear no relation to what Jesus said. He may have been a harsh, uncompromising character who generated more fear and dislike than love. If he came today he would look nothing like the popular image of a soulful shepherd. Indeed we still wouldn't know what he looked like, because he'd be a textile worker in a Thai sweatshop. Or maybe he'd be a small Columbian farmer. He'd create some trouble for the local multinational subsidiary. We'd hear about him after he was murdered by the military.

So why bother with Jesus today? It's not the miracles that made Jesus significant then or now. In his time miracle-workers were two a penny. They were as common as wise women and witches in the villages of medieval Europe, or along the River Ganges today. It's what he said that made him significant, and still does. People who accept the status quo don't change anything, don't get crucified, and don't found religions. As someone who makes Julius Caesar or Alexander the Great seem relatively insignificant you would expect him to have something new to say, to be upsetting. And perhaps what Jesus had to say was worth the disciples putting up with him as a person, with the way he ripped apart their livelihoods and families. What was it?

Clearly, in the Gospels we only have a tiny fraction of the words of Jesus. The 60,000 or so reported words that we have, including duplication and later additions, could have been spoken in a couple of days. About half of these are given in the canonical Gospels (those in the New Testament), the other half in the non-canonical writings. It's a shame we don't have more, and better sources. He needed a Boswell to his Johnson, taking the words down. But we have to work with what we have.

Most scholars would say we are closest to Jesus' own words when we read the parables and the "sayings." Jesus was a countryman from Galilee, which was a fertile place, with a moderate climate. The countryside comes alive in his stories: wild flowers, weeds amongst the crops, wheat to be separated from the chaff, fig-trees and grapevines, ripe harvests, the farmer with his seed, baking bread, fishing. It's a world away from the theology of Paul, or Greek philosophy. It's different from the bombast of revelation and apocalypse, common at the time.

Having said this we still have to be careful: we can't assume we have the parables word for word as Jesus gave them. They vary from Gospel to Gospel according to the agenda of the writer.

Mark's parables tend to be ones of nature, set in the world of the villages. Some of them have an allegorical meaning, like the parables of the sower and the fig tree. Luke avoids allegory, even when repeating one of Mark's parables. He lets the meaning look after itself and focuses on Jesus' teaching on prayer or the danger of wealth. Matthew uses allegory and emphasizes the teaching on hell, which hardly occurs in Luke.

But there's enough to get a general impression of what Jesus was on about. At the age of about 30, he set out to preach the kingdom of God.

What is it?

42 THE KINGDOM

"God has no religion."

GANDHI

The subject of almost all the parables is the kingdom of God: 40 speak of what it is like, 25 of the fate of those who are unprepared for it. The kingdom is the "economy" of true Christianity, the heart of the message. The Christian faith is not a process of moving from sin to salvation. It's not moving from a lower to a higher state. It's not about God coming down to earth and living on it, or people going to live with him in heaven. There's no angelic cavalry or magic wand to sort out all the problems. In the kingdom, there are no priests, or temples, or sacred books, or liturgies. There are no divine rules. Questions are answered with more questions. When asked: "Art thou he that should come?" (Luke 7:20), Jesus does not answer, "This is who I am," but, "What do you see?" Contrast this with the warrior God of Moses detailing how he should be worshipped to the last lick of gold leaf, grabbing the last inch of obedience out of the 600 plus laws. The kingdom Jesus describes is at the opposite extreme. It's about how people should live on earth, by themselves. He is stepping away from the traditional "God religion" of sacrifice and worship, not into it. His impact on the people around him was because of his message that God is ours. He is us. He doesn't belong to the priests. Jesus was not a political but a religious revolutionary.

We're so used to the parables and the Sermon on the Mount that we forget how non-religious the language of Jesus is. The Christian God-language we use today, the language of doctrines, is the kind of language the Pharisees and Sadducees used. What Jesus says over and over again is that his message is simple, but you have to take it in. This is made explicit in the parable of the sower (Matthew 13:18-23; Mark 4:3-20). Only those who hear the word and follow it, bearing fruit in their lives, are really listening. If it doesn't change you, you haven't got it.

One of the most frequent parables says that the kingdom of heaven is the most valuable thing you can have. It's worth everything (Matthew 13:44-45). But you can't buy it. You can only enter by letting go (Matthew 11:29-30). It's always open for you (Matthew 10:5-7; 20:1-16). Indeed it seeks you out. If you've got it, you will be given more, you're on your way (Mark 4:25). It will grow and take over (like the mustard seed, Mark 4:30-32). But you have to be ready for it (Matthew 25:1-13). And it's not incremental, a question of doing a little bit better, it's a different way of living (Luke 5:36-39).

The Jews (and everyone else) saw life in terms of distinctions. At the top was God, holy and separate. At the bottom were Gentiles and lepers, those whom God had cursed. These distinctions were embodied in the Law, the Temple, the purity rituals, the structures of the family, of every aspect of society, right down to the details of what you wore and ate, how you behaved, whether you were healthy or ill, how you lived every minute of the day. Avoiding contamination by "impure" touch was taken to the point of obsession. The penalty for violating the purity code in relation to the Temple was execution. But in the kingdom distinctions are abolished. Jesus walks through the Gospels as if he is oblivious to society. He mixes happily with lepers, who everyone believed must have committed the most terrible sins to be afflicted with such a horrible illness. Every individual is of supreme worth (Matthew 20:30-34; Luke 15:4-7). It's what you are in yourself that matters, not how you look, what your family is, what your race is, what you believe, what you think of yourself. It doesn't matter if you're ill, poor or criminal (Luke 14:16-24; 19:1-10). The gospel is not about repenting for past sins, it's repenting because the kingdom of heaven is at hand – turning to a new reality (Mark 1:14-15; Matthew 4:17). Jesus is not here to restore a lost state of union with God but to show a new one. Love, joy and peace: you already have them, if you can realize it.

This is why the economy of the kingdom is the reverse of that on earth. Those who are ahead in the social exchange have more they need to lose. The first will be last, the last first (Luke 14:7-11; 18:10-14). The more you have, the further from God you are (Luke 14:16-24). God is embodied in the powerless, not the powerful. It's not the fittest, or cleverest or richest who get to the kingdom. It's those who renounce the game of survival of the fittest. Forsake all that you have (Luke 14:33). Free yourself from all ties of obligation and family (Matthew 8:21-22). It's those who suffer now who will be blessed (Matthew 5:3-12). If you're rich, forget it (Matthew 19:16-24; Mark 10:24-25; Luke 12:16-21; 16:13, 19-31).

The kingdom is a feast, a wedding (Matthew 22:1-14). Life is a party. It's "good." What you have is not yours (Matthew 18:23-35), it's given to you. So live openly and freely. Enjoy every moment. Don't worry – be carefree (Matthew 6:25-34; 10:29-31; Luke 12:22-34). If you say thank you for what you want, you'll find you have it. If you believe you have it, you will. Belief is creative. It can move mountains (Matthew 17:20-21). Anything you ask for you'll get (Mark 11:24). If two or more believe the same thing, and ask for it, the power is multiplied exponentially (Matthew 18:19). Make it true in your life, and it will be true. The universal Father wants you to have everything.

God loves the good and the evil in creation without distinction (Matthew 5:43-45). Loving your neighbor is a given (Luke 10:25-27), but this is not enough. You must love your enemy too (Matthew 5:38-45; Luke 6:27-34; 10:28-37). We are all God's children, so love is the only option. Those who love their enemies have no enemies. The kingdom is about renouncing power. Forgive people what they owe you (Matthew 18:23-35). The more forgiveness, the more love in return (Luke 7:41-43). It seems not

too far from the law of returns, called karma in the East. The energy we give comes back to us. If we give love, we are enriched
beyond measure. You have to forget calculation, the measurement
of benefit to yourself. It takes the unselfconscious love of a child to
enter the kingdom (Mark 10:14-15).

The Jews (and virtually everyone in the first-century world)
saw tolerance as weakness, open-mindedness as sin. The more you
gained and the more powerful you were, the closer you were to
God. The kingdom turns this upside down. You must take up your
cross, and follow Jesus (Matthew 16:24-25; Mark 8:34-36; Luke
9:23). You must not only give what you have away, you must give
your very self. Let it die (John 12:24). Forget about saving your
self, you find your salvation in offering it up.

Understand this, and you will live in the love of God, as Jesus
does (John 14:21). Freud called loving your enemy the most
impossible commandment ever written. It outrages our sense of
boundaries. But Jesus says there are no boundaries. It's only when
we realize this that we see the kingdom. It's only when we forget
ourselves that we find God. Because God is to be found in everyone else. We are in him, and he in us (John 17:21). The Jews
regarded God with such reverence that they did not address Him
by name. Jesus calls Him "Dad." We are all sons of God (John
20:17). We are all one (Matthew 25:40). We can never be separated
("I am with you alway, even unto the end of the world" Matthew
28:20). Jesus models the way to live in conscious union with God
(John 14:6). When we see this we no longer need divine beings
"up above." The kingdom of God is "spread out on earth," and
made real in ourselves, by forgetting our selves (Mark 1:15; Luke
4:43; 17:21-23; Matthew 4:17). The "scandal of particularity" in
Christianity is not that this particular human being was God, but
that he said all people could become like him and be God. God is
as much like our twin brother as He is like an almighty deity up in
the sky.

We have no idea why Jesus came to think in this way. Unlike the Buddha, Jesus' reasons for thinking as he did have not been passed on in terms we can understand. It's the lost story of Christianity. But we have seen that this idea of the kingdom is the key to his message. It's evidently not what the Jews were expecting. His disciples could never quite get the hang of it. Maybe Jesus himself wasn't sure where it was leading. Perhaps he had no plan, no purpose, and was going with the flow. Perhaps he would have developed his ideas if he had lived longer. All we know is that the material in the Gospels that is most likely to have been said and enacted by him revolves around the kingdom of God. He may have believed that in giving up his own life he was bringing it about.

Jesus probably knew what he was doing when he took on the establishment in Jerusalem. He didn't need to do this – he could have remained an obscure teacher in Galilee. He went to the cross because he wouldn't compromise his vision. He talks about the new and better world that is around us if we can make it happen. Take these values as your own, and follow him, and it will be realized. But we have to make this conscious effort. We have to break down the walls we've put up between ourselves and our true natures, between ourselves and everyone else. We have to become self-aware to the point where we forget the self. And the impossible odds paid off. This obscure teacher with an outlandish dream of everyone being equal in the sight of God set a ball rolling.

Of course other people see Jesus differently. Most Jewish scholars would see this as extravagant speculation. For them he is one of a line of itinerant preachers and would-be Messiahs, who at best had the same concerns as Hillel, with maybe a sprinkling of Essene thought.

The writer of the Gospel of John saw him differently. So did Paul. The Church came to see Jesus differently. He's the judge who will return in clouds and glory, condemning unbelievers to hellfire.

So is he basically a divine figure of wrath and punishment, or a powerful teacher and exemplar of mercy and tolerance? It's possible to read it either way. It seems most likely that unconditional love is at the core of his teaching, with the apocalyptic second coming and judgement (particularly as expressed in the nightmare of Revelation) being added later by the Church. The latter tradition came from John the Baptist (whose followers some of the disciples were) rather than Jesus. Maybe he would have been appalled at the religion the Church created, and horrified if he knew that even one heretic had been tortured in his name.

Maybe it's not so much a question of what Jesus taught as what you're prepared to believe.

43 Is this relevant today?

"No one can be redeemed by another. No God and no saint is able to shield a man from the consequences of his evil doings. Every one of us must become his own redeemer."

SUBHADNA BHISHU

Surely it's not possible that the Church could have got Jesus so wrong? But why not when each bit of the Church says the other bits are wrong? Protestants say the Church had the wrong message for most of the last two millennia. Roman Catholics have doubted the validity of the Orthodox Church. Churches like the Nestorians have looked on both as mistaken. All say that all the followers of all other religions are wrong.

Jesus was mugged by the Church. It turned the kingdom of God for everyone into the kingdom of heaven for the salvation of a few, to which it alone held the keys. It controlled the gates and charged for entrance. Most people, in the UK at least, don't believe in the kingdom of heaven any more. In losing our faith in that it has become more difficult to believe in God, or find a meaningful way of expressing Him. But does the kingdom of God on earth still have any relevance? Isn't it a smaller, less significant kind of an idea?

Religions exist in the uncertain borderland between our selves and the world. We're aware today of the extreme difficulty of saying that a revelation genuinely comes from "out there," and is not generated or shaped in our own heads. To illustrate this take a quick look at a religion that does claim this. One of the most curious on earth is that of the Dogon people in South Mali. They believe that fish-like aliens brought knowledge to them from a star later identified as Sirius B. In the 1930s they provided French anthropologists with a detailed working knowledge of the solar system, down to the rings of Saturn and the four moons of Jupiter.

They described the type of star it was, and traced its path around the sky. The odd thing is that Sirius B is not even visible to the naked eye. Its existence was not confirmed by telescope till the 1860s. The orbits of which they appeared to have detailed knowledge were not confirmed till the 1970s. Now *that's* confirmation. And the idea that aliens stopped off for repairs in Mali and spoke to a few Africans is just as plausible as God sending His Son to earth to speak to a few Palestinians.

I expect there's nothing in the story told by the Dogon people. It's like the Gospel writers and the resurrection. A story was circulating which the writers wanted confirmed, and some individuals were happy to oblige. It's heading along the right lines though. If Jesus or Christianity had given us one single fact about the heavens (or anything at all really) which was not known at the time but was proved right later, this would be a different book.

As soon as we start to express what we mean by way of spiritual reality we are shaping our experience in our own terms, not the terms of what might be "real." We project our thoughts across and shape what we see. But this is not just an optional extra, a Sunday occupation for those who have the time to be "religious." It's fundamental to the way we think and act. When humankind became self-aware it found itself in a dilemma. Rather than act in the interests of the group individuals could override their biological programming and act in the interests of the self. But to act solely in the interests of the self is self-destructive in the longer term. Religions grew to connect us again with the larger whole. It's our "big idea" that ties us together. The one that stops the self getting drunk on its own appetite for power. A solid religion creates structures that encourage inspiration, service, transcendence, and controls the appetites of the self. But we corrupt the insight. Control turns into oppression. Inspiration turns into deceit. We threaten to drown in our own creations. Every now and again a teacher picks up the original manual and says: "This is how we're meant to do it. We're on the same side. Love each other." Then we sink again.

Of all the world religions this is perhaps illustrated best of all in Christianity, due to the short life of its founder, the suddenness of his death, the lack of any original or contemporary records. First comes the dynamic master teacher, turning the establishment upside down, blowing away the cobwebs and structures that self-interest has created, bringing people back to universal themes of truth, justice, freedom, equality, "oneness." After his death there's a vacuum. The awed disciples, without the same intensity of vision but with an average mortal's share of self-interest, scurry around stitching up the hole and re-creating the world as it was before. With time the bureaucrats parcel out the vision into prescribed chunks called doctrine, the leadership types organize groups into communities called churches, the salesmen go out with the one and only true original product and knock everyone else's, the accountants start to look for profit. It's true of business and governments as well: the path from vision to VAT. Much the same happened in Islam, where Mohammed's followers proclaimed him the last prophet soon after his death.

If Jesus came back today he'd see that the Church is like the Judaism of his own day: nothing much has changed. The Church created a new religion of blood sacrifice out of the ashes of his efforts to say that no sacrifice is needed; a religion of fear and obedience out of his attempts to say that fear and laws are what we need to put away. He was turned into what he rejected.

This explains something about orthodox Christianity. It gets steamed up over subjects on which Jesus says nothing, and the Bible little – subjects like sex, homosexuality, keeping women out of the priesthood, drugs, abortion, church finances, infant baptism, remarrying divorcees, liturgy, etc., mostly questions of authority and control. It insists it's following the laws of God rather than social trends, though these invariably seem to reflect the conservative social position of the time, and are held in common with similar conservative positions in other religions. When the position becomes untenable on basic humanitarian grounds the Church moves, a century or two late.

This happens even when the Bible is quite explicit on the subject. Slavery is an example. It's clear that the Bible approves of slavery. God gives the Israelites detailed instructions on how long slaves can be kept, how to go about selling your daughter as a slave, what to do with the children of slaves and how it's okay to beat slaves to the point of death as long as you don't actually kill them (Exodus 21:1-21). In the New Testament, Paul tells runaway slaves to go back to their masters and behave. There's no hint anywhere that slavery might be wicked, or not part of God's plan for humankind, though you can find this in "pagan" literature. We might guess that slavery is not part of Jesus' view of life, but he never refers to it. In the nineteenth century, the arguments for abolishing slavery were humanitarian rather than biblical. The founders of twentieth-century evangelicalism and the doctrine of biblical inerrancy – Charles Hodge, Robert Dabney, James Thornwell – believed in slavery as "some of the plainest declarations of the Word of God" (*Presbyterian General Assembly Report* 1845). After all, the USA had been built on slave labor. How could it not be approved by God? The Vatican defended slavery as part of natural and divine law as late as 1866.

Similarly, the divine right of kings to rule, the inferiority of women, capital punishment for minor crimes, the persecution of Jews – these have also been accepted by most Christians through history as biblically obvious, and they are, according to one way of reading the Bible. You can believe from scripture that women are the property of men, that polygamy, concubines, sex with slaves, prostitution, are all normal and fine with God. Far more easily in fact than you can read support for the nuclear family. In the past century, the Bible has been used to support apartheid, the Nazi program and nuclear weapons. You can find approval of any evil in the Bible if you want to.

So what can Jesus' idea of the kingdom of God on earth, his contribution to the Jewish people and to us, still mean today? Jesus didn't know it, but it's taken millions of years for consciousness to evolve, for us to be aware of ourselves as separate. Maybe we can't continue for much longer without striking a new balance, acknowledging that we are not truly separate after all. Maybe the next step for consciousness is to control the ego, to transcend the self. To abolish the boundaries and see our selves as "one," in the kind of way he described.

Maybe we need a big idea to make sense of the world we live in, to make it a better one, to provide a large enough incentive to act in the interest of everyone rather than ourselves. Maybe just loving our neighbor isn't enough to get us going. Maybe if we don't have this bigger idea to aim for, this idea of truth and love that we call the kingdom of God, we'll end up in an evolutionary dead end. We'll die the death of a thousand wars and pollutants, till the crust of the planet we live on runs out of patience.

The idea of the kingdom in Jesus' teaching only survived in fragments that found their way into the early Gospels. Given the progressive dilution of the teaching from the first three Gospels (a generation after Jesus) to the Gospel of John (a generation further on) to the writings of the Church Fathers, it's possible to guess that the teaching was more radical at the time he gave it.

How does it work in practice?

The kingdom is not easy to define because it comes across in the life of Jesus as not so much a "state" as an "attempt." He is unstoppable in his pursuit of it. Family, disciples, Pharisees, Romans, none of them could persuade him out of it. It's not a search that can easily be mapped out in steps because it's internal. It's what you make of it. It challenges you in so far as you're open to being challenged. He never tried setting it down in writing.

When he talks it is in puzzling stories, which ask you to "go deeper." He never turned it into laws; the point seems to be that laws are there to be broken. He didn't set up a community or suggest working arrangements for living together. He virtually destroyed whatever living arrangements he could find. There's no practical advice. There's no mission statement. It is just "go further." If you've given some of your money away, give it all away. If you've forgiven your enemy seven times, forgive him seventy-seven times. If he hits you, encourage him to hit you again.

It's perhaps the most demanding teaching of any spiritual master. It even offends the evolutionary logic of altruism – that co-operation works in the long run because cheats will be punished. It asks us to shed all our instincts for self-preservation, developed over millions of years. Living in the present, not worrying about the future. Untying the laws that keep society sane and ordered. It asks us to abandon the rational mind, the one asset that distinguishes us from the animals, and instead just trust. Have faith. No matter how tough it gets. It's faith that makes us what we are. Faith and love. They can achieve the impossible. Don't worry about the evidence all around you that they don't exist. Believe in it and it will be true.

It's not history that is important, it's the myth. If we could really follow it, it would change our selves, and the world. But we can't. We can manage it in pieces. Individuals can manage it between themselves to some extent. Many of the best relationships are based on the idea of sacrificing your own interest for the benefit of your partner. And it's possible to extend that to the family. Some saintly individuals manage to extend it further, to communities of the disabled, or the poor. But for most of us it's an ideal that never happens. Nevertheless it's there, as an idea. And that's the real power of Christianity, the power of Jesus, today, that he rediscovered this wonderful idea that would make us all happy if only we could all take it on board at once. But none of us can be the first to let go of what we have. We don't believe we have the courage, or the love. We're content, more or less, with the image we have. The one we've inherited, absorbed from our peers, developed for our protection. We would feel stupid. The kingdom is for the fools of this world.

But this is all very general. What does the kingdom mean today?

44 THE RUB

"We have just enough religion to make us hate, but not enough to make us love one another."

JONATHAN SWIFT

If a teacher is worth following it's because we believe he or she gets closer to the heart of the human condition than anyone else. Because our condition is one of separation and only fitful happiness the teaching is likely to be more challenging than any other. There are many aspects of the kingdom teaching that we could cover – freedom from the self, equality, closeness to God, inner peace, nature, love, forgiveness – but this is a book of snapshots. Let's just look at one aspect, the teaching on money, and see if it's still challenging today.

Money is a big issue for all of us. How much money we have defines what we can do, where we can live, what kind of holidays we can take, maybe even the friends we have, how we think of ourselves.

Jesus has a lot to say about money. In the first three Gospels there are about ten times as many verses on money as there are about going to the cross (for example, Matthew 6:19-20, 24; 10:8-13; 19:18-21, 23-24; 25:41-46; Mark 10:21, 23; Luke 6:20-34, 38; 12:15-34; 14:12-14, 31-33; 16:13, 19-31; 21:3-4). There's also a large body of teaching in the Old Testament about the just distribution of wealth, and, with the possible exception of Isaiah 53, nothing at all that's clearly related to Jesus' death on the cross. Are these verses relevant today? You may say that society is fairer now, that we still have poor people, but not as many as before, and they're unlikely to starve. We live longer, there are more of us, life is better. Admittedly the evidence suggests that once we've got beyond a certain minimum level of income having more doesn't make us any happier. But what we have is what we've earned. It's ours by right. There's no good reason why Christians should have less money than anyone else. Many say we should have more.

But it's not our neighbors down the road we should be comparing ourselves with. In the time of Jesus Palestine, and every small region of the world, was self-sufficient. The relative discrepancies in wealth between different regions and nations were close to zero. The world today is a global economic unit. Most of what we purchase in the shops comes from abroad, as food and manufactured goods, or as raw materials to have value added, often by a multiple of several hundred times from cost to retail. A cappuccino can cost $3 in the West, while the coffee grower gets a cent. We have exported our cheap labor and the associated hardships.

Two hundred years ago the ratio of wealth between rich and poor countries was 4 to 1 and 100 years ago it was 10 to 1. Today it's 60 to 1. Today it's we in the developed world who are "rich." The overall percentages in the global economy are worse today than they were in Palestine in the first century AD. Then the top sixth of the population (governors and priests) owned around 60% of the wealth. Today, globally, the top sixth control 80% and have an average income of $70 a day. Today, 60% of the world's population live on less than $2 a day; 25% on less than $1 a day, the United Nations' official minimum survival level. This translates into harsh realities as shocking as anything you could find in the first century. Four out of five people in the world live in substandard housing. Over one-third are malnourished; half have no decent sanitation; one-third have no drinkable water. Every day 30,000 people die of starvation, while 100 billion dollars of food gets thrown away every year in North America alone.

So if Jesus were around today he would probably have had as much to say on wealth as he had then. What are his words to the rich? Wealthy people cannot enter the kingdom of God, full stop. Christian commentators consistently water down the message by saying that it's the love of money he condemns, not money itself.

That's not there in the text. It is by the time Paul writes to Timothy (1 Timothy 6:10), but Jesus doesn't say that. He never says: "Money's okay if you use it for good, if you give a portion to charity, if you don't let it take you over." He says if you have it, give it away. "Give to every man that asketh of thee; and of him that taketh away thy goods ask them not again" (Luke 6:30). If you hang on to money you'll be corrupted; you don't understand how dangerous it is. There's no ambiguity here. You simply can't be rich and follow him in a world of poor people. If you really treated the poor as you would like to be treated, if you saw God in them as well as yourself, you couldn't be rich. You couldn't live with yourself.

The most vivid teaching is given in the parable of Lazarus (Luke 16:19-31), the only parable character to get a name. He lives on the crumbs from the rich man's table. The rich man doesn't do anything wrong in the parable: he comes across as a decent guy, concerned about his family. He's just rich. He probably thought he was doing Lazarus a favor by leaving him the crumbs. After all, he'd earned his wealth, created it, and wealth trickles down from the top to help everybody. No doubt Jesus' listeners thought, as we might, that Lazarus' poverty wasn't the fault of the rich man. Maybe the fault was even with Lazarus. Perhaps he should have found himself a job. If the rich man had given him more he would probably have frittered it away on gambling, drink or tobacco. Not a bit of it. The condemnation of the rich man is complete. He doesn't get a chance to repent, not even a chance to warn his wealthy brothers what's waiting for them.

The parable is crackers, isn't it? That's just what the wealthy ruling priests thought. In case we haven't got the message, it's repeated many times. We're saved not by faith but by how much we give to our neighbors. On judgement day the people God rejects are not the ones who aren't saved or born again, but those who haven't helped their neighbors: "I was an hungred, and ye gave me no meat: I was thirsty, and ye gave me no drink: I was a stranger, and ye took me not in: naked, and ye clothed me not: sick, and in prison, and ye visited me not . . . Inasmuch as ye did it not to one of the least of these, ye did it not to me" (Matthew 25:42-43, 45). The rich young man who does everything right is told to do just one more thing: to give away all he has (Matthew 19:16-22). The words, "For ye have the poor always with you" (Matthew 26:11) are a judgement, a curse, not an excuse for laissez-faire capitalism. There isn't a clearer message in the Bible.

It's a parable for our time. But the wealthy top sixth today are largely distributed around North America and Europe, with the huge bulk concentrated in the USA and Western Europe. As 75% of Americans say they have made a personal commitment to Jesus Christ, the wealthy are mostly Christian. The majority, living on under $2 a day, are outside the gates. If you're in the top sixth today, earning $25,000 or so a year, there's little doubt about it: if you take the Gospels seriously, you're damned. Most of the Western Christian Church is going to hell. If you're earning more than $10,000 or so a year you're on the slippery slope.

Is that too harsh? It's hard to live on $10,000 a year in the West. That in itself is a judgement on the kind of global society that the Christian West has largely shaped. Most of us live in and support a system that Jesus would have condemned. The disparity in wealth in the world today is obscene. The richest 200 people in the world increased their income last year by $100 billion. That increase alone is roughly equivalent to what the poorest 500 million people earned. In other words, just one of these rich Christians, by foregoing one annual increase (not the basic income) could have doubled the income of five million starving people, several times the population of a country like that of Palestine in the time of Jesus. So perhaps giving a proportion of our wealth, whether 1%, 10%, 50%, is a sop to our consciences, not a "kingdom style" response. If it were 90%, or in some cases 99.9%, we could claim to be getting serious.

But individual responses are not enough. A kingdom of God with a few individuals present is as meaningless as a heaven with a few saved souls. A true kingdom response to the inequalities in the world would mean redefining what we mean by society. Rethinking the definition of money. Maybe we should think about abolishing the idea of an economy based on debt and individual success altogether. Get rid of "interest," which was morally condemned by most religions up until around the sixteenth century. Perhaps this is too extreme. Perhaps we should tone down the anarchist elements of Jesus' thinking and not worry about giving all our money away, but think about creating a society where the income all round the world is nearer the average of $7,000 a year. Extend basic human rights to cover education, clean water, decent housing, and keep any surplus for the benefit of the environment. Recover the Old Testament idea that decisions should be made for the benefit of the "seventh generation." Perhaps we should be wary of people who want excessive wealth in the same way we are of those who want excessive power.

Would this simply be redistributing wealth to people who haven't earned it? The parable of the vineyard (Matthew 20:1-16) says we shouldn't worry about that. But have we really earned it all anyway? The question of reparations is going to loom ever larger over the next few decades, and the sums involved are, potentially, astronomical. To take an example from chapter 11, perhaps we should repay the 20 million or so kilos of gold and silver looted from Central America in the sixteenth and seventeenth centuries? At a rate of interest about half that we charge Third World countries today for debts incurred largely for the benefit of Western businesses (particularly arms manufacturers) the accumulated debt would run to several hundred digits.

Maybe life just doesn't work this way, and this is too simple an approach. But Jesus' message *is* a simple one. That surely is the point of the gospel. He went the whole way. That's why his message has inspired individuals down the ages to act against their own interests. That's why he was crucified. Of course the gospel is an ideal that we're not going to live up to, but it's there to remind us that, left to ourselves, we'll weasel our way out of our responsibilities to others. Maybe even if we're not going to sort out the past, we should try and sort out the future. Because after all, there *is* enough food and fresh water to go around. If we acted in love and treated everyone equally, we could all live as if we didn't have to worry. The kingdom of God on earth is not that far away. But we all want that bit extra for ourselves, to put more into our cupboard than into our neighbor's, to protect our own interests. "The world has enough for everyone's need, but not enough for everyone's greed," as Gandhi said. We all want to hang on to what we have, or maybe we'll give up a bit, but only if everyone else does too. Few are prepared to go out on a limb. Perhaps that what Jesus meant by taking up your cross and following him.

This is not to suggest that Jesus was some kind of radical socialist, though it's hard to understand how Christians can vote for political parties whose emphasis is on increasing the private wealth of the few rather than improving public services for the many. Jesus was driven by a vision of the whole person, how we relate to each other and to God, not by economics. These comments are trying to bring out a modern application of his teaching on one topic. Again, it's not saying that Christians are worse than Muslims or Hindus or whoever. There are many millionaires in Bombay driving in Mercedes to dieting clinics past people literally starving to death. And the teaching is not unique to Jesus. Buddha underwent a greater degree of deprivation. But going further than you might think reasonable or possible in the cause of people in need seems central to what Jesus was about.

Of course others select different texts and come to different conclusions. It's fair to say that if this kind of kingdom really was at the heart of Jesus' teaching it was short-lived. The kingdom of God turned into the kingdom of gold leaf, with the Church being the richest organization in the world over most of the last millennia rather than one of the poorest. But perhaps it's been heading off in the wrong direction since the first century. Perhaps in turning Jesus into God it missed what he had to say as a man.

PART 6

SHAPING THE
CHRISTIAN GOD

45 So why did Christianity succeed?

"Intellectually, religious emotions are not creative but conservative. They attach themselves readily to the current view of the world and consecrate it."

JOHN DEWEY

So how did the religion of this poor itinerant preacher, in an obscure province of the Empire, become the state religion of the mighty and godless Empire itself? How did Jesus, who defined closeness to God as powerlessness, crucified as a criminal, turn into the living head of the wealthy and powerful Church, a God himself who through his priests on earth was instrumental in torturing and murdering millions? It's a strange story. Following the twists helps us to understand the way in which religions start, change and decline. It shows us something about how societies work, and the measure of the problem we have with our selfish egos. Along the way we find ideas that can still work for us today. But if you're getting bored and are not interested in the history of the Church go to chapter 54.

Some Christians will say: "But despite everything, Christianity did survive and flourish. We're here, aren't we? One-third of the world's population today are Christians. How did frightened disciples turn into dynamic apostles if the resurrection didn't take place as the Bible says? Something clearly happened to the disciples to galvanize them into action."

Yes, but there's no relation between truth and numbers of converts. In any case, it took 300 years for Christianity to be adopted as the official religion of the Roman Empire, and even then Christians were only about 10% of the population. In contrast, Islam took only 100 years to completely control – albeit with the help of the sword – a much larger area, stretching from India to Spain. And Islam started from an even more remote and backward region than Palestine. In the eighth century Islam was even touching China, and for a moment seemed as if it might carry the entire Old World before it. So if we are to measure truth by numbers, we should all be Muslims. Or perhaps Hindus. Or perhaps we should go back to hugging trees and praying to the sun and moon.

So why did Christianity succeed in the Roman Empire?

You may have an image of heroic Christians being martyred for their faith, inspiring others to take up the torch, until the whole Empire was converted. Of course there's an element of truth in that. A small one. But the ability to endure persecution for our faith is no guarantee of its truth, or we would all be Jews. Or gypsies. Or hunter-gatherers. It's the same with martyrdom. Islamic suicide bombers don't persuade us to become Muslims. Some people get to the point where they want to be martyred. Through their suffering they come closer to their God. Sometimes it seems the last and only remedy for injustice. Sometimes it's self-indulgence. In the Philippines today some Christians willingly undergo mock-crucifixions, though not to the point of death. There's some scary stuff lurking around at the bottom of the brain.

The simple reason why Christianity succeeded is that it evolved into a belief that made sense to a lot of people at the time. It did not emerge clear-cut, as a new, distinct religion with a worked-out creed. It changed into what people wanted. At first, Jesus was one of many intermediaries between humanity and God whom people followed. It's hard for us to understand this today because we're so used to thinking that there is only one God, with one right interpretation. The Roman view of religion was maybe more sophisticated. They were aware of many gods, both of their own tradition and of the many peoples they had conquered. They judged them on their merits. They were aware that religion was a two-way street, what you got depended on what you put in. Gods were not gods if they weren't worshiped, offered sacrifices. The Romans were in some ways more credulous than we are, in others more skeptical.

Over dozens of generations these intermediaries, their writings, their worship, merged, separated again, created new forms, much like businesses today. The different religions and temples in the Empire competed for custom and revenue. They often specialized in niches for particular crafts or classes. The average Roman might sacrifice to several deities for different purposes, just as today we turn to doctors, lawyers or priests for different personal needs. Over a period of centuries Christianity absorbed existing traditions and turned them into a belief system that most people could identify with. It rolled up the specialist providers into one divine package headed by a single almighty God. The followers of Jesus overlaid Him with aspects of other gods and heroes and the Church took over their temples, festivals, symbols, and the Old Testament itself.

This is why there are so many similarities between Jesus' actions and those of other heroes. And why there are so many parallels with the Old Testament. Jesus continues the tradition of water miracles by calming the waves and walking on the sea. Where Elisha heals one leper (Naaman), Jesus heals ten. Where Elisha multiplies twenty loaves and feeds 100 men, Jesus manages to feed 5,000 from five loaves (and two fish) with twelve baskets of leftovers. Indeed, some Jews believed Jesus to be one of the old prophets returned to earth (Luke 9:19). Maybe he was consciously modeling himself on Moses and Elijah. Maybe the Gospel writers selected some miracles out of the many available that showed a similarity. Maybe they elaborated on the events to heighten the similarity. Maybe they invented them. Maybe it was a mix of these things.

But Jesus became more than an outstanding Old Testament prophet. He evolved into a God-man of the kind that Romans were used to. There were many of these in the Empire. One was Dionysos who was eaten by the Titans when he was a baby. For this crime Zeus struck the Titans down with lightning and created people out of the ashes. The symbolic act of eating the flesh and blood of the god (John 6:54-55) at a special meal brought union with Dionysos, who granted eternal life. His specialty was turning water into wine. The Church adopted these traditions into their texts. At a wedding Jesus turned water into a thousand bottles of wine, a Dionysian-style quantity, the purpose of which must have been to help the guests get drunk.

Asclepius, another god-man, with hundreds of cult centers in the Empire, heard prayers and healed people. His symbol, like that of the early Hebrews, was a snake coiled round a pole. But, unlike Jesus, he could not overcome death. Asclepius raised a man from the dead but Zeus killed him for it. In contrast, God rewarded Jesus by raising him from the dead and bringing him back to heaven.

Hercules, the deliverer and protector, was perhaps the most popular god-man of all. Born of Zeus, he had to struggle through a human life on this earth without knowing his parentage. He was overcome by his fate and died horribly, but ascended into heaven where he was taken into the company of the gods. Jesus trumps him more spectacularly still. As God, Jesus himself descends from heaven and lives here on earth, the hero and savior, though few recognize his divinity. He dies crucified, descends into hades and opens the gate for his followers. According to the writer to the Hebrews, he does the same to death itself (Hebrews 2:14).

These parallels have been recognized for over a century. The dispute is over the interpretation. One populist view is that the myth of Jesus as the God-man came first, and the historical background of the Gospels was added later. But it's very unlikely that the Gospel writers, with their prophetic Jewish background, came from this starting point. Most scholars would say that Jesus was a historical figure who was interpreted later by his followers in the idiom of their time, as a dying and rising God-man. Most

Christians though would take it the other way around. They would say that the parallels are coincidental. Jesus is the only true God-man. The fact that there are many similar stories around may reflect our need to believe such stories but doesn't mean that the Christian story isn't the only real one.

What all scholars would agree on is that what really provided the impetus for the new faith was the relationship of Jesus to the Jewish idea of God. Judaism was already making converts in the Empire, but to follow the God of the Jews you had to take on the dietary laws and restrictive practices of Judaism. The fact that many were prepared to do this is a testimony to the attractiveness of the Jewish idea of God as a single, all-powerful Spirit. It swept away the clutter of minor gods. When Christianity came along, it opened out this idea of God, making Him available to all people, not just to the Jews and Gentile proselytes. And through His Son Jesus, God spoke to the individual. The dramatic force of the Gospels lies in the individual confrontations. In following Jesus, believers not only had a leader through whom they could be blessed, forgiven and healed while on earth, they could also defeat evil and gain eternal life.

And the clincher was that Christianity was not just for the rich. In fact, being rich and powerful was a positive liability. The new faith was for the 90% who did not have "rights" in the form of citizenship. Christianity gave people a new sense of worth, a new dignity. It inherited the Judaic idea of caring for widows and orphans, the poor and oppressed. Christians looked after each other. This didn't last, of course. In a few centuries the Church was the largest slave-owner in the Empire. But in the meantime not being noble, or wealthy, or a famous soldier, was a positive virtue. Through Jesus the poor had the chance to save themselves. They might not have the villas and the slaves but their souls were secure and they would be rewarded in the next life.

46 WHAT DID THE FIRST CHRISTIANS BELIEVE?

"To die for an idea: it is unquestionably noble. But how much nobler it would be if men died for an idea that were true!"

H. L. MENCKEN

This process of establishing a divine identity and purpose for Jesus didn't happen overnight, it took tens, hundreds of years. In that time people experienced him and defined him in many different ways.

We see him today through the prism of the creeds, the papacy, the Church, the Bible. But all these took several centuries to reach their present form. Perhaps that doesn't sound much, out of two millennia. But imagine yourself back several centuries – say to around 1700 AD. The ship's wheel has just been introduced to replace the tiller. The Swedes are defeating an alliance of the Russians, Danes and Poles, and capture Warsaw. The French gain control of the English forts around Hudson's Bay in Canada and settle in Texas. George Washington wouldn't be made the first president of the USA for another 100 years. Virtually everyone in the West still believed in a divine order of being that had kings at the top and slaves at the bottom. The difference between first and fourth-century Christians is of the same order.

We tend to assume that first-century Christians thought and practiced as we do. We think of "pure Christianity" as a blend of the New Testament and the local church. But the first Christians had neither. In fact today they would probably feel more at home in a Sufi mosque than in a Christian church. Today, the closest you'll get to an experience of the early Church is in West Syria, which contains one of the most flourishing of the Christian communities in the Middle East. Damascus and Jerusalem are both about the same distance from Galilee. In Damascus you can still find Christian services in Aramaic, the language Jesus spoke. The worshipers still pray in lines with their foreheads touching the ground, bottoms in the air, a practice which was later largely dropped in Christianity but continues in Islam.

Christians were first known as "Nazarenes." "Christians" was a name given to them later by non-Jews at Antioch (Acts 11:26). Romans who were opposed to the faith first used the word "Christianity" in the second century. We don't know much about the Nazarenes, but there is no doubt that for the first generation or so they were happy to be seen as Jews. This wasn't just a question of race; they saw themselves as practicing within the Jewish faith. They kept the law, the Sabbath, they circumcised their children, ate no pork, worshiped in the Temple. Most didn't attempt to convert Gentiles.

What did the Nazarenes think of Jesus? According to most scholars, they thought he was an ordinary human being, but one who managed to follow the Law perfectly. They did not believe in the virgin birth: they knew his parents. They probably believed in the resurrection, but not as a unique saving event. Jesus was taken up into heaven in the same manner as Elijah, a similar divinely anointed prophet with a special relationship to God. Jesus' message for them was that the literal interpretation of the laws had become a burden that oppressed people rather than pointing them to God. A new kingdom of love, of fellowship, of healing, was more important. He was in the radical, uncomfortable tradition of the prophets, nudging Judaism in a different direction. But he was a good Jew. If we're to be literally true to the earliest traditions of Christianity we should be circumcised as Jews.

The first leader of the Nazarenes in Jerusalem was James the brother of Jesus, succeeded by Simeon, Jesus' cousin. James had a long-running dispute with Paul, believing he went too far in extending the Christian franchise to Gentiles. In Galatians 2, Paul criticizes James for trying to reconvert Paul's converts back to following the laws of Judaism. By AD 56 James had even gained favor with the Pharisees. But the Sadducees killed him in AD 62, which may have been the point of departure between the Jews and Jewish Nazarenes. By AD 85 the Nazarenes were excluded from synagogues, and synagogue liturgy included a condemnation of them.

The "James group" of Nazarenes centered on Jerusalem were scattered, along with all other Jews in Palestine, by the failure of the Jewish revolt against Rome in AD 70. They became known as the Ebionites, which means "the poor," perhaps staying true to Jesus' teaching on wealth. In exile they prayed facing Jerusalem, as the Muslims today face Mecca. They were still strong in Palestine and Syria 300 years later. But they had become an embarrassment to the Gentile Church, which had moved away from Judaism. As they still had the Jewish ceremonial and Law they never produced much in the way of scripture. They may have had a forerunner of the Gospel according to Matthew, and probably had a rival to the Acts of the Apostles. They rejected all other Gospels.

There were other groups of early Christians though. One developed around the shores of Lake Galilee with Peter as their leader. Matthew's Gospel originates from here. Peter believed in the resurrection but did not go as far as Paul in seeing Christianity as a universal faith. For him Jesus was still a Messiah for the Jews, which as we have seen did not mean that he saw him as God.

The apostle Thomas started a further group. His supporters claimed he was the twin brother of Jesus. They didn't believe that Jesus came to die for our sins on the cross – they said he came to enlighten those who would hear his words. We don't know much about them; the *Gospel of Thomas* itself wasn't discovered till 1945. It's believed to be of an early date, probably older than the New Testament Gospels.

Incidentally, the teaching of Thomas was carried to Persia, where an individual called Mani developed it to the point where it became a separate religion. Mani was born around 217 AD and grew up a Christian. He combined his teaching with elements from Zoroaster and Buddha to create a universal, gentle religion that foreswore violence. In many ways it was an improvement on Christianity. The Manichean clergy were sworn to tell the truth, avoid violence, to be celibate, vegetarian, and poor. In this form it spread to India and China, where it survived for a thousand years. In its early days it spread back to the Roman Empire. Augustine, the most important figure in developing Christian teaching after Paul, was a convert from Manicheism to Christianity late in the fourth century. Being a peaceful religion, it didn't stand much of a chance of becoming dominant, and got up the noses of the establishment everywhere. Mani was hanged by the Zoroastrian magi, and his followers were persecuted in the Roman Empire first by pagans and then by Christians when they had the power. Manicheists survived Christian persecution in Europe till the seventh century, when they disappear from the record.

Another group of Jerusalem Christians moved to Antioch after the destruction of Jerusalem and became known eventually as the Nestorians. They believed that Jesus had two natures, one human and one divine, and they took this to the point where he appeared to have a dual personality. They spread through Persia to India, central Asia and China. By the seventh century there were Nestorian churches in most Chinese cities. The Mongol Khans nearly converted to this form of Christianity, which would have made them a more powerful Church than the Roman Catholics. A few groups still survive. The liturgy of the Eucharist which they use – *The Anaphora of the Apostles Addai and Mari* – is the oldest in use anywhere.

There were many other Christian groups that also traced their teaching back to the first disciples. Early Churches were established in Egypt, Syria, Ethiopia and Armenia. Some groups thought of Jesus as the reincarnation of the prophet Moses, others thought of him as an angel, or a divine being. The flavor of the times is caught by Paul: "Every one of you saith, I am of Paul; and I of Apollos; and I of Cephas; and I of Christ" (1 Corinthians 1:12), and that's just in the one church Paul was writing to.

Reliable records of what Jesus said or thought were so brief that Churches and individuals could interpret their ecstatic experience of the Spirit pretty much anyway they wanted. We're just skirting the surface here. Think of any combination of Jewish, Pauline, Gnostic, Buddhist, pagan belief, and there was a Christian sect believing it. One of the earliest, for example, was the Elchasaites in Syria and south-west Turkey. Compared with the foreign offshoots of Christianity springing up in far-away places like Rome, they were just down the road from Jesus' home patch of Galilee. The Elchasaites retained the Jewish law, circumcised their children, rigidly kept the Sabbath, and didn't accept the heretical innovations of Paul. But they believed that two huge angels had appeared to their founder, Elchasaios, and told him that Jesus was reincarnated anew every century, and born of a virgin on each occasion. There were a dozen other Churches in the area, each with their own angle. The most exotic beliefs of Christian cults around the world today are no more bizarre than those in the first century.

47 FOLLOWERS OF PAUL

"It is the customary fate of new truths to begin as heresies and end as superstitions."

THOMAS HENRY HUXLEY

Think of the Nazarenes as one of many side branches slowly breaking off the tree of Judaism. There were many similar ones. The Essenes, for example, had many themes in common with Christianity. They considered Temple religion to have become polluted and had withdrawn to the desert. And another group, the Mandeans, who were baptizing in the Jordan around the time of Jesus, had similar themes of death and rebirth, cosmic ascension, and a cultic meal of bread and wine. After the destruction of Jerusalem by Rome in AD 70 they fled to the marshy areas of the southern Tigris and Euphrates rivers. In the last century they became known as the Marsh Arabs and still survive today, just; they're being destroyed by Saddam Hussein. Another group were followers of Simon the Magus, a Samaritan teacher who was a contemporary of Jesus. He had a more God-like idea of the Messiah than the Jews and was perhaps an influence on the early Christians. He's mentioned in Acts 8:13. The Church Fathers later reviled him as the fount of all heresy.

These groups and many others influenced each other when they met. Some changed the course of Christian churches, or were changed themselves. As they spread, the teaching increasingly diverged. Journeys were carried out largely on foot, in difficult conditions. Teachers had to support themselves as they went along, teaching and making converts on the way. Many of the widely dispersed Christian Churches, like that of Ethiopia, continued in relative isolation till modern times.

Of all these Jewish groups it's the Christian offspring that grew to overshadow its parent. And of the many Christian groups the most influential became the churches shaped by the influence of Paul. Among the early disciples his interpretation of Jesus was the most powerful, and it's hard to think of Christianity today without him. Paul was a Pharisee, believing, like all the Pharisees, in the imminent coming of God's kingdom on earth and the resurrection of all believers, a line of thought going back to Daniel. On the road to Damascus he had a vision of Jesus (apparently it's him) who questioned his actions, and as a result he was converted to Christianity.

Some say Paul is the co-founder of Christianity. The New Testament is largely written from his perspective. Thirteen of the twenty-seven books are attributed to him, though four or five of those are probably the work of others. Paul didn't have as much success in his preaching to the Jews as Peter, James and others, but he was outstandingly successful in preaching to the Gentiles (a word the Jews used for everyone who wasn't a Jew). The Jews ended up rejecting the Nazarene cult whilst the Gentiles accepted it, and ironically it's Paul's teaching that we Gentiles are most familiar with.

Ironic, because for first-generation Christians Paul's words would not have carried much weight compared with the disciples or brothers of Jesus. The Church increasingly laid most emphasis on "apostolic" oral and written traditions on the grounds that they were likely to reflect most closely what Jesus actually did and said. Paul himself had never met Jesus, or heard him speak. He doesn't show any real interest in him as a person, rarely quoting him, or referring to events in his life. He doesn't seem to have heard of the miracle stories or the virgin birth. And he spent his time traveling and preaching to people who knew nothing about Jesus. In this connection, it's important to understand that the New Testament is presented back to front. Because the Gospels are placed before Paul's letters we tend to assume that his listeners already knew them. We think of Paul's letters as theological reflections on the life of Christ as presented in the Gospels. But it's the other way round. The Gospels were written after the life had been interpreted. Again this is an over-simplification. But virtually all scholars, conservative and liberal, agree Paul was writing within 18 years of Jesus' death, finishing 16 or so years later, before any of the canonical Gospels were written.

Paul saw Jesus as more than a prophet come to renew Israel's faith. He scaled up the historical figure of Jesus, making him the Lord Christ, a key player in the cosmic drama of humankind. It was Paul who sowed the seed of the doctrine of original sin, linking Adam to Jesus. Adam was the first man, from the earth. Jesus was the last, the spiritual "man of heaven" and we're transformed into his image (1 Corinthians 15:49, Romans 5:12-19). Jesus lived such a life of service that God "designates" him to be His Son (Romans 1:4). Jesus is not equal to God: he shows the way. (Paul wasn't a Trinitarian, the concept hadn't been thought of yet). But it is through surrendering ourselves to God through Jesus and understanding our total dependence on him that we're saved.

This adoption of Jesus as God's Son seems to happen at the resurrection. Mark, writing later, moves it forward to the baptism, when the Spirit of God descends on Jesus in the form of a dove. Matthew and Luke, writing later still, bring it further forward to the birth. John, the last of the New Testament Gospels, says that there was no time in history when Jesus was not God's Son. But it was Paul who started the ball rolling. He sees Jesus as bringing the gift of the Spirit to humankind. We can become "one with him in spirit" (1 Corinthians 6:17 NIV). The dwelling-place of God is no longer the Temple (1 Corinthians 6:19). God has come down from heaven into us. He now dwells within each individual Christian. The divine image in the human race is restored, proved by the defeat of death in the resurrection. By believing in Christ and being baptized we can all share in both Christ's new humanity and his immortality. Paul's teaching on the new importance of Jesus was taken on board by the churches and introduced into the story of his life when the Gospels were written.

So in a generation Paul turned Christianity from a local Jewish sect, which followed a historical Jesus, into the "cult of Christ." The healer and miracle-worker preaching the kingdom of God became God's designated Son, born to save humankind from the penalty of its sin, and coming again in judgement.

Paul also tried to control the new churches. In his letters he lays down the law about what should be believed. You can trace the tension in them (particularly in Romans) between the first Christians, for whom obedience to the Jewish Law was an essential part of their faith, and Paul, who saw Christianity as a religion for everyone and taught that non-Jews could be Christian without submitting to the Jewish legal code.

By the end of the first century the idea held by the first Christians that Jesus was a Messiah for the Jews and had come for them only (Matthew 10:5-6) had gone. So had the idea that the disciples had a role in establishing a new kingdom and judging it (Matthew 19:27-29), and that a new Temple was going to be built (John 2:19). The heartland of Christianity had migrated from Jerusalem and Palestine to the major towns and seaports of the eastern Mediterranean and its appeal was to Gentiles rather than Jews.

In the first century, Jews account for all the main Church leaders and writers (with the possible exception of Luke); thereafter, none are Jews. In the view of the Jews, the Nazarenes/Christians had betrayed both faith and people, selling themselves to the Roman enemy for converts and cash. Christians retaliated by saying that Jews had murdered God. This state of one-sided war continued for two millennia until its appalling climax in the twentieth century.

48 THE EARLY NEW-AGERS

"The supernatural is the natural not yet understood."

ELBERT HUBBARD

By the end of the first century, Christianity had come a long way from the days when the first worshipers met in the Temple at Jerusalem. But it's an over-simplification to say that it was predominantly a new faith rather than a Jewish sect. Different interpretations co-existed for centuries. The letters of Paul's opponents have not come down to us, but we can tell from other letters, for instance, from the letter written by the first-century Clement of Rome, that Paul's view took generations to get the upper hand. Clement assumes that Christians naturally followed the Jewish Law and way of life. From him we see that early Christian services were only slight adaptations of the synagogue service. There's none of Paul's extreme salvation history.

Christianity though at the end of the first century still wasn't a religion we would recognize today. Most people in the Roman Empire understood it to be a new kind of mystery religion, of which there were several around, the most prominent being Mithraism.

Few scholars would dispute that, as with parallels between Jesus and other divine figures in the Empire, there are close parallels between Christianity and other mystery religions, particularly with Mithraism. Mithraists worshiped the old Iranian God of light (still followed in Hinduism today with the god Mitra.) They had rituals similar to those of Christians: baptism, anointing with oil, a Eucharist, Sundays. Like Jesus, Mithras was worshiped as "the way, the truth and the life," as redeemer and savior. He was born to a virgin on what is now 25 December, a date which the Christians took over in the fourth century. The shepherds and the magi visited him as a baby. He performed miracles, healed, was buried in a stone tomb and rose on the third day, in March, at the time of the spring equinox. The similarities were such that Augustine said the priests of Mithras worshiped the same God as he did.

Believers in these mystery religions were often referred to as "Gnostics" (meaning roughly "those in the know"). Gnosticism was more a way of thinking than a belief: there were pagan and Jewish as well as Christian Gnostics. Up until recent times it was assumed that Gnostic Christians were an unimportant offshoot of the main – "true" – Christian trunk. They describe themselves as an enlightened minority, and the Church Fathers are dismissive of them. They've been so effectively buried that most of their writings have only been discovered in the last century. Now they're increasingly seen as playing a far from insignificant role in the life of the early Church. Maybe Gnostics were even in the majority, depending on how broad a definition you use. We'll probably never know, and it doesn't matter, unless you define truth in terms of numbers of supporters.

The Gnostics took religion seriously. They saw themselves as moving beyond the gods of mountaintops and rivers, beyond laws and doctrine, to the worship of God as Spirit. The Jewish God appealed to them – they tended to monism. Their message was that you can know God directly; He is within you. Self-knowledge is knowledge of God. But their reading of God in the Old Testament tended to be the opposite of what became orthodox Christianity. They saw Him as a vengeful, arbitrary deity, favoring the Jews for no good reason, periodically threatening destruction and doing evil. He was a demonic being who imprisoned man in his material body. Some worshiped the villains and "anti-heroes" of the Old Testament, like Cain. Jesus sprang from God fully grown as it were, a more advanced God, a new redeemer God to put things right and free us into our natural state of spirit. Some went so far as to say that all gods and demons are figments of our imagination. According to the *Gospel of Philip*, "Human beings made gods, and worship their creation. It would be appropriate for the gods to worship human beings" (see 71:35-72:4).

Christian Gnostics thought the physical existence of Jesus was unimportant. They did not believe in the resurrection, or even that Jesus died on the cross. Some thought that Simon of Cyrene changed places with him when he carried Jesus' cross. Others believed that Jesus had a separate spiritual form that descended on him at baptism as a dove, and left him to go back to heaven when he was on the cross. What mattered to them was their direct, ecstatic experience of Jesus – a "living Jesus" who speaks of enlightenment from illusion, not sin and repentance.

How did Gnosticism develop? It may have originated in the churches of Asia Minor, which looked to John as their leader. In John 5:17-18 Jesus refers to God as his own "private" Father, making himself equal with God. And in verse 21 Jesus says, "The Son gives life to whom he is pleased to give it" (NIV): he gives all his followers what he himself is and has. Revelation is progressive, not a one-off (John 16:12-13). But all can become special, enjoying the same relationship, becoming pure spirit like Jesus.

Or Gnosticism could have developed on a line of teaching from Paul. The leading Gnostic of the second century, Valentinus, was reportedly taught by one of Paul's students, Theudas. There are passages in Paul's letters that imply there is more revelation to come, for example Romans 16:25-26. In 1 Corinthians 15 Paul implies a belief in the spiritual rather than physical body. In 2 Corinthians 12:2-4 he refers to a time when he was physically transported to the third heaven (there were seven), and also to paradise, where he "heard unspeakable words, which it is not lawful for a man to utter." In 1 Corinthians 2:6-16 Paul uses the sort of terminology that was later taken up by Gnostics: "We speak the wisdom of God in a mystery, even the hidden wisdom, which God ordained before the world unto our glory" (verse 7).

Or it could be that Gnosticism predates the orthodox tradition.

The basic idea of Gnosticism, that the material world is inherently evil and each person is imprisoned within it, to be freed by the spirit of Jesus, comes in the *Gospel of Thomas*, which is earlier than the New Testament Gospels, and probably Paul's letters also.

If many Christians were Gnostics, it may partly explain the lack of interest by the early Christians in the Holy Land itself. If we had been around then we'd want to go and talk to Jesus' family. We'd visit his hometown, the villages where he preached. But the early Christians didn't think of Jesus as a historical figure in this way. Only when Constantine, the pagan sun-worshiper, made Christianity the state religion, did it become fashionable to search for places that were "sacred." The tomb was "discovered" in AD 327, and from then on Jerusalem was transformed, with churches over any site that could be important.

And the extent of the persecution is more easily understood if many Christians were Gnostics. Gnostics – and practitioners of the many mystery cults that were common in the Empire – tended to believe that the heart of knowledge was secret. Initiates who passed through the system got the opportunity to identify with the divine through rituals that involved simulated death and resurrection. There were similarities with Christian Gnosticism. When Christians compounded their secrecy by refusing to worship the emperor, Roman authorities regarded them as x-rated. In the public mind Christianity may have had the connotations that witchcraft and sex orgies have today. Christians were accused of incest (marrying their brothers and sisters in Christ) and cannibalism (eating and drinking divine flesh and blood in private suppers) as well as atheism (refusing to honor the gods). Elements of this secrecy linger, as in the way Greek Orthodox churches still celebrate the Eucharist behind a screen, where not even the congregation can see what's happening.

There was never a clear-cut divide between Gnosticism and what was to become orthodox Christianity, any more than there is between conservatives and liberals today. Some Gnostic traditions were simply assimilated, their origins quietly forgotten. Take the sacraments as an example. They early on become the center of Christian worship and identity, as they are today for the huge majority of Christians. But considering their later central position in the life of the Church they do not feature strongly in the New Testament. Jesus performed no rituals. There are references to the Eucharist in 1 Corinthians, and references to baptism (which soon became a rite for infants), but Paul scarcely mentions the sacraments, and neither do the other New Testament writers, with the exception of Luke in Acts. There's a vast chunk of early Christian experience and practice that's simply not covered in our New Testament. The importance of the sacraments in the early Church probably originates with Christian Gnosticism where membership rituals were highly important – and secret. The sacraments owe less to the New Testament and more to works like the early *Gospel of Philip*, which was probably learnt and chanted by the early initiates into the Christian faith. One of the reasons this gospel didn't make it into the canon was because it stressed the earthly nature of Jesus too strongly. In particular, it suggested that his relationship with Mary Magdalene was sexual.

In the choice between the Gnostic idea of Jesus as a teacher of wisdom and God within you, or Jesus as the almighty Son of God coming to rule and deliver judgement, the Almighty won. But it may have been a close run contest. The divine Emperor Diocletian outlawed the Gnostics in AD 295, and their influence diminished. If it had gone the other way Christianity might have ended up much closer to the Eastern religions of today. There were Buddhist missionaries in the Near East at the time of Jesus, at the port of Alexandria, and the two religions could have developed a fruitful interchange of ideas. In the *Gospel of Thomas* you can comfortably substitute the word "Buddha" for "Jesus" without greatly altering the sense. You can see this line of development in later writings like *The Book of the Blessed* by Justin the Gnostic, which draws on a range of religious experience including the Hindu Lord Shiva, before pointing to Jesus the Son of Man as the fulfillment of divine purpose.

Gnosticism never entirely died out. It resurfaced in the Cathar movement in Southern France in the eleventh century, until the population was massacred by a Church crusade. Centuries later, it can be seen in the philosophy of William Blake. In some ways it's coming back into the frame today. The "anything goes if it feels right" flavor of New Age thinking is reminiscent of Gnosticism. Many of their best-selling books are "kind of Christian." Perhaps in the next millennium Christians will increasingly think of themselves as the Gnostics used to, seeing "orthodox Christianity" as a wrong turn that led into the sands for a couple of millennia.

49 ORTHODOX CHRISTIANS

"The vision of Christ that thou dost see
Is my vision's greatest enemy.
Thine has a great hook nose like thine,
Mine has a snub nose like to mine."

WILLIAM BLAKE

So the idea that there was ever a "pure" early Church holding a clearly-defined set of beliefs, a single body believing in a common doctrine, is simply not true. What we now think of as orthodox Christianity was gradually established by a succession of bishops and teachers known today as the Church Fathers (Irenaeus, Clement of Alexandria, Origen, Justin Martyr, Tertullian, etc.). But they did not all hold the same opinions and were not always orthodox themselves. Origen was the most prolific and original, and got the worst of both worlds. He died from the effects of torture during the persecution of the Emperor Decius. Then in AD 534, 300 years after his death, he was excommunicated by the Synod of Constantinople for believing that hell was finite, and that all could be saved from it: so he was sent there retrospectively. He also believed that the Father was greater than the Son and the Son greater than the Holy Spirit; that creation was continuous; that the sun and moon and stars received commands from God and probably had souls; and in reincarnation. Tertullian, crucial in developing the doctrine of the Trinity, ended his life as a Montanist, believing the "new prophecy" that the kingdom of heaven would shortly descend on what is now Turkey. Clement believed that Jesus had a semi-divine body, not actually needing to digest food and drink.

Perhaps the most important of the early Church Fathers was the first, Justin Martyr, of the second century. He developed the teaching found in John's Gospel and Hebrews, blaming the Jews for rejecting Jesus, and suggesting that Christians were the "new Israel," and the rightful inheritors of the "Old Testament." God, the supreme transcendent Being, operated through His Word, the Logos. This Logos had scattered itself around the world, so that all people had traces of it. Justin Martyr made Christianity acceptable to many in the Roman Empire by distinguishing it from Judaism and opening it up to Greek philosophy. For Justin any lover of truth counted as a Christian – Greek philosophers were Christian without knowing it. Philosophy continues to mold Christian thinking for the next two millennia.

The Church Fathers would have been surprised by the beliefs of many Christians today. For example, as a general rule they didn't take scripture "literally," they didn't see that as making sense. The purpose of scripture was to convey spiritual truth, in multiple layers of meaning. The literal, historical sense was secondary, even irrelevant. They began the tradition of seeing the Bible as a closed book, a mystery to be interpreted by the Church. This idea prevailed for the next millennium and more until some brave individuals decided to translate the Bible into the vernacular, risking being burnt at the stake. When the Europeans managed to catch up with the Chinese and develop printing (in most technologies the Chinese have been a hundred to a thousand years ahead, up until recent times) the Church's monopoly of the sacred word was over. The mass production of print, taking over from the laborious hand-copying of the monks, led to the discovery of the Bible by the masses and the rise of biblical literalism in the Protestant community.

But to return to the third century AD, if it hadn't been for the Emperor Constantine, Christianity in its different forms would probably have remained one of many cults in the melting pot of the Empire, to be forgotten or absorbed in the others. Constantine, an able and energetic ruler, gained control over his rivals from AD 306–324. Like a corporate empire builder of today, he wanted a new mission statement. The "Roman Way" of the previous centuries no longer provided the driving force that had created the world's most remarkable Empire ever. The resolution of the Empire was weakening: too many different peoples and cultures had been assimilated from the bottom up; too much corruption and wealth had come from the top down. Energetic tribes on the borders were threatening. The old Roman gods had lost their sway. There were still the mysteries of Eleusis and Orpheus, and the more intellectual faiths of Platonism, Stoicism and Epicureanism from Greece. But these were remote, abstract. As in the West today a gap was left in the popular imagination into which numerous intermediaries of divine or semi-divine character flooded; the cults of Isis from Egypt, Cybele from Asia Minor, Astarte from Syria, Mithraism from Persia, Judaism and Christianity from Palestine. Now Constantine was looking for a unifying force – he needed unity in matters of state and religion.

Incidentally, if you think of Constantine as a nice, statesman-like character who was persuaded by the virtues of Christianity to lead a better life, forget it. He was a violent and nasty individual, executing his rivals rather than imprisoning or exiling them. He even executed his eldest son, Crispus, and his brother-in-law. He had his second wife Flavia killed by immersion in boiling water. In the now unstable Empire it was only the most able and ruthless who could gain power and hold it.

Christianity had advantages for candidacy as the state religion. Its appeal was geared to everyone, not just to particular sections of class, tribe, or craft. It was organized in a three-fold ranking of bishops, presbyters and deacons, following the structure of the Empire. We still talk about "dioceses," which originally referred to a Roman province. Perhaps most importantly Constantine saw it as giving him a personal edge. When he adopted Christianity, he partially took it over. Eusebius, the major Christian historian of the time, tells us that the Emperor began to exercise functions that had previously been seen as the province of Jesus.

The choice of state religion wasn't clear-cut. Nor were the religions themselves. Choosing a religion was similar to choosing a political party. Think of making a choice between Democrats and Republicans, Labor or Tory. Over generations they borrow each other's ideas, even switch positions on major issues. Mithraism, associated with the army, looked for a while as if it might become predominant. Another cult, equally associated with the East, possibly of a pre-Jewish, Canaanite origin, and centered on the winter solstice, was that of the sun god, "Deus Sol Invictus." His symbol was the halo, which the Church adopted for its saints. Constantine, whose reign was also spoken of as a sun emperorship, found it difficult to choose between the Christian God and the sun god. He swung between the two, sometimes appeasing both at the same time. Indeed many Romans, including Constantine, may have confused the two. Christ, after all, is spoken of in the Old Testament as the "sun of righteousness," and Clement of Alexandria describes him as driving his chariot across the sky like the sun god. This conflation of Gods is seen today in the names of the days of the week. The Christian practice, inherited from the Jews, of resting on the seventh day combined around this time with popular astrology to give us our Sundays and weekdays named after the pagan gods of the heavens.

So Constantine converted to Christianity, the key moment apparently being at the Milvian Bridge in Rome on 28 October 312 AD when legend has it he saw a flaming cross in the sky during the decisive battle with his rival for the throne, Maxentius. At that point Constantine became divinely ordained as the ruler of the earth, the friend of God, and interpreter of the word. There were approximately ten million people in the Empire at the time, about 10% of the world's population, and about 10% of them were Christians – one million is the best guess we have. About three centuries after the death of Jesus 1% of the world's population were Christian. It's around now that we start talking of Christianity as a religion rather than a cult.

50 THE CREED

> *"Religion may have been the original cure. Freud reminds us that it was also the original disease."*
>
> **P. RIEFF**

At first Constantine may have believed that Christianity was a unified Church, but he was soon disillusioned on this point. It was split in many ways. By now there were Docetists, Adoptionists, Gnostics, Apollinarianists, Montanists, Nestorians, Monophysites, Arians, and many others, sounding today like so many Pokemon characters, all believing different versions of how Jesus was man, or God, or what kind of mixture. Constantine summoned a general assembly of bishops to meet at Nicea, near Nicomedia. To Constantine it seemed simple. They were to talk through their theological difficulties and agree on what they believed. This wasn't the first council of bishops, but it was the most important. They produced a creed, which is more or less the one spoken in churches around the world today.

Here it is:

> *"We believe in one God, the Father, Almighty, maker of all things visible and invisible;*
>
> *"And in one Lord Jesus Christ, the Son of God, begotten of the Father, only-begotten, that is, from the substance of the Father; God from God, Light from Light, Very God from Very God, begotten not made, of one substance with the Father, through whom all things were made, both in heaven and on earth; who for us men and for our salvation came down and was incarnate, was made man, suffered, and rose again on the third day, ascended into heaven, and is coming to judge the living and the dead;*
>
> *"And in the Holy Spirit.*
>
> *"And those who say: 'There was a time when he was not,' and:*

'Before he was begotten he was not,' and: 'He came into being from nothing,' or those who pretend that the Son of God is 'of another substance, or essence' [than the Father] or 'created' or 'alterable' or 'mutable,' the catholic and apostolic church places under a curse."

(The last paragraph is usually missed out.)

This is less the foundation of Christianity than a late travesty. Which is perhaps not surprising, after all it's 300 years after the death of Jesus. The most interesting things about it are what it leaves out, which is pretty much everything that you would think should go in. It doesn't, for example, quote Jesus, or refer to the events of his life. It doesn't give any indication of how we should live. It only refers indirectly to the big questions of sin and eternal life. Above all, it doesn't mention the core of Jesus' message: "Love the Lord your God . . . love your neighbor as yourself." The kingdom has disappeared. Most of its ritual chant revolves around Jesus' relationship with the Father, how he was begotten by God and no one else, of the same, and not a similar, substance. The Creed reflects the intensity of the disagreement on these matters at the time. The historical Jesus has been displaced by the Lord Christ, raising more questions than answers as to who exactly this being was. The Church has by now completely lost the plot.

For the last 1,500 years the nature of Jesus and his relationship to God has been defined in the doctrine of the Trinity, to the point that the only proper Christians are "Trinitarian." It's like saying the only true English people are those living in the USA. It seems bizarre, as there's no mention of the Trinity as such in the Bible. There's one reference: "baptizing them in the name of the Father, and of the Son, and of the Holy Ghost" in Matthew 28:19, which is probably a later addition. There's an oblique reference in 1 John 5:7-8, which does not appear in the oldest and most reliable manuscripts and is almost certainly a later addition. There's an implication of it in John's Gospel, where John has a more developed theology on the "Word." There are incidental references in some of Paul's letters. But that's all. There's no coherent theology of the Trinity. It certainly doesn't feature in Jesus' teaching. He wouldn't have known what was meant by it. It's one of the Capital Letter Doctrines that the early Church invented, and it took centuries to become generally accepted.

We're so used to the idea of the Trinity that we forget what a strange notion it is. The Christian Trinity makes rather less logical sense than, for example, the Hindu trinity of the three forms of God: Brahma the Creator, Vishnu the Preserver and Shiva the Destroyer. That at least reflects more of the rhythm of creation, the reality of life as we know it.

Today Christians explain the Trinity in different ways, for example, by saying it represents God outside the world, God acting in the world (Jesus), and through the world (Holy Spirit). Much as Hindus talk of the knower (*Rishi*), the act of knowing (*Devata*) and the object known (*Chhandas*). Similarly we have mind, body, spirit. Or subconscious, conscious, super-conscious. It's like having a God for the sky, the earth and the sea; or rocks, trees and water. To make sense of the Trinity today we have to see it as a metaphor rather than as three different aspects of the divine reality, but it's an open-ended game. For instance, perhaps we could view it progressively: the Hebrew religion centered on God as Father; Christianity centered on the Son; today we focus on the Spirit. Or perhaps we can characterize them by different functions. There's the Creator Father who gave us life; the Son who came and showed us what matters in life; the Spirit who enables us to do something about it. There's scope here for endless rewriting.

But how did the idea of the Trinity develop? Are the three "Gods" separate centers of consciousness or not? Theologians still argue over this, 2,000 years later. This issue goes to the heart of the complication of Christianity, which evolved as a compromise between the Jewish view of a single omniscient God, and the

Roman/Greek pantheon of many gods and their different families and relations. A muddle ensued, which is still with us.

The difficulty for the early Christians began with the introduction of Jesus into the divine equation. The early Christians came to see Jesus as embodying God in human flesh. The central ritual that developed, the Eucharist, even involved worshiping him, and only God could be worshipped. But the whole of God obviously could not have been present in Jesus, or heaven would have been empty. So there was God, and the bit of God that was present in Jesus, and Jesus.

There was also an idea that had been present for some centuries in Jewish and Greek thought, that it was an "aspect" of God that had created the world, often called *Sophia*, or Wisdom. The early Church Fathers, following John and Paul, interpreted the divine presence in Jesus as this Wisdom, or creative Logos. They regarded it as begotten of God, and thus God, rather than created by God like an angel. *Sophia* features more strongly in some of the non-canonical gospels.

So the Trinity idea in Christianity was a means of shoehorning Jesus in with God and Spirit. But it was still no easy matter for the early Christians to establish what kind of person Jesus really was. Do we now really have one God, or two, or three? If Jesus was God's Son, there surely must have been a time when God existed and Jesus didn't? So wasn't he then of secondary importance? If he was not secondary, and had always been around, and was God, then did he have sex with his own mother? That must logically be the case, and the *Epistula Apostolorum*, a book considered canonical by parts of the early Church, thought so:

"Do you not remember that I previously said to you that I became like an angel to the angels?' And we said to him, 'Yes, O Lord.' And he said to us, 'At that time I appeared in the form of the archangel Gabriel to the Virgin Mary and spoke with her, and her

heart received me; she believed and laughed; and I, the Word, went into her and became flesh; and I myself was servant for myself, and in the form of an angel; so I will do after I have gone to my Father.'"

To reconcile those who thought Jesus must be man, and those who thought he must be God, the doctrine of "hypostatic union" (the union of persons) was developed: he was man and God in one. But this also led to problems. If Jesus and God were the same, what was the point of the different entities? A neat and popular attempt to explain this conundrum was given the name "modalism." This solution, which appeared around 200 AD, may have been followed by the majority of Christians. It said that God was one deity with three different phases. God the Father changed into God the Son at the virgin birth, and then became God the Spirit at the resurrection. Modalism kept both the one God and the deity of Jesus intact. But it caused problems too. If God the Father turned into God the Son, leaving heaven empty, then who was Jesus praying to when he was on earth?

You may begin to get the drift of how complicated all this is, and understand why many turned with relief to Islam in the seventh and eighth centuries, a faith that simply regards Jesus as a very enlightened prophet. Many at first saw Islam as a new Christian movement. Some Christians converted to it as a Roman Catholic might convert to Protestantism, shedding a cartload of doctrines and practices for what seems to be a return to the pure original truth. For Muslims the very idea that God needs to go around begetting bits of Himself to get things done is heresy, reducing His divinity and glory. Within a century or two the heartland of Christianity in the Middle East and North Africa was largely Muslim, and has remained that way.

At the Council of Nicea the positions consolidated around three key players: Arius, Athanasius, and Marcellus.

For Arius, Jesus was sinless, but was not God. If he was God he couldn't be wholly human, and if he wasn't wholly human he couldn't wholly identify with humankind. If he couldn't wholly identify with humankind his sacrifice was not complete and humankind is not saved. And after all how could God literally "die," even if only for a few days?

Athanasius and his followers, on the other hand, came at it from the other angle: that if Jesus was not God his sacrifice on the cross could not be completely effective. It wasn't a "big" enough sacrifice for God. So they believed that God and Jesus were of the same nature, and co-equal with the Spirit, giving us what we think of today as the Trinity.

Jesus as subordinate to God or equal to God? The Empire was roughly equally divided, with the followers of Athanasius predominating in the West, Arians in the East.

There was a third, compromise position, that of Marcellus. This was that God was one, and only manifested Himself as three in creating and redeeming the world ("And when all things shall be subdued unto him [the Father], then shall the Son also himself be subject unto him that put all things under him, that God may be all in all." 1 Corinthians 15:28).

It's hard today to get an idea of the intensity with which these positions were held. The divisions over the linguistic subtleties threatened to tear the Empire apart. At the Council of Nicea, called to settle this subject, the followers of Athanasius combined with those of Marcellus to win the day, fighting it out in the streets, but the controversy continued for 60 and more years afterwards. It was touch and go who would win. Support for one side or the other changed according to fluctuating political and military fortunes, with Athanasius being exiled five times. It was an Arian bishop who baptized Constantine as he lay dying. Success for the Trinitarian formula came down to the toss of a political coin.

Indeed, after Constantine's death Arianism became the accepted doctrine in much of the Eastern, Greek half of the Empire and looked as if it would take over the whole. It spread to the Germanic tribes of central Europe who were baptized as Arians. It was carried by the Visigoths back into Italy when they conquered the capital Ravenna (after Constantine's death the capital of the Western half of the Empire had been moved from Rome to Milan, and then to Ravenna which was more defensible). Their war cry on going into battle against the Athanasian West was, "The Father is greater than the Son."

The debate continued over the next 600 years. This subject was discussed in a series of councils, of which seven are recognized as canonical. They often led to splits in the Church and mutual charges of heresy. The last council to discuss Arianism was that of Constantinople in the ninth century. It remained as one of the key differences between the two halves of Christianity, the Roman Catholic West and the Orthodox East, which have never been resolved. Relations between the two reached their lowest point when the Crusaders sacked Constantinople in 1204, plundering the churches, raping the nuns, slaughtering the civilians. They didn't cancel their mutual excommunication of each other till 1965.

In the West, Arianism lives on today in the Unitarian Church, one of the more admirable of modern Churches. It forgoes creeds and believes in the right of individuals to work out their own belief system. In the UK today the Trinity is a meaningless idea to 95% of the population.

To brand this particular version of establishment fourth-century Christianity as the only authorized one is the kiss of death.

51 WHO WAS RIGHT?

"The most scandalous charges were suppressed; the Vicar of Christ was only accused of piracy, rape, sodomy and incest."

EDWARD GIBBON

ON THE CONDEMNATION OF ONE OF THE THREE RIVAL POPES IN 1415

Opinions among Christians in the first few centuries ranged from the view that Jesus was an ordinary man, a teacher of wisdom, right through to Jesus as God, with a dozen steps in between. Until the Council of Nicea in 325, you could believe at any one of these points on the spectrum and be a Christian.

The grounds for making the Nicean decision on the Trinity binding on all Christians down the ages are very weak. Maybe this bunch of soldiers, clerics, politicians, theologians (who were unrepresentative of the Church at the time, and mostly came from the Western provinces) at the first council were all godly men led by the Holy Spirit. Perhaps they simply needed the prompting of a godly emperor to ascertain the will of God. Or perhaps they were just your average power-hungry politicians – or more likely the usual mixture of both. Early Church councils were sometimes vitriolic, bloody affairs. Power, both religious and secular, was at stake. Defeated opponents were exiled, not pensioned off. Athanasius, the eventual winner in the Arian controversy, was hesitant about attending the Council of Tyre (AD A335) as he feared for his safety. One of his supporters, the presbyter Makarios, had been accused (falsely) of the kidnapping and murder of Bishop Arsenios. Arius was ultimately struck down by a mysterious illness – caused, some believed, by poison – and according to Athanasius himself ended his life "split in pieces in a public lavatory."

Catholics nevertheless say that we can rely on the Church to have kept the teaching of Jesus intact. They maintain that Jesus authorized a line of leaders to whom he gave the authority to decipher the intentions of God on earth and provide rulings on them. So no matter that there were conflicting beliefs and always have been, whatever the Vatican says to be true at the time is true.

This authority is based on two verses in Matthew 16: "And I say also unto thee, That thou art Peter, and upon this rock I will build my church; and the gates of hell shall not prevail against it. And I will give unto thee the keys of the kingdom of heaven . . ." (verses 18-19). Most scholars say Jesus didn't speak these words. There's nothing comparable elsewhere in the Gospels and the style is different. And it does seem unlikely that Jesus planned for a long succession when he believed the end of the world was imminent. The general tenor of his teaching seems to be against hierarchies and titles (Matthew 23:5-12). But in any case it was not until the late fourth century that they were significantly used as a reason for claiming primacy of the church in Rome. The churches with the closest links to the apostles were in Asia rather than Europe.

The main justification for the idea that the bishops of Rome rather than any other city are the successors of Peter stems from a legend that Peter went to Rome and was crucified there, upside down, during the persecution of Christians by the Emperor Nero in AD 64. This in itself, even if true, doesn't seem to prove the point. Peter visited many places. He spent far more time in Jerusalem. Why should where he was killed be relevant? But it was an attractive story for the Roman bishops. In fact, several other bishops in the main centers of Christianity – like Alexandria and Antioch – began to call themselves pope. For several centuries, though, none of them, including Rome, claimed power over the other bishops. The first pope to say he could overturn decisions reached by other bishops was Pope Julius in AD 340-341, when he was supporting Athanasius against the Council of Tyre. Again, as with the creeds and the Bible, it's a 300-year gap from the time of Jesus. The first pope to exercise much authority in the West outside Italy was Pope Leo I, AD 440-61.

As well as the lack of evidence for the idea that the popes were authorized by Jesus to interpret God, there's the more significant problem of the popes themselves. Out of the 265 popes there have probably been many good men. Equally, there have been popes you wouldn't trust to mind your daughter if you were out of the house. Popes you wouldn't even want in your house. Corrupt, evil men who poisoned relatives, raped, murdered, committed every conceivable kind of crime. At least one, Pope Stephen VII, was mad. He had the body of his predecessor, Pope Formosus, exhumed from his grave, dressed up, tried in court, his blessing fingers cut off and the body thrown into the River Tiber. Stephen himself was strangled by the Roman mob. The papacy finally reached the pits in the fifteenth century, when popes were called "Antichrists," with good reason. Alexander VI (1492-1503) was a man of unbridled immorality. He obtained the papal throne through bribery, openly advanced his bastard children, and eventually died of the poison he had prepared for some of his cardinals.

That popes can in any sense be regarded as correct in their judgements by virtue of their position is a disturbing relic of a past way of thinking. In the twenty-first century it is as bizarre a belief as that kings rule by divine right, that slavery is divinely ordained, or blacks are naturally inferior to whites. It is surely just as likely – far more likely – that this series of individuals, hampered as they have been by the trappings of wealth and power that Jesus so strongly condemned, have consistently led the Church in the wrong direction, further away from his teaching.

52 WRITING THE NEW TESTAMENT

*"Jesus said: 'It is I who am the light which is above them all. It is I
who am the All. From me did the All come forth, and unto me did the
All extend. Split a piece of wood, and I am there. Lift up a stone, and
you will find me there.'"*

GOSPEL OF THOMAS

By the sixteenth century dismay with the venal Church was so
deep and widespread that Christianity in Europe split in two. The
Protestants found an alternative source of authority to the Church
by going back to the Bible, particularly the New Testament. But is
this any less compromised by the efforts of man? The New
Testament is a selection of writings generated in the first 100 to
150 years of the Church's history. The texts of the books we have
were a battleground, with alterations and rewriting continuing for
the first century or so of their existence. But the more general
problem was the difficulty of deciding which books should be in
the New Testament. The argument goes that the books in our
New Testament reflect the early apostolic tradition. But it's not as
clear-cut as that. Luke wasn't an apostle but his books are in;
Thomas was but his is not. We don't really know whether the
Gospels of Matthew, Mark and John were written by apostles. It's
even uncertain whether these are the names that should be
attached to the Gospels since there's no record of them before AD
185. Most scholars would say it's unlikely that any of the New
Testament writers had met Jesus. So who decided which books
should be included? Were they right? More significantly, who
decided on the need for a New Testament in the first place?

Many quote Paul's letter to Timothy: "All scripture is given by
inspiration of God, and is profitable for doctrine, for reproof, for
correction, for instruction in righteousness" (2 Timothy 3:16).
What we've got is what is right. But what we've got isn't what

Paul had. Those who quote this verse assume that Paul is referring to the Bible as we know it. But this evidently can't be the case. The Gospels hadn't been written yet. In the preceding verse, 2 Timothy 3:15, Paul refers to Timothy as he was 20 or more years earlier: "From a child thou hast known the holy scriptures" – which pre-dates the whole of the New Testament. Not even the Old Testament had been established yet.

Why did it take so long for the early Christians to write the Gospels? How did they get through the first couple of generations without them? The delay is understandable. At first there was no hurry to write down the words of Jesus. Hadn't he said, after all, that the disciples would not have time to visit all the cities of Israel before the end comes (Matthew 10:22-23)? That it would come in the lifetime of his listeners (Matthew 16:27-28; Luke 9:27; 21:32)? But by around AD 70 there could have been very few people still living who had ever seen or heard him. For a common faith to survive the Church needed to make a record of what Jesus had said. So many churches began writing their own "gospels," which were a mixture of stories they had been told and the subsequent interpretation.

The earliest gospels are probably "Q" (a lost document which most scholars agree was a major source for Mark, Matthew and Luke) and the *Gospel of Thomas*. Both reported only the sayings of Jesus. The happenings, miracles, passion narrative and the language of resurrection and apocalypse in Mark, Matthew, and Luke came later. John comes later still. But there were many more accounts of the words and deeds of Jesus. Luke himself refers to a number, since lost (Luke 1:1). The first Gospels were not necessarily seen as "inspired". And as late as the end of the second century there was an oral tradition of the words of Jesus which was regarded as having independent authority, separate from the Gospels.

As more Gospels were written things became confusing. They pointed up the differences between the churches. Because the gospels reflected their different beliefs, the churches found it impossible to agree on one Gospel. Some preferred Matthew because of its Jewishness and insistence on adhering to every jot of the Law (Matthew 5:18). Gentiles preferred others that supported non-observance of the Jewish Law. Gnostics liked John, with its rejection of the world, or the *Gospel of Thomas*. In the mid-second century Tatian proposed and, indeed, produced, a definitive, brilliantly harmonized account (the *Diatessaron*). This was accepted by the Syrian but not the Greek and Latin churches. No one party was strong enough to impose its will on the others. Hence the need for a collection.

It took many generations for the need of a collection of authoritative writings to outweigh the desires of different churches to go their own way. And what should go in? If letters, then which writers were "qualified"? Just the disciples of Jesus? Some thought yes. Otherwise how could you decide who to include? Should it include the Jewish scriptures, as an "Old Testament"? Some thought no. Wasn't Christianity a separate religion from Judaism? The use of simple word counts alone shows the difference between the Old and New Testaments – "faith," for instance, scarcely gets a mention in the Old Testament, but occurs about 250 times in the New. And if you're going to have a collection, which way should it bend? To favor the Jews or the Gentiles, followers of Peter or Paul, Gnostics or Apocalyptics?

The first attempt to draw up a definitive list of Christian scripture was made in the middle of the second century by Marcion, a key figure in the early Church. He wasn't what we would today call a Trinitarian Christian. And like many Gentiles, he found the morality in the pagan writings to be better than that in the "Old Testament."

Marcion thought that there should obviously be only one authoritative Gospel, and he chose that of Luke, but edited it to remove all mention of the Jews and references to the Old

Testament. Whilst respecting Jewish scripture, he saw Christianity as a new, independent religion that had no need of it. He also edited the letters of Paul to make him show Jesus teaching a God of love, not fear.

Valentinus was a leading contemporary of Marcion. He hated the idea of a definitive list. Each believer had the truth within himself, so why shouldn't everyone write their own gospel? He showed the way, with his own *Gospel of Truth*.

Many Christians in the second century identified with the teaching of Valentinus or Marcion, rather than Paul, or James, or Peter, or Thomas. Marcionite communities were still flourishing in Syria 300 years later. As the Church grew in importance over the next couple of centuries, the pressures to create an established official scripture increased. When Christianity became the state religion the impetus was overwhelming. The Church needed a single "belief" and a "history." It wasn't defined any more by race, like the Jewish faith, and it wanted to separate itself from the pluralist collection of stories that made up Roman religion.

Power became concentrated toward the middle ground. The lead was taken by bishops who were prepared to define a religion broad enough to include a history going back to creation, taking over the Jewish heritage, but more limited than that promoted by the Gnostics. They borrowed a history from the Jews, drew up their definitions of belief, and fought for the position that the stories they selected were "historical" while everyone else's were not. The emperor needed a pedigree for his authority, and this was established by creating a dynasty of "apostolic succession." Peter, as one who had spoken with and touched Jesus, replaced Paul in the hierarchy, and his power became invested in the Church of Rome.

Throughout this period scripture proliferated. By the second century there were at least a dozen gospels in existence. Over the first three centuries there may have been 70 or more. There's a whole library of other texts – letters of Jesus to foreign kings, letters of Paul to Aristotle, histories of the disciples and of many other characters from the life and times of Jesus. Most of these have been lost: the Church did its best to burn all those that didn't fit in with its teaching.

Here are some of the major works that we know of which record the words of Jesus, in rough alphabetical order:

Bartholomew, Gospel of

Clement of Alexandria

Dialogue of the Savior

Epistula Apostolorum

Exegesis on the Soul

Great Seth, Second Treatise of

James, Apocryphon of

John, Acts of

John, Gospel of

John, Apocryphon of

Kerygmata Petrou

Luke, Gospel of

Mark, Gospel of

Mary, Gospel of

Matthew, Gospel of

Peter, Apocalypse of

Peter, Apocalypse of (Ethiopic)

Philip, Gospel of

Revelation, Book of

Sophia of Jesus Christ

Thomas, Gospel of

Thomas, Apocalypse of

Thomas the Contender, Book of

Titus, Epistle of

Many have only come to light in the last half-century. This

would suggest that there are many more that may be found, or may be lost forever. Of these, which do you think are the most important, and how do you justify it? We know virtually nothing of any of the writers. Some of the non-canonical material is identical or similar to the teaching of the New Testament Gospels. Sometimes it elaborates, using similar language, repeating points or extending them. Sometimes it makes them more forcibly, for example:

> *"Jesus said: 'Whoever does not hate his father and his mother as I do cannot become a disciple to Me. And whoever does not love his father and his mother as I do cannot become a disciple to me. For My mother gave me falsehood, but My true Mother gave me life.'"*
>
> GOSPEL OF THOMAS

This is close to a saying of Jesus recorded in the Gospel of Luke, but it introduces the important idea of God as Mother as well as Father. Or perhaps we should say, as it is probably earlier than Luke, that Luke takes that idea out. A less patriarchal God is also commonly seen in other non-canonical gospels. In the *Gospel to the Hebrews* Jesus speaks of "My mother, the Spirit." In the *Apocryphon of John*, he says, "I am the Father. I am the Mother. I am the Son." And in the *Gospel of Philip*, "Spirit is both Mother and Virgin."

Sometimes, though, the other gospels have a totally different feel from the Gospels in the New Testament:

> *"But they, the archons, those of the place of Yaldabaoth, reveal the realm of the angels, which humanity was seeking in order that they may not know the Man of Truth. For Adam, whom they had formed, appeared to them. And a fearful motion came about throughout their entire dwelling, lest the angels surrounding them rebel. For without those who were offering praise – I did not really die lest their archangel become empty."*
>
> SECOND TREATISE OF THE GREAT SETH

We can make a good guess that Jesus didn't actually say this – the tone is too far removed from the bulk of the Gospels. But who can really decide? And after all, the idea behind the *Treatise of Seth* – that the God of the Old Testament is one god amongst many, inferior to some, and that Jesus comes from the true heaven above – is not without merit. Would it have appeared any more fanciful to many of the early Christians than the idea that Jesus was the Son of the God of the Old Testament? Probably not. We live with the assumptions of two millennia. It's quite possible that in the early days a sizeable proportion of Gentile Christians saw Jesus as a true God revealing truth to humankind, and the Jewish God of the Old Testament as a deceiver.

So what was it to be? Was the Church going to splinter into a number of different sects or religions, or were Christians going to stick together and exercise power? Numbers or truth? Impact or purity? It's the problem that bedevils all religions down the ages.

The letters of Paul had widespread support – he was the "missionary to the Gentiles," the guy who got it going. They could be read by the now-orthodox as supporting Christ as savior, and by the Gnostics as supporting a non-historical view of him. They were accepted as canonical by around 200 AD, and the bulk of the New Testament as we understand it today had general acceptance by 300 AD. Early in the fourth century, the 300-year gap again, a similar period from the founding of the USA to the present day, Eusebius drew up what came to be the list that most agree on today. He leaves out the *Acts of Paul*, the *Shepherd of Hermas*, the *Revelation of Peter*, the *Epistle of Barnabas*, which up till then many churches had considered authoritative, and he includes the Revelation to John and the epistle to the Hebrews, which had previously been excluded. The first "Bibles" now begin to appear.

But it wasn't till the fifth century that Eastern and Western Churches finally agreed on the selection, with the former accepting Revelation and the latter accepting Hebrews. Agreement was never universal. The Syrian Church today still recognize only 22 of our 27 New Testament books; the Armenian Church includes a third epistle of Paul to the Corinthians; the Ethiopian Church has a different selection again. These may be minor Churches in the twenty-first century but at the time they were as significant as any other. The Syrian Church covered the heartland of Paul's missionary endeavors. For the first few centuries more Christians lived there than anywhere else. Ethiopia was one of the first significant Christian areas, and Armenia was the first Christian state. They certainly can't all be right, maybe they all got it wrong. Maybe, for instance, all Paul's letters should have been excluded. Who's to say? Why shouldn't we write a "new" New Testament today?

53 WHY HAS CHRISTIANITY SUCCEEDED SINCE?

"The fact that an opinion has been widely held is no evidence whatever that it is not utterly absurd."

BERTRAND RUSSELL

We've seen how much beliefs and structures can change over three centuries. Christianity has now been going for a further 17. Think of how much England has changed over the same period – the length of recorded history is about the same. England first features significantly in written history when Julius Caesar wrote up his invasion in his *Gallic Wars* just 50 years before the birth of Jesus. But it was another 13 centuries before there was a recognizable English language, and even then the English upper class still thought of itself as French. England has been a constantly shifting mix of peoples and boundaries, shaped by victories and defeats, immigration, emigration and chance.

The story of Christianity is similar. Sometimes it goes through phases of wholesale change. And so do all religions. Like animals, plants, people and everything else, religions survive by adapting themselves to new conditions; if not, they die out. All societies in history that are isolated by circumstance – losing long-range contact with others, the exchange of ideas, rivals to emulate – wither and fossilize. Hinduism has worked for 5,000 years and more by virtue of its flexibility, adding gods faster than the Hebrew kings added wives. Buddhism, originally an offshoot of Hinduism, developed different forms as it spread: first into Theravada (Ceylon) and Mahayana (Tibet), then with further offshoots like Madhvamika, Tantric, Vajrayana and Zen. Christianity has had to change more than most. Like Buddhism it has lost its original heartland, and has had to put down new roots in foreign soils. And perhaps more than most it was also "lucky."

The fourth century was the most remarkable ever for

Christianity, the turning point. At the beginning of the century it was a minor cult in the Empire. At the end it was the only permissible religion. This meteoric rise in status drove the creation of the creeds, the establishment of the papacy as supreme power in the Church, and the creation of the Bible. Constantine had accorded Christianity equal status with the pagan religions. The Emperor Julian (AD 361-363) tried to turn the clock back and restore paganism, but failed. Theodosius (379-395) made it the only religion, banning the worship of pagan gods in AD 392. In the *Codex Theodosianus* he declares other religions to be "demented and insane," and states that their followers can be punished and executed. This starts the period known to historians as the Dark Ages, when civilization in Europe went down the chute and Christian persecution of the Jews and other religions began. The doctrine of the Trinity, developed through dispute and war, became the yardstick by which heretics – particularly Jews – could be persecuted.

The Church also tried its best to tear itself apart with doctrinal disputes. We're not talking polite disputing in the Synod here: mayhem and murder make a regular appearance. You may recall Athanasius (chapter 50), who won the argument over the definition of the Trinity. His successor at Alexandria, Bishop George, was lynched by Donatist (Christian) mobs. Alexandria was at that time the center of power of the most flourishing area of Christianity (which was in North Africa, then a well-populated, fertile stretch of territory), and Donatists were the most numerous of the Christian groups. They were suspicious of emperors, of Rome, of everything to do with the world, and believed in a pure version of the Church, upheld by suffering and martyrdom. Augustine (354-430), the most influential of the Church Fathers, made his name by defeating them in argument and they were driven underground or exiled. Donatists were the first Christians to be murdered in significant numbers by other Christians. In the fourth and fifth centuries Christians probably killed more of each other than had been killed by the pagans in the previous three centuries.

It was Augustine who made this possible by creating for the Church a sacred status of its own. Salvation could now only be obtained through the Church. Sacraments were even valid if administered by unholy priests. The laws of God, as interpreted by the Church, were superior to the individual conscience and it was okay to force people into belief. Only God knows and chooses who will be saved. Augustine drove the nails into the coffin of the kingdom, granting the Church a monopoly on permissible belief that lasted for the next millennium.

In this way the Church began to fill the power vacuum left by the collapse of the Empire. The German barbarians, who had been left unconquered in their forests, came under pressure from tribes migrating from further east and swarmed across the frontiers. Rome itself was sacked by Alaric the Hun in AD 410. Many blamed the Christians, with some truth − turning one's back on the world to assure your salvation did not help man the defenses and many Christians would not serve in the Army. Augustine wrote his major work, *The City of God*, to counter the accusations of those who blamed Christians for the collapse. The Empire survived in the East, but over the coming century it was swallowed in the West by various Germanic tribes − Huns, Visigoths, Osogoths, Vandals, Franks, Saxons, Angles, etc.

Christianity in the West managed to survive, converting numbers of the new pagans. The Bible became the foundation document of the Holy Roman Empire, a quasi-religious feudal and fairly ramshackle organization that the barbarians created out of the ashes of the old. And eventually the Bible also became the basis of the self-identity of the new nation states that arose out of feudalism. Christianity achieved this by bending to its own purposes the beliefs and traditions of the newcomers.

Let's take another snapshot. We'll move on half a dozen centuries to the land we now call England. The Empire has been long forgotten. The locals look wonderingly at the remains of the grassed-over straight roads, the ruined amphitheaters, temples, aqueducts, palaces, and muse on the race of giants that could have built them – even wondering what they were used for. London has reverted from a powerful metropolis and European trading center to a ramshackle village. The buildings are small, smelly constructions of wood, daub and wattle (cow dung and straw), rather than the grandly-engineered works of brick, stone, and marble of Roman times, with fountains and mosaics, under-floor heating, baths and murals.

In the smoky, dark chieftain's hall the elders and heads of families are listening to a powerful preacher-poet chanting one of the major hymns of the time, a hymn that expresses their Christian faith:

> *Therefore for every warrior the best*
> *Memorial is the praise of living men*
> *After his death, that ere he must depart*
> *He shall have done good deeds on earth against*
> *The malice of his foes, and noble works*
> *Against the devil, that the sons of men*
> *May after praise him, and his glory live*
> *For ever with the angels in the splendor*
> *Of lasting life, in bliss among those hosts.*

THE SEAFARER (TRANSLATED FROM OLD ENGLISH BY R. HAMER)

This is one of the finest hymns of the period. But there's no dealing with sin here, no awareness of divine justice, of good and evil, no ideal of holiness or salvation. The imagery that works for these Anglo-Saxons is military. Jesus has been adopted as a Rambo-type figure that helps warriors conquer their enemies. Heaven is an adaptation of the Nordic Valhalla, where the dead warriors drink and toast their victories – those heads we hewed off, limbs hacked, villages plundered, that spear-thrust, that courage we showed in the face of greater odds. It's in warfare and comradeship that we fulfill our destiny and find our meaning.

It's hard to find a great deal in common between this and the teaching of Jesus, but it was a driving force behind much of Christianity for a millennium or so.

Does the idea of Christianity changing down the centuries seem strange to you? It's obvious when you come to think of it. What you believe is a product of who you are, what your grandparents thought, how your tribe thinks. Religious beliefs work with what they have to hand; they don't appear out of thin air. Most of the practices, rituals and events that we think of as Christian (baptism, the sacraments, icons, the Virgin Mary, Christmas, feast days, Sunday, incense, prayer, the Eucharist, the festivals – the list is endless) have been absorbed from other cultures and beliefs. The rosary managed to travel through several traditions, starting off as an aid to meditation in Buddhism, adopted by Islam, and arriving in Europe through the crusades. The cross itself is a pre-Christian icon, a symbol of the sun god in Assyria. It also represented life to the Egyptians and Aztecs, and later became the hammer of Thor in Scandinavia. As late as the twentieth century it was adapted to form the crooked cross or swastika of the Nazi party. Much of what passes for Christianity in many parts of the world – statues and altars, the worship of saints and icons – is more akin to polytheism than the abstract Trinity of the theologians.

It's the same with Christian doctrine. Take away the kingdom and there is nothing original in Christianity. All its later themes are ancient, universal beliefs that it has adapted in a particular way. Salvation, eternal life, the second coming, heaven and hell, prayer, speaking in tongues, churches – anything you can think of. The idea of a man–God being raised from the dead is one of the oldest and most central themes of all.

Christian doctrine has undergone major sea changes. The first came when Paul turned the historical Jesus into the cosmic Christ. The second was with Augustine, giving authority on earth to the Church, setting up the framework of Church and state, predestination and free will, grace and works.

The third was with Luther in the sixteenth century. By this time the worship of relics played a major role in the lives of Christians, and in churches and monasteries stolen relics were exchanged for large sums of money. There was another large trade, the trade in "indulgences" – paying cash in return for forgiveness from the Church. Luther cut through it all, teaching that God could be known directly through the scriptures, that you were saved by your faith rather than through the Church, and that the evolution of tradition through the councils of the Church was not a legitimate expression of the will of God at all. The system of sacraments was largely an invention of the Church to control the people; the Bible was the only central sacrament, but God's promise was also communicated through the signs of baptism, penance and Eucharist.

After Luther, Protestants continued to disagree and to split off from one another over the significance and nature of the sacraments. Many individuals and groups tried to take the Reformation still further, returning to the Gnostic idea of every individual worshiping God directly, without the need for any organized Church at all. Broadly known as Anabaptists, these sects were persecuted by Protestants and Catholics alike. Their teaching still survives in communities like the Mennonites, Brethren, and the Quakers.

The Roman Catholic Church effectively took on many of Luther's criticisms in the Counter Reformation of the seventeenth century. The rivalry between the two Churches helped drive the motor of colonization up to the twentieth century.

The high-water mark of organized Christianity was probably the end of the nineteenth century, when European and North

American societies were dominant in the world. In the twentieth century two world wars, Fascism and Communism, the Cold War, have destroyed the seemingly overwhelming superiority of white Christian civilization. The Far East has narrowed the technology gap.

At the beginning of the twenty-first century Christianity is strongest in the Third World, weak in its millennia-old heartland of Europe. Fundamentalist Christians have retreated into a faith that denies much that we know to be true. The insistence of fundamentalist and conservative Christians on Jesus as the only path to God is tugging at the seams of the Church and pulling it apart. They are shepherding it gently into the grave. In Europe most people have effectively left the Church, and many look to the East for spiritual consolation, if they look anywhere at all.

PART 7

BELIEVING IN
GOD TODAY

54 A NEW CHRISTIANITY

"Religion is a defence against the experience of God."

CARL JUNG

Imagine if in this century aliens make contact with us. They are intrigued by this idea of God, seemingly unique to humankind, an omniscient Being who even sounds superior to them. It's the only interesting idea on the planet. They want a single-page definition – who He/She is, how to find Him, how to approach Him. But there's a proviso that they'll only take it seriously if representatives of all the peoples who believe in God agree to the wording – they don't want to get drawn into internal "god politics." If they don't hear, they're exploding the planet to make room for a new galactic space station. Could we email?

At the moment Christian Churches can't agree with each other, far less with Muslims and Jews who believe in the same God, far less still with those of monist and animist beliefs. The threat of nuclear war, or of using up the planet's resources, or declining credibility, hasn't yet been enough to bring about a shift in positions.

The chances are that nothing much is going to change. The old orthodox Christianity with its view of an omnipotent Trinitarian "God out there" who sent His Son to die on the cross for our sins and establish a Church to worship Him will continue for a long time yet. Many will always want their closely-defined faith and their labels. Some will even insist on keeping the same kinds of services, much as some still want the mass in Latin. The Roman Catholic hierarchy is perhaps the most conservative on earth, exceeded in the past only by the Egyptian priesthood. The accumulated teaching, tradition and wealth of 2,000 years aren't going to be jettisoned in a hurry.

But today, in Western Europe at least, culture and faith have parted company. It's growing in other parts of the world, particularly the less developed ones. They're taking on board Western technology, and sometimes its political and economic systems, like parliaments and McDonalds' franchises. They don't have the background of a couple of centuries of critical thinking that has occurred in the West, and are maybe throwing out cultural traditions that would suit them better.

In some respects, for Roman Catholics under the present pope, and in conservative Protestant circles, the Church is going backwards. The early Church Fathers would be surprised to see today's Christians interpreting literally many things in the Bible that they interpreted allegorically. A great theologian like Aquinas, who was happy to take on board Greek thinking via Muslim scholars like Averroës, would be astonished to see the Church denying knowledge rather than working with it to create a better natural theology.

The Church has been in worse places before. At times in the Dark Ages it threatened to disappear. Then just a century ago it promised to dominate. But today it's hard to imagine it having the same legs as say, Hinduism, which has been around nearly three times as long. It is too closely tied to a world-view that has disappeared. It lacks the inclusiveness that characterizes the Eastern religions. Maybe the existing Church is past reviving. It's part of the problem rather than the solution. The time to change was earlier in the twentieth century, after the shock of the world wars and the Holocaust. Most of those prepared to change are already outside the Church. The "kingdom shoots" are found in secular and humanist agencies as much as Christian ones. Conservatives have been left in charge, and won't let go. And conservatism must be a dead end in the long run. The most secular places in North America and Europe today are those where extremist forms of Christianity like Calvinism had the strongest hold.

Perhaps we need to find our own paths, and create a new

language of God and the self. Maybe Christianity hasn't really developed into a "proper" religion in the best sense of the word yet. It's still at the cultic stage of making impossible truth claims, venerating the leader as God, commanding blind obedience. It's time to move on. It may be centuries before the traditional Church as a whole takes a more enlightened view of the Bible. Maybe parts of the Church will change enough for us to be able to live within it. Perhaps we'll end up with one Church for Protestant conservatives in the Americas and Africa where they still follow sacred scripture, and a second, informal Church in Europe and parts of the rest of the world. There might be a similar split (perhaps in reverse) among Roman Catholics.

For those who suspect that we are already too far removed from the world of the Hebrews to make traditional Christianity work we need to create something that is as different from the Christianity of today as today's is from the warrior-based, relic-worshiping Christianity of a thousand years ago. It will mean turning Jesus back from a god into a man, and God back from a personal deity into the Unknown. Otherwise Christianity will eventually wither like all other religions before it, perhaps muddling along with followers numbered in the millions rather than the billions. Something like the Zoroastrian religion today (the followers are now called Parsees).

What does this leave us with? Not much in terms of an orthodox Christian viewpoint, but maybe we can change the definition of Christianity. The particular interpretation we follow today is one concocted by Paul and the priesthood. They turned the teaching of Jesus into another religion of sacrifice. As we have seen, most religions are based around this idea. God/gods are something "other," fearsome, angry, holy beings who need to be placated. Offerings are made to ensure that the sun will rise again, the seed will take root, the crops grow, that spring will follow winter, the waters won't flood, the lightning won't strike.

Virtually everyone in the Mediterranean area in the first century thought this way. The Greeks, Romans, Jews, all offered sacrifices. Their religions were all temple religions. Sacrifice and law dominated the lives of the Jews. Every hour of the day, in every way, God had to be propitiated. But life itself was still a burden. The Jews were oppressed by the Law, by poverty, by the Romans. They awaited a deliverer, a savior, who would raise their status to what it should be as God's chosen people. Paul, in a stroke of religious genius, had a new vision of the spiritual world. He turned it upside down. God shows Himself through weakness and shame, not power and strength. He doesn't demand sacrifice, He offers it. In a literal flash of insight Paul saw Jesus as being the sacrifice God Himself had sent as an offering for the sin not just of Paul himself, or the Jews, but of all humankind. The deliverer had come, and humankind had crucified him, in line with God's plan. God Himself had freed humankind from the burden of sin and oppression, and all each person had to do in return was realize it.

Paul was going on hearsay. He'd never actually met Jesus or heard him speak. A generation or two later and John was writing his Gospel as if Jesus had said all this himself. But he hadn't. As far as we can tell the teaching of Jesus went in the opposite direction. His message was that you don't *need* to sacrifice. His arrest was prompted by his throwing the money-changers, who controlled the sacrifices, out of the Temple. Priests and temples don't help, they hinder, creating barriers. God is not an angry, remote figure who needs propitiating. He is all consciousness. His image is in all of us, seen most clearly in lepers and children. They are free from what we have created. Religion should break down these distinctions, not support them.

Today the Trinitarian orthodox God is a glass ceiling on the growth of Christianity, much like the laws of Judaism were for the first Christians. It's a ceiling that has to be broken for the religion to develop. True followers of Jesus are those who transcend the self in favor of others, who recognize God everywhere. All of life is sacred, it has chosen to be so by coming into being. That's the fundamental religious impulse.

> *"Jesus said:*
> *'It is I who am the light which is above them all. It is I who am*
> *the All. From me did the All come forth, and unto me did the All*
> *extend. Split a piece of wood, and I am there. Lift up the stone,*
> *and you will find me there'"*
>
> GOSPEL OF THOMAS

Maybe religion is at best a useful human construction, one that is up to a million years old and part of our mental make-up. At this level it provides part of the framework for building societies, for relating to each other, a ritual for the key moments in life. It's a way of organizing our perception of the world, of relating "self" and "other," of recreating a "whole." It's one way of navigating around the streets. But maybe there's more to it than this.

Scientists now say what people have instinctively felt since self-awareness developed. That mind and matter are in some way related. That how we see the world is as important as the world itself. We not only read the map, we create what it images. "We" is not just you and me. Consciousness is a line that stretches back millions of years and forwards for billions. We shade into chimps on the one hand, into angels on the other: one day we'll all play like Beethoven, draw like Michelangelo and calculate like a computer. We're moving out into this new world as tentatively as the first humans moved out of Africa, going on into a world of riches and diversity they knew nothing about. We'll look back and see the "savants" of today as the equivalent of our "Archaic Humans." We'll unravel matter down to the fundamental atomic level where it somehow makes a choice, to be or not to be. All these trillion trillion choices add up to the incredibly complex universe we live in, defying the laws of probability at every point. We'll find our-selves exercising the choice to create this universe. A choice to be loving. We'll live and move in this loving universe like whales in the ocean, rather than amphibians living half in the world of spirit and half in the body. We know this is going to happen, because we're here. The line is a circle; it exists "now."

Religion has called this process "God," and has called God by a thousand names. All are ways of sharing momentarily in the larger universal mind that's behind matter.

Is this true? Any talk of "God" is more autobiography than documentary. As much fiction as fact. It circles back to "me," another creation of my "self." Any truth we create is only relevant to ourselves. It makes it hard to explain to anyone else. The cave-men of 30,000 years ago probably couldn't have explained exactly what they were about when they painted their beautiful drawings in inaccessible places. But that's what we remember them by. Seeing beauty, investing the world with meaning, that's the way we can choose to live. It's where faith comes in. It gets us moving, exploring. If it is true, what image of God reflects it best? Does it matter? No. This doesn't offer assurance in the kind of way that a more orthodox faith does, but certainty always seems to come at the expense of truth or love.

So from here on it's more personal. But is this larger, universal mind "nice"? Is it "good," "friendly"? If there is indeed a unifying purpose to existence orchestrated by this "mind," why is there so much evil and suffering?

One answer to this question is used by some Buddhists, namely that evil and suffering, along with all material things, are an illusion. They don't exist. There are not even accidents in life. Everything is cause and effect, created by your karma, your accu-mulated deeds. Much New Age teaching takes a similar view. All suffering and illness are self-created. All disasters are a result of collective decisions. Everything can be improved if we can raise our awareness high enough.

I think there's an element of truth in this, but it's like original sin, not the whole truth. Some illness, for instance, is psycho-somatic, self-generated, more than Western medicine gives credit for. But bodies do fall ill, regardless of the mind. Children, healthy people with positive attitudes, all fall ill. Our cousin chimps fall ill. The world was no different when there were no people or chimps around to create karma. Every living thing fights for survival, and has to. It's in doing this that life has created the planet we're on, right down to the air we breathe. Nature is profligate and inex-haustible, but not gentle. Species that don't eat die. Every species exists at the expense of another.

Maybe the Semitic view of God as "One" rather than "good" is closer to the truth. Goodness can only be realized through self-awareness. "Nature" is neutral. The Islamic view of "fate" can help us here. A large part of suffering is unavoidable. In the process of creation, of matter becoming mind, it is continuously broken and remade. The atoms that constitute our bodies have been through trillions of "incarnations," and will do again. Over a few years every cell in our body is different, we're losing 200 billion every day. Earthquakes, floods, disease, their effect can be minimized but not avoided. We have to see ourselves as part of the ongoing process of creation, not the end product that gets upset if the process doesn't stop at a time that suits us.

Maybe there's a deeper truth that nature is not "neutral," but a violent communion. The need to act is the irreducible fact of life. Our guilt at eating other life is transformed into the higher act of eating God, and being eaten in our turn. Maybe all religion, from God's sacrifice of Jesus on the cross to Arjuna of the million mouths, is a way of accepting responsibility for what we are.

Another idea to help us is that suffering is part of self-aware-ness. Great artists, musicians, are often suffering individuals, on the edge. They create out of pain. Happy robots don't. A central religious insight is that suffering is creative. It's through our developing awareness of it that we grow. Christianity goes furthest with this. God Himself is the embodiment of suffering, taking it all on Himself. Jesus on the cross is a symbol of a suffering God, of a universe working through death to create new forms of life.

Evil is harder, but can be seen in the same light. There's no "answer." It's not just that some good people suffer at the hands of some evil people. A usually selfish individual can do something heroic, jumping into freezing water and rescuing a child. Generous and well-meaning people can connive in policies of genocide. One of the paradoxes of religious history is how often extremes of good and evil are demonstrated in the same individual – saints who are happy to torture heretics, for example. We are all capable of extremes of selfishness and evil given the right conditions. Experiments have shown that average individuals are easily capable of inflicting suffering on patients if they have been told to do so. Evil is our choice to inflict suffering, to reject love, to destroy relationships.

But we can "choose" to be better, to grow in love. We can forgive ourselves for having damaged our "selves" through our own actions. We can ask forgiveness from those we have hurt. This capacity has been hard won over a million years, but we can exercise it. Zoroaster got it right when he divided the powers of the world into twin brothers of good and evil, between whom we have to choose. And the nature of the quantum world suggests that at some level this choice has already been made. Whatever the universal mind, or God, is, it is the outcome of trillions of choices that have already happened, and are going to happen. We cannot sin against God, because God is self-determining, at every moment. This is the moment. Don't blame it, it is us.

An objective real evil force? Demons, possession? I try not to think of them. Sometimes it's individual and collective wickedness. Sometimes it's clearly in the mind of the beholder. I've read enough reputable accounts to believe it happens in some form. But equally it seems to be more common in the past than today, more common in societies that believe in it than those that don't. The obsession with it creates the conditions in which it flourishes. Like Freudians having a disproportionate share of Freudian dreams, we wish it into existence. It's the same with the paranormal. It happens to those who believe in it. If you try and evaluate it objectively, you're not going to see it. If our minds create, perhaps they create evil. Maybe hell exists for those who want to believe in it badly. Maybe Christians who preach damnation long enough and hard enough find out what it's like.

So how do I relate to the Church? For me, being a Christian means rejecting the capital "C" Church as it exists now. It means working backwards through the last two millennia, undoing the damage it has caused, the wrong myths it has created. The first hurdle to be jumped is the Reformation: the infallibility of scripture, the doctrine of justification by faith. The second is the "establishment" of the Church by Augustine, the sacraments and priesthood. The third is the cosmic theology of Paul. Along the way go the papacy, Capital Letter Doctrines, original sin, guilt, buildings and wealth. Indeed the whole religious sphere of life goes. Life is a whole, not to be directed for us by priestly specialists. It will only work if we can live it as a whole. In the Christian tradition the Quakers have come as close to this as anyone.

I go back to the first and second centuries. I think the Gnostics got Jesus (and God too) more right than Paul, though they lost sight, as Paul did, of his teaching as a man. If we follow them we can see a non-theistic God everywhere, in everyone, in a similar sense to some Eastern religions. I think Christianity has to migrate again, this time to take on board the insights of these religions, if it is to survive in the West. But it will remain different from them. The Buddha, for instance, is calm but remote. He is beyond the suffering of the world, the concerns of the individual. Krishna (the

Supreme God for many Hindus, who visited earth around 5,000 years ago) is similarly immune from suffering, living in constant bliss. Jesus is at the other extreme. On earth he laughed, partied, wept and suffered. He engages with individuals rather than detaching himself. He died in agony on the cross. In him God has shed His divine remoteness and become human.

My understanding of being a Christian is that it starts with the death of Jesus as a vulnerable human being, who believed in putting the divinity into humanity, and taking religion into the real world of doing good. God is the ideal of the best we can do. He may even exist as the universal mind of which we are fragments. We may be at the beginning of the process that brings Him into being. The closest we get to Him is by embodying love. Jesus saw himself as pointing the way to reconciliation between humankind and God, between one person and another, and within each person, because all are essentially one. In loving our neighbor we love ourselves. In loving the world we love God. The world *is* God. It's that simple.

55 A NEW CHURCH

"He who steadily observes those moral precepts in which all religions concur, will never be questioned at the gates of Heaven as to the dogmas in which they differ."

THOMAS JEFFERSON

What's left? What sacred scriptures would we have in this new world, where would we go to Church? Maybe none, and nowhere. When you set ground rules like this you start excluding people. Only a belief that everyone can assent to in principle will work. This won't be achieved in centuries, but seems the only way forward.

A new Christianity will probably not have a "Holy Bible" at all. The new Church will have a collection of writings that are more important than others in expressing faith, but a changing one, and different for each community, as in the first centuries of Christianity. In the new Bible we would edit out much of the Old Testament, leaving it for the Jewish faith, where it belongs. We would add passages from the scriptures of other religions where they complement Christianity. We would add new writings. This would not be too difficult if the will and imagination were there. The compilers of the Jewish Old Testament had less promising material to work with and a selection of texts that had been lying dormant for centuries. The traditions they merged were as contradictory as many of those in different religious traditions today.

The Bible stories are there to prompt our understanding, not as historical truths. Genesis tells of our dawning consciousness, accounting for our sense of separation. Noah's ark with the saving of all earth's species is a model for the future. The birth of Jesus with the shepherds and stable is a celebration of life and love. It tells us that the lives of the weakest and most helpless are of supreme value. The measure of how we treat them is the measure of our love. God is to be found on earth in humility and service, by giving up what we want, not gaining it. The resurrection says that the human spirit will triumph and live for ever, because we are part of a greater spirit that we call God, and are not on our own. A reading of Paul today says that worship is a state of gratitude for the way we are created and supported every instant of our being. For the paths we have been shown.

These stories collectively represent our highest ideals and values, our deepest awareness, which we describe as our faith. Faith includes the practice of religion, but also doubt and unbelief. It's in the process of questioning it that we deepen it, and come close to "God." This belief will always be like "yeast." It helps us to keep growing, to keep questioning. There may not be any perfect answers. But God is the expression of our faith that we are not alone, shouting into the void. The answer is all around us, if we have the faith to see it.

The Church will change again, if there is one at all. Jesus said nothing about the need for a Church. Most Gnostics didn't want one. Perhaps it's the packaging that can now be left behind. Jesus would want the Church, if there were to be one, to model the kingdom. Maybe he'd say something like – "Make yourselves redundant, all of you. Take the average notice period for workers in your area, and its equivalent in salary, and go. Throw yourselves on the mercy of the community. If they want to support you, they will. If they don't, find a job. Give your church buildings to the community. Open them for the use of all religions, and all uses that the community decides are appropriate. Encourage them to be used for playgroups, dance centers, meditation, counseling, community business centers, meeting places, coffee mornings, parties – let the community decide. Have Sunday services where the community feels they are appropriate. Let the community decide the form of the services."

The churches that are kept would be open to all, and adapted to make sense for each locality. Many festivals – the Hindu festival of Diwali, for instance, and the Muslim festival of Eid to mark the end of the annual fast (another good idea) – could be adopted. The festival of All Saints and remembrance days could be resurrected for those who have died. Mothering Sundays could develop into services to renew commitments amongst families. Funerals would come back into the Church, and baptism could become more frequent as a commitment of the parents to bring their children up as part of the spiritual as well as the social life of the community.

I love the old churches in England with the ancient yews, surrounded by fading gravestones, with the butterflies amongst the wildflowers (in the more deserted or enlightened ones), the rooks nesting in the trees. You can sense the worship of a hundred generations in the stones, a record of the lives and deaths of the community. There's still a sense of the sacred and of belonging that sum up the meaning of *religio*. This is a Little England fantasy, I know. But perhaps we can create new rituals that bring *religio* back to life for more people. Ones that leaves space for the participants to think their own truths, rather than telling them what to think. Effective rituals create the atmosphere for reflection. They use images and symbols – crucifix, landscapes, incense, art, music, ceremonies – to encourage meditation. The key is for the ritual to become "personalized" and meaningful to the individual.

This is already happening in a small way. Worship is no longer so formal. It is more human-centered, with people sitting or standing to pray rather than kneeling. Ministers face the congregation more. They don't dress up so often, or pray for national victory. We pray more for others than ourselves. Affirmations work just as well. I would guess that meditation will become as integral to Christianity over the next few centuries as prayer has been. (It has always been a part of Christian tradition, at least since John Cassian of the fifth century.) Ecstatic experiences will also continue to play a part. All practices that work will be embraced.

This leads to the question of who will hold authority, if not the self-appointed priesthood. Authority is best left to the local congregations. They can affiliate with whomever they want to. Centralization attracts to itself power, which demands control in the form of creeds. If the congregations can't agree amongst themselves they split. The ones that come up with the most credible teaching and practice will survive.

A new religious language is needed, one that doesn't rely on the old categories of "God out there" and Capital Letter Doctrines, one which works for everyone, in the same kind of way that Shamanism worked for everyone before we had Revealed Religion. If Jesus was here I think he'd say something like this:

"You are part of everything. I am in you, and you are in me. I and the Father are one. You and the Father are one. We are all in each other, and in every bird, insect and stone. We are all made of stardust. We are all energy, materialized. We are on our way back to the beginning to find our end. So don't worry about the moment. Forget who and what you are. Forget pensions, houses and mortgages. Forget hierarchies, job descriptions and salaries. As soon as you have something, give it away. Live happily in your own skin, for the present moment. Live at one with creation. Live at one with God. We are all divine.

"Follow me, do as I do, and we can realize the kingdom of God on earth. But it will only happen by taking risks. You have to risk other people, other countries, taking advantage of you, and be happy if they do. You have to risk scorn and poverty, loneliness. Don't protect yourself. You have to be the one to take the first step. If everyone hears this and does it, the kingdom has arrived."

It sounds impossible, and perhaps it is. Perhaps that's why the world hasn't changed since Jesus' time, why the poor are still with us. In reality few practice this, the Church less than anybody. Maybe it should make a start, set a small example.

Is that challenging enough? Perhaps you feel that it isn't, and that Jesus should be God as well. It seems to me that the best thing to do is to start practicing the second of the commandments, the commandment, to love our neighbor, which we can understand, and see how it leads to the first. Rather than define God, and then apply Him to our neighbor.

Maybe this isn't distinctive enough to be characterized as "Christian." But then I see it as truer to Jesus than a religion that puts dogma before love. I would just redefine Christianity to be inclusive of truth from wherever it appeared, given the qualifications of the next chapter, in the same way that the more enlightened sections of Buddhism and Hinduism do. Just because Judaism was a "tribal" religion of chosen people doesn't mean we have to live with that mindset for ever. The religion you choose to operate in is one that suits the culture you are part of and the temperament you have developed. It is not "truer" than another. God has no interest in your theology. By all means have an orthodox Christian faith, have your personal relationship with God, believe in your personal salvation, or however you want to describe it. But recognize it for what it is, a working model, not a final truth. It's the psychological equivalent of the "household gods" of Abraham. The personal God of Moses, or Jesus, not the Godhead. It's the 99 names of Allah, not the hundredth that is unattainable. The Tao that can be spoken, not the Tao that is beyond words.

The almighty, creator God-beyond-God, whoever or whatever it is that holds every atom in His hand, is beyond our reach, for the moment. But He is the end of all our journeys.

"If you know who you are, you can become as I am."

GOSPEL OF THOMAS

56 A NEW TRINITY

"The ecstasy of religion, the ecstasy of art, and the ecstasy of love are the only things worth thinking about or experiencing."

DON MARQUIS

But we need something more than this. "Doing good," "loving your neighbor," these are large parts of life but not a defining vision. Spiritual "wholeness" needs stronger "measurements." It needs spokes tying it to the larger picture rather than being a point on the line of human relationships. What's the basis for ethics today? As a first-century Jew, Jesus had a conception of God that we can't relate to. His God of the Old Testament, of Abraham and Moses, Ezekiel and Daniel, is not ours. His was part of the tradition of the Jewish people, tied into their historical experience and family memories. We can see this God from a distance, as we can see many others. They are all revealed in fragments of ourselves, both good and bad. The side that aspires to light and goodness, and the side that wants blood and sacrifice. But how do we link what Jesus was saying to our understanding today?

There are many defining visions of the good. Taking on board a ready-made scheme of the world from some group or other – Christian, Buddhist, Hindu, whatever – helps us a little way down the road. This is the transport that happens to be available. Whether you're in car, limousine or bus makes no real difference. The particular form your belief takes is largely irrelevant, so long as it doesn't harm others. Don't mistake the journey for the destination. Nothing that happens in this life is the destination, unless you're absolutely certain that there's no life of any kind afterwards. But how do we go further when we feel we've reached the limits of our particular religion? If we want to take a further step of faith that we can't define in traditional religious terms, how do we give it flesh?

Jesus is one of many teachers who point forwards. Perhaps the best, but others claim differently, and who's to know?

What Jesus had, and other religious teachers have, is a moment of insight when they see the real underlying patterns in the relationships between people and the world. It's the same kind of insight that mathematicians have when uncovering a new formula, or musicians finding the right chord. Great discoveries don't happen just by logic, they're the result of finding new combinations of things that hadn't been seen as part of the same pattern before. Scientists talk of the "beauty" of a discovery. The more beautiful and simple the answer, the more likely it is to be true.

This gives a clue as to how we should respond to different teachers. We're not going to know whether or not what they say is "true." They're not operating at a level where they can "prove" claims. They can point you in a direction, but the best wisdom traditions say that the only true wisdom is the one you find within yourself, because we're all different. Every truth is different. But truth is an aspect of beauty, and vice versa. I think it's the same with love. All the forces in the universe (gravity, electromagnetism, strong and weak nuclear forces) are trying to bring things together again, to create the universal mind out of fragmented matter. In so far as we play a part in bringing things together, creating rather than destroying, loving rather than hating, we are fulfilled. In rising above our "self" and becoming aware of the patterns at the heart of the universe we are practicing religion. If it's not beautiful, if it's not loving, it's not true.

"Beauty," "truth," "love," these are in some sense "real." More "real" at any rate than God the Father, Son and Holy Ghost. The universe is not random, it has unfolded from these principles like a flower from a seed, separating out into the 10 to the power of 72 atoms that have formed galaxies, stars, plants and people. The "how" of this we are beginning to understand. The "why" – why it has developed into the thing of beauty we know rather than one of the trillion other options that lead to chaos or destruction – this we do not know. But it has created beautiful patterns in doing so – circles, spirals and helixes. It's seen in the Fibonacci ratios, sequences of numbers which dictate the patterns in nature, from the spread of leaves, through the spirals of shells, to the structure of sub-atomic particles. It's at the heart of the universe.

"Beauty is truth, truth beauty,' – that is all
Ye know on earth, and all ye need to know."
JOHN KEATS

We imitate these patterns in everything we create. The golden mean, for instance, where the whole is to the larger part as the larger is to the smaller, is a guiding principle in art and architecture. Similarly with music, the chords that we enjoy listening to are those that can be divided by whole numbers. We instinctively move towards the golden mean. We instinctively believe that the golden rule is right in relationships. Whether or not these are "divinely sanctioned" in some way, I don't know, and don't ultimately care. They work. That's my religion. The defining characteristics of this religion are the search for truth, the appreciation of beauty and the practice of love. Much of what we already appreciate in Christianity is motivated by these. But often one is pursued at the expense of another. There's also a lot of "noise" that drowns out the heart of it, a concern to prove things that cannot be proved, to say this piece of music is better than that piece. There is no such "absolute" truth that we can see or realize, any more than there is absolute beauty. We recognize them, but we can't describe them. To be "real," what is one must be the others as well. They are aspects of each other, possibilities that will come true when the universe completes itself. It's an evolving work of art, in which we are parts, which we may one day perceive as a beautiful whole. It will be "whole" and completed when matter has returned to mind. We call it "God."

There's nothing scientific in this. It just represents to me what the best of being alive means. Within the Christian tradition itself there have been many who have thought this way. There's nothing original here. In the Middle Ages it was highlighted in a dispute over whether the ultimate vision of God was primarily one of love or of knowledge, with Bonaventura preferring the former and Thomas Aquinas the latter. In the Renaissance period Marsilio Ficino maintained in his *Theologica Platonica* that the highest Platonic ideals of the Good, the True and the Beautiful could be found in the human soul. For him this "theology" was at the root of all religion. He concentrated on Greek and Persian religions, but another Italian, Giovanni Pico della Mirandola, extended this to embrace Jewish and Muslim wisdom. He was condemned as a heretic.

Story-telling is a good way of communicating all three. It's why there are so many sacred scriptures around the world. The Bible itself is a baseline on which many further stories have been built, like *The Brothers Karamazov* or *Daniel Deronda*. If you're bored with Obadiah and Nehemiah, read Dostoevsky or George Eliot instead. Don't get stuck on the Bible. Think of religious truth like a great novel. The main characters are the different religious leaders down the ages. Their sidekicks are the great theologians, mystics and philosophers. Who's the narrative voice? It's you, all of us. We create our story out of these past lives, much as they have created us.

Funnily enough the great era of Western fiction coincided with the passing of Christian belief. The first atheists and the first novelists are roughly contemporary. The eighteenth-century novel took the idea that characters could explore their own destinies under the controlling pen of the author far further than previous literary forms. The great flourishing of the novel in the nineteenth and early twentieth centuries seems too remarkable in relation to changing belief patterns to be coincidental. The great Victorian novelists knew what they were doing. George Eliot translated liberal German theologians with tears streaming down her face as she saw the basis of Victorian faith disappearing – "The personality of God is nothing less than the projection of the personhood we find in humankind" etc. (*The Essence of Christianity*, Ludwig Feuerbach). Charles Dickens created the sentimental Victorian Christmas as a partial substitute for the meaning the Victorians had lost. Thomas Hardy turned the almighty God into a bleak vision of indifference to suffering humanity. In Russia Tolstoy tried to create a new synthesis of rational Christianity and Russian psychology, and Dostoevsky created a Christianity that would survive despite its destruction by reason.

Writers, musicians and artists are often a generation ahead of their time. Scientists, centuries. Founders of religion, millennia. We need all of them.

57 WILL WE PULL THROUGH?

"Behold, I come quickly . . ."

REVELATION 22:7

That's my best shot at it. I know it doesn't all hang together, I'm still working on it. Thanks for reading, and for asking the question.

So have I answered it? Do I believe in God? Is He a Santa Claus for grown-ups, dealing out reward and punishment? Or is He the sum of all the relationships that are, of everything that is? Does God exist? When the Buddha was asked this he didn't answer. When Pilate asks: "What is truth?" Jesus doesn't answer. Perhaps there is no answer. If the universe is infinite God will always be a bigger question than we can find an answer to. If it is finite there are always further questions: Why is it made the way it is? Why is there something rather than nothing?

There will always be a "beyond," and there's no reason why it should be within the grasp of the human mind. But I do believe the question is worth asking, that it's not an academic exercise. That if we keep questioning we progress. That a vision for the "whole" is what we're about.

In the process of writing this I've cleared away some of the clutter in my own mind. I've tried asking myself with every sentence, "Do I really believe this? Am I simply afraid to lose the investment I've placed in the idea of God to date?" I can't answer that. I know I'm at a different point than when I started this, a year or two ago. I know I don't believe in the God I believed in as a teenager, who had "saved" me from the person I was, from all the sins I hadn't yet committed, and laid on me an obligation to convert everyone around me to this point of view. It took about ten years to lose belief in that God, about the same length of time it took to believe in Him. I don't think I'm any the worse person for the change, perhaps a little less frenetic, though my family might dispute that. But I do find myself being drawn back to the God that is the other side of myself, that sums up the wonder, love and mystery of life. These are qualities of infinite depth. Certainty is shallow.

But maybe this is just playing with words. It's not difficult to swing the argument one way or another. What I've been trying to say here is that it doesn't matter what you believe. It's like your language or your skin color. It's who you become that's important. Better to be a happy and loving Hindu or atheist than a mean and intolerant Christian, and vice versa.

What does this mean for me today, in a few sentences? Imagine a soap bubble. It materializes out of space-time foam and floats free. For a fleeting second, threads of biology, history, culture are knitted together by personality. I have this moment to enjoy and through a few simple actions hope to leave the world a fraction better than I found it. The actions are defined by love, which represents the fullest form of self-awareness that we know of. In my case that spills out to you and your mother, family and a few friends. I don't have the strength to go much further. Developing this is cultivating a state of mind we call prayer. Worship is gratitude. The flip side of awareness is accountability. We're responsible for what we become and do, for this second of time. The kingdom of God is the measure that I don't live up to. Faith is the belief that the bubble dissolves again back into the mixture we call God, that the awareness we have developed somehow survives in the bubbling ferment of creation.

I believe this because we're here, because we're having this conversation. Because through 15 billion years the universe has been evolving toward consciousness, and will continue to do so. We're part of this. And you will be a fraction further along the line. Where's our line heading?

The very idea of progress is itself a relatively new one. Every generation since the year dot has tended to think of their grandparents as more upright, less prone to crime and trivia, wiser than they are. Throughout recorded history most societies have looked back on a past golden age rather than forwards: the Garden of Eden, the Age of Perfection, the *Krita Yuga*, from which we are slipping. And maybe they're right. History suggests we're just as likely to spend the next couple of centuries going backward as going forwards. It's taken us 2,000 years and more to recover the understanding of the solar system the Greeks had, the flushing toilets of the Cretans, the motorways of the Romans. The average citizen of New York or London today is probably more ignorant and less cultured than the average citizen of Athens 2,500 years ago. In Athens citizens who did not regularly engage in lengthy public debate were classed as "idiots."

The problems generated by twentieth-century capitalism may overwhelm the successes. Today we redefine our problems rather than solving them. We no longer leave girl babies out on mountainsides to avoid the cost of extra children, but we redefine the starting-point of life instead. In the latter half of the twentieth century the number of abortions was greater than the totalitarian murders of the first half. Instead of lots of little and not-so-little wars we invest in nuclear stockpiles. Rather than resolve the inequalities of wealth we increase them, strengthening the national and regional boundaries to keep out the poor.

What's the place of religion in this? I divide religious practice into three: the bad, the neutral and the good. Bad religion fosters division and resentment. Indifferent practices are those only concerned with the individual soul. Good practices are those that lead to an awareness of responsibility for self, neighbor, community and planet.

The Church has not been convincingly enough on the side of the good to make it worth keeping, at least not in anything like its present form. Dark undercurrents keep resurfacing. It taught for centuries that Jews were outside the faith, that it could be a

Christian thing to do to persecute, exile, kill them. Hitler was an evil individual, but he was also the end result of some evil Church teaching. There's a disturbing new "final solution" emerging today in fundamentalist thinking on Armageddon (the apocalyptic imminent return of Jesus, which involves the destruction of most of humankind). The best-seller of all books in the 1970s in the USA was *Late Great Planet Earth*, which through a crude identifi-cation of the biblical land of Gog with Russia placed nuclear Armageddon in the immediate future. Ronald Reagan believed it. Most Americans did. I confess to having published it in the UK. The equivalent today is *Left Behind*, a best-seller of the 90s (over 35 million of this book and its sequels have been sold in the last few years) in which all the "saved" suddenly disappear, leaving cars crashing and planes falling out of the sky. It's scary that there are people running the world's largest power who believe in these apocalyptic fantasies of world destruction.

The fundamentalist ideas that the world is about to end, that Christians are a persecuted minority, that you can take the Bible literally, that what is not "Christian" is in some way evil, breeds the extremist "survivalist" groups. "Christian Identity" and "Aryan Nations" in the USA prepare for holocaust and anarchy. Admittedly fundamentalism is only one strand in the tapestry of Christian thinking, but the doctrines that have allowed it to flour-ish in different forms over the centuries are central to the faith. Today their more mainstream counterparts are closer than ever to having the power that could make their wishes come true. In this respect only do prophecies come true, when they are self-fulfilling. It's the Garden of Eden scenario – given enough time, if there's a wrong decision to be made and the capacity to make it, someone, somewhere, is going to press the button. If the world is about to end anyway, and if it will bring God to earth, why negotiate? Why compromise? Why bother to look after what we have? Why waste time on love?

There's a seeming inevitability today about the prospect of nuclear war, or cataclysmic plague. One slip of the finger on the button and we'll be back in the Dark Ages, or worse. The possibility of blowing ourselves to pieces must be high. Maybe not in the next 5 years, but 50? 5,000? 50,000? These are still drops of time in the life of a species. Will fingers stay off the trigger (nuclear, biological, or whatever comes next) for that long? It's not difficult to imagine a situation where increasing fundamentalism in the Islamic world collides with increasing geo-political dominance by the Christian West, maybe itself led by fundamentalists in the White House. It will be fuelled by pressures of population growth and ever-increasing consumption of diminishing resources like water, all highlighted and concentrated in the flash point of Jerusalem, sacred to three religions.

It's tragic because it's the Garden of Eden scenario over again. We're actually in it if only we could see it. The world is wonderful if only we could realize it. There's enough food for everyone if only we could share it. But it only takes one bad guy, or one madman, or one mistake, or one computer error, and we're all history. You have more trust in our leaders than that? Look at the US government today (supported by the UK). It's won the arms race of the twentieth century, is only spending half a trillion or so dollars a year on the military, has no major enemies in sight, so what's the obvious thing to do? Start another arms race, stupid. And make it bigger and more expensive than the last. If the earth isn't big enough, extend it to space. The Klingons from *Star Trek* are us.

If the apocalypse that we risk creating by our own efforts doesn't arrive then we have the chance of surviving, but on a planet that by definition has limited resources that are rapidly being used up. We have the example of past civilizations to show us what happens when the soil, or fuel, has run out, only this time there is no virgin territory to move into. The Easter Island scenario then beckons. It's the only case in history of a totally self-contained society, living in isolation. As the trees and soil disappeared the fishhooks got smaller because there were no canoes to get to the fishing grounds, the crops ran out, warfare between the villages increased, till an extraordinary society collapsed and disappeared. 110 out of the world's 138 living Nobel Prize winners signed the *World Scientists' Warning to Humanity* in 1992 that we're at the same point.

Maybe with the wisdom of hindsight future galactic historians of another species will simply say our brains grew too fast. A couple of million years ago the brain spurted to its present size, pushing out the skull to allow room for the skills of communicating and organizing that went with the development of language. Like the insects too heavy to turn themselves the right way up if they fall over, and the arthropods whose brains grew around the food channel and stifled it, we're an evolutionary dead-end.

The human brain got too big for the body, leading to the pains and dangers of childbirth. We have too many teeth for our jaws. Worst of all, the newer and older parts of the brain haven't integrated well. We've lost many of our natural instincts – like regulating breeding rates according to food supply – without developing an intelligence large enough to compensate. And indeed, there you have the Catholic Church in the forefront waving us, lemming-like, over the cliff edge. Having lost the biological imperative of sharing food along certain genetic lines, we haven't developed enough compassion to avoid absurd inequalities in the distribution of wealth. The result is crime, social unrest, revolution, legacies of suffering and bitterness. We can't even find sufficient self-control to avoid over-fouling our own nest. Maybe the third millennium will be a time of disaster, human-made, on a scale we haven't seen before.

So hold the idea of God in your head as a possibility. Live it as if it's true. We need a big idea to aim for, something to carry us through the next million years, or we won't make it. We need to grow to the next level of consciousness. It's in living by faith that we grow. Imagining that we can get to the next step, overriding our genetic programming. It's in growing that we meet God. Maybe He exists out there, maybe He's all in our heads. Maybe it comes to the same thing. It's worth believing, but it's not worth a moment's argument, a single wrong action.

58 THE FUTURE

"Space travel is bilge."

BRITAIN'S ASTRONOMER ROYAL, IN THE YEAR BEFORE SPUTNIK, 1956

H. G. Wells early in the twentieth century saw humanity as in a race between education and catastrophe. But education doesn't make us less selfish. It enables us to consume and throw away more, to produce more deadly weapons. There are plenty of educated people in the World Bank, the International Monetary Fund, the World Trade Organization, who are speeding us along on the path to Easter Island; more growth, more pollution, more inequity. I see the religious sense of "spirit" as more important. "Either the next century will be a spiritual century or there will be no next century at all," as Robert Muller, former deputy secretary general of the United Nations said. For me the best summary of the world of spirit, the alternative path to catastrophe, is the teaching of the kingdom of God. The idea that you treat other people with the same respect that you would treat God. The idea that we can realize heaven on earth if we can die to our selves. Is there any more chance for it than over the last couple of millennia? If enough individuals can follow it to make it work, what's the future likely to be?

To look on the bright side, at least four-fifths of the people in the world theoretically follow the Golden Rule of treating their neighbor as they would like to be treated. If they all managed to live by the teaching of their founders the planet would work. For this to happen some kind of effective world parliament for religions is essential, a forum where disputes can be settled, or at least agreements made to disagree. It could act as a restraining influence on fundamentalism of all varieties much as the UN should do on rogue states. It would encourage toleration, diversity of practice, and treat cross-cultural evangelism with the same kind of distaste meted out by the UN to cross-border gun running.

The first time representatives of all the world's religions got together was just over 100 years ago, at the World Congress of Faiths in Chicago in 1893. It was influenced by Narenda Nath Datta (Vivekananda, 1863-1902) who emphasized a strain of Hinduism that can accommodate a variety of religious belief. Eastern religions are more open to acknowledging truth in other religions. The practice of the "Great Church" (*tai chao*), for instance, of the Chinese blends Taoism, Confucianism and Buddhism.

Vivekananda considered that the Divine worked on two levels: the higher level is beyond description, but can be known through meditation. At the lower level God has qualities that are imaged in different ways, through different religions. All rituals are imperfect responses to a partly seen Divine Reality. We can know this from within because divinity permeates everything, and it is by recognizing the divine in other people that we are spurred on to love and good works. His teacher, Ramakrishna, had intense spiritual experiences of union with Christ, the Mother Goddess, Kali, Muhammad. All represent different ways to knowledge of the divine. Most of us struggle to realize one.

There was another world parliament in 1993 in Chicago. There are many inter-faith organizations, but the establishment Churches support them as a matter of peripheral goodwill rather than seeing them as central to their vision. A successful world parliament for religions might help promote the idea of the UN as a world parliament for nations and peoples. This may all seem absurd, but the League of Nations seemed absurd to many at first, so did the Olympic Games a century ago. Go back a millennium and the idea of nation states would have been incomprehensible. But go back ten millennia and there was probably little basic difference between people's beliefs and the way they organized themselves in different parts of the world. Go back 50 millennia to when Cro-

Magnon man first came out of Africa and there was little difference between humankind physically or culturally. Now go forward
50 millennia and the wheel will come full circle again. The distinctions that have developed between races as they settled around
the globe will be blurred through intermarriage. It's started to
accelerate in the last few centuries. The differences between religions will have diminished in the same way. Why not start
preparing for it?

Maybe Christianity can reconfigure itself in the next century as
a religion that works for the kingdom of God on earth rather than
the salvation of the few in heaven. It would then take us forward
into the next millennium. In the West, Unitarianism is the strand
most open to this, and creates a context for a "do it yourself" religion where individuals can be encouraged to follow their own
spiritual journey. A nineteenth-century offshoot of Islam, the
Bahai faith, preaches world peace and the unity of humankind. But
these movements are small. The religious "market" is wide open
for a progressive Christianity that is based on tolerance and mutual
respect.

If we avoid killing each other off, over-exploiting resources, and
continue for millennia, we will change. For one thing, we're going
to end up looking a lot different from how we look now. Even in
the short span of recorded history the average height of human
beings has decreased and risen through changes in lifestyle and
diet. As we create our own environment and have the power to
genetically manipulate our own bodies the rate of change will
increase. It is likely to prove impossible to resist the drive to
improve human beings genetically, much as we have already been
improving crops and dairy animals, breeding dogs and cats, apples
and tomatoes, for thousands of years. The replacement of human
organs and tissue by that of other species or with man-made materials is already advanced. The ability to clone people may be just a
few years away. There's every reason to suppose that the science of

genomics will be able to fashion human beings in every conceivable form. But will this be a democratic process, undertaken for the good of everybody, or will it lead to different classes of people more extreme and rigid than anything Hinduism or the Hebrews could have dreamt of? If you successively replace different parts of the human body with organs from other people, or animals, or mechanical devices, how far can you go? Where does a "person" begin and end? How will a thousand-year life expectancy change our view of life? Maybe this is where our problems will really begin. If we can't get our act together now, defining what it means to be human, how we relate to each other fairly, how will we cope with a world of a few million-dollar-super-humans who are genetically and physically superior to the rest of us?

We're as yet just a blink of an eyelid in the planet's history. If we can overcome tribal desires to rule, conquer, and convert, the future will open out, and we'll shape our environment to enable consciousness to continue and develop, rather than be driven by it to a dead end. The world of science fiction will then increasingly become fact. Think of life on earth as a giant game of snakes and ladders. We've crept past a couple of dozen snakes to get this far. Religious fundamentalism is one of the next big perils. Just a few thousand years ago it didn't exist. Now it's one of the threats to the planet. If we go down, it's back to cockroaches and rats. If we get past that snake and keep going we'll start to tap the resources of the planet's core, rather than scratching at the surface. Then we'll tap the energy of the sun, and be able to manipulate and create planets. Later the galaxy, manipulating stars. Maybe by then "mind" will be cased in forms other than the organic – maybe electrical energy, who knows what. The brain will then be free to grow to an indefinite size, freed from the restriction forced upon it at present by the need to fit through the birth canal, taking it to 10 to the power of 11 neurons, or 12. Maybe then we'll be free of the guilt of flourishing at the expense of other species. We'll encourage life rather than destroy it. Maybe we'll develop a more collective kind of consciousness of the kind already possessed by some other species, like the termites. Maybe we'll go back to the sea and talk over family matters with our far-distant cousins, the whales, asking forgiveness for the last few centuries of one-sided slaughter. If this took a million years, or ten million, that is still an infinitesimal amount of the time the universe still has to run. If we stay in the game we may be part of the consciousness that in ten billion or so years' time, when the universe comes to an end, finds itself at the beginning, ready to play again.

The biggest question of all is that of life on other planets. Think of the many billions of planets there probably are in the universe, and how rapidly life has evolved on earth in the last billion years or so. There may be millions of life forms elsewhere who would see us as barely out of the slime stage. If life is not unique to earth, then we should be preparing ourselves to confront another image of God that is less like our own. We have no idea how they would look, or whether we could see them at all. In films we tend to make them look something like us, with a head and limbs, as we do with God. But though all life on this planet is related, any life on other planets would have developed separately, in different conditions it is likely to be nothing we could recognize or communicate with. We can't talk to whales on our own planet who have the same kind of brain ratios that we have, the same genetic make-up, breathe the same air we do.

Or maybe it takes ten billion years for the conditions in which life and intelligence can form, and we're part of the first wave. Or maybe the frequencies of mass extinction through meteorites or exploding stars and gamma rays are too high for such civilizations to last.

We probably won't know in our lifetimes. We've only just got to the point of being able to tell that there are indeed planets around nearby stars, and that most of the 100 billion stars in our galaxy probably have them. It will be another generation or two before we're able to view them through telescopes. But if out of the trillions of possible planets in the universe only the earth supports life then life itself is "religious" in the highest possible sense. Every form of life on the planet relates to every other. Every one is "sacred." Any religion that doesn't see this isn't worth the name. At the moment we're destroying species at the rate of a million or so a year. We've no idea even how many there are, probably somewhere up to 100 million. Shake any tree in the Amazonian rainforest and new species fall out. Humanity has upped the average extinction rate by a hundred to a thousand-fold, leading to the kind of mass destruction of life that the planet hasn't seen since the dinosaurs disappeared 65 million years ago. The history of life over the last billion years suggests that any one of them could hold the key to the future.

Maybe our story has come full circle. We've found the keys to the Garden of Eden. We can clone species, we're on the edge of creating them, of fashioning ourselves in new forms. We've unpicked the metabolism of life and death, pulling its fruit down from the tree. But we don't have a new story for this. We seem to have lost the facility for writing new chapters. We're still living with the old ones. The old story is essentially that to be self-aware, to gain knowledge, is to transgress against God. Thinking is bad, obedience is good. The Church still promotes this. Jesus offered a new story, where personal growth and sharing takes priority over law. He called it the kingdom of God.

But the Christian nations who claim to take their morality from him and dominate the world economy have in the last century invented concentration camps and nuclear bombs. Roughly half the scientists in the world, mostly Christians, work at least part-time for the military establishment. In the ultimate ironic twist it is God-believing Christians, if anyone, who will destroy the planet, and the life on it that God has spent 3.5 billion years shepherding through to consciousness.

There's a story about the grand project of the third millennium, which is to produce a quantum computer. This would be made of electrons existing in the "in-between" state, in which they haven't yet decided where to appear. In such a system the electrons would calculate probabilities in all the possible universes simultaneously. It's been calculated that a microscopic quantum computer with just 300 electrons would have more components in its parallel states than there are atoms in the universe, and the power of larger ones would increase exponentially. In principle it could simulate the universe. It's a difficult thing to build, because organizing electrons that don't exist yet is a hard act. But it's made. The greatest human achievement ever.

The world leaders gather around it for the opening ceremony. The Pope is allowed to ask the first question: "There's only one question worthy of this historic moment," he says. "Does God exist?" The machine whirrs, and after a moment comes back the answer, "He does now."

"Believe nothing because a wise man said it.
Believe nothing because it is generally held.
Believe nothing because it is written.
Believe nothing because it is said to be divine.
Believe nothing because someone else believes it.
But believe only what you yourself judge to be true."

THE BUDDHA

Simple Timeline of some of the dates mentioned

BC

15,000,000,000	Universe created
8,000,000,000	Indian estimate for age of universe
5,000,000,000	Earth formed
3,500,000,000	Life begins
24,000,000	Primates diverge from hominids
5,000,000	Human ancestors diverge from chimps
500,000	Persian estimate for age of universe
250,000	Oldest cave rituals
100,000	*Homo Erectus* dies off
34,000	Fossil of last Neanderthal Man found
30,000	Venus figurines
8,000	First cities
4,000	Hebrew estimate for age of universe
3,500	Writing invented, first pyramids built, first *Vedas*
2,000	Epic of Gilgamesh written
1,500	Zoroaster, first revealed religion
1,400	Abraham
1,200	Moses and Exodus
1,000	David
Eighth century	First books of the Bible written, including Genesis 2:4-3:24
Seventh century	Thales, first scientist
722	Fall of Northern Kingdom to Assyria
621	Josiah finds the Books of Moses
Sixth century	Buddha, Confucius, Lao Tsu, Mahavira, Pythagoras, Socrates
	Bhagavad-Gita, Genesis 1:1-2:3 written
586	Fall of Southern Kingdom to Babylon, Exile
Fifth century	Histories of Thucydides, Herodotus, the first historians
	Compilation of much of Old Testament
445	Nehemiah returns to Jerusalem

AD

4 BC–AD 26 . . . . . .Life of Jesus

50s . . . . .First letters of Paul

60s . . . . .Last letters of Paul, *Gospel of Thomas*

70s . . . . .Gospels of Mark, Matthew

80s . . . . .Gospel of Luke

. . . . .Increasing separation of Christians and Jews

90s . . . . .Acts of the Apostles

. . . . .Jewish Old Testament agreed

100 . . . . .Gospel of John

Second century . . . . .Christianity a separate faith, Gnostics, Justin Martyr

295 . . . . .Gnostics outlawed

312 . . . . .Constantine converted

325 . . . . .Nicean Creed

380 . . . . .Worship of pagan gods banned in

. . . . .the Roman Empire

Fourth century . . . . .Roman popes begin to claim authority

. . . . .over other bishops

. . . . .First list of all 27 books of the New Testament

410 . . . . .Rome sacked

354–430 . . . . .Augustine

Seventh century . . . .Spread of Islam

. . . . .Text of Jewish Old Testament agreed

Eleventh to fourteenth Crusades

Fifteenth century . . .Renaissance, papacy in the pits

Sixteenth century . . .European expansion begins

. . . . .Reformation

1633 . . . . .Galileo faces Inquisition

Seventeenth century .Enlightenment

1781 . . . . .War of American Independence

1854 . . . . .Doctrine of Immaculate Conception

1893 . . . . .First World Congress of Faiths, in Chicago

1993 . . . . .Roman Catholic Church admits Galileo was right

1993 . . . .*Fatwa* against "round earth" teaching

1998 UK . . . . .Regular Church attendance 3.7 million

10,000,000 . . . . . . .End of humankind if we survive for the average

. . . . .lifetime of a species

5,000,000,000 . . . . .Sun burns up, life on earth ends

10,000,000,000 . . . .Stars disappear

SHORT READING LIST:

After God, Don Cupitt, Orion
The Awakening Earth, Peter Russell, Arkana
The Book of Nothing, John Barrow, Jonathan Cape
Christianity; a Global History, David Chidester, Allen Lane
Civilization, Felipe Fernandez-Armesto, Macmillan
Climbing Mount Improbable, Richard Dawkins, Viking
The Complete Jesus, Ricky Mayotte, Steerforth Press
The Death of Forever, Darryl Reanney, Souvenir Press
The Disappearance of God, Richard Friedman Little, Brown and Company
The Five Gospels, Funk, Hoover, Harper Collins
From the Holy Mountain, William Dalrymple, Flamingo
Gnosis, Andrew Welburn, Floris Books
Gospel Truth, Russell Shorto, Hodder and Stoughton
The Historical Figure of Jesus, E.P. Sanders, Allen Lane
Images of Eternity, Keith Ward, Oneworld
Jesus: A revolutionary biography, John Dominic Crossan, Harper San Francisco
Jesus: the Evidence, Ian Wilson, Weidenfeld and Nicholson
Just Six Numbers, Martin Rees, Weidenfeld and Nicholson
Life: an Unauthorised Biography, Richard Fortey, Harper Collins
Mapping the Mind, Rita Carter, Weidenfeld and Nicholson
The Meaning of Jesus, N.T. Wright and M. Borg, SPCK
Myth and Ritual in Christianity, Alan Watts, Thames and Hudson
One Jesus, Many Christs, Gregory Riley, Harper San Francisco
The Origins of Virtue, Matt Ridley, Viking
The Phenomenon of Religion, Moojam Momen, Oneworld
Q is for Quantum, John Gribbin, Weidenfeld and Nicholson
Religion, Leszek Kolakowski, Fontana Press
Rescuing the Bible from Fundamentalism, John Shelby Spong, Harper San Francisco
The Rise of Christianity, W.C. Frend, Fortress Press
The Runaway Brain, Christopher Wills, Harper Collins
Testament, John Romer, Michael O'Mara Books
The Unauthorized Version, Robin Lane Fox, Viking
The Wisdom of Bones, A. Walker and P. Shipman, Weidenfeld and Nicholson
The World's Religions, Ninian Smart, Cambridge University Press

SOME OTHER TITLES FROM O BOOKS

GLOBAL SPIRIT LIBRARY

Robert Van de Weyer

The first comprehensive collection of the spiritual literature of the whole world presented in accessible form.

It is aimed at people who belong to a particular religious community and wish to broaden their spiritual outlook, and also at the much larger group who have little or no attachment to a religious community, but seek spiritual wisdom. Each volume in the series contains the major writings of one of the world's spiritual traditions, presented in the form of an annual cycle of daily readings.

The editor, Robert Van de Weyer, was raised by atheist parents who were active socialists, was introduced to religion by Hindus and Muslims in India, studied Christianity in Ethiopia, and became a priest in England. He serves a church near Cambridge committed to global spirituality.

384pp, 180/122mm, hardback with jacket, 2 colour illustrations, £14.99.

Titles already available:

366 READINGS FROM TAOISM & CONFUCIANISM

0 85305 456 8

Included are:

- the profound and enigmatic sayings of Lao Tzu
- the wit and irony of Chuang Tzu
- the spiritual adventures of Lieh Tzu and Yang Chu
- the gentle wisdom of Confucius and Mencius

366 READINGS FROM JUDAISM

0 85305 455 X

Included are:

- the life and history of the ancient Hebrew tribes
- the visions and ideals of the ancient Hebrew prophets
- the wit and wisdom of the Jewish rabbis
- the insights of the Jewish philosophers and mystics

366 READINGS FROM CHRISTIANITY

0 85305 454 1

Included are:

- the life of Jesus Christ in the Gospels

- letters to churches from early leaders, including Paul, John, Clement and Ignatius

- writings of Christian philosophers, applying reason to the mystery of religion

- accounts by Catholic mystics, monks and nuns of their spiritual experiences

- testimonies by Protestants of the spiritual journey

366 READINGS FROM BUDDHISM

0 85305 453 3

Included are:

- teachings of the Buddha, taken from the Pali Canon compiled soon after his death

- *The Dhammapada*, the famous summary of the Buddha's wisdom

- stories, poems, sayings and spiritual insights of the Mahayana sages from Tibet, China and India

- jokes and stories from Zen

366 READINGS FROM ISLAM

0 85305 452 5

Included are:

- The Life of Muhammad by Ibn Ishaq, written soon after the prophet's death

- The Quran, received by Muhammad, which is the sacred text of Islam

- stories, poems, sayings and spiritual insights of the Sufi mystics

- philosophical reflections of the great Arab thinkers

366 READINGS FROM HINDUISM

0 85305 451 7

Included are:

- the Vedas, the ancient hymns which form the basis of Hindu spirituality

- the Upanishads, the collections of meditations and stories embodying Hindu thought

- The Bhagavad Gita, the sayings of Krishna which embrace all spiritual life

- the original instructions in the practice of yoga, and its underlying philosophy

- the devotional poems and meditations of the Indian mystics and the Sikhs

TIME AND TIDE-

Sea of Faith Beyond the Millennium 1 903816 00 9

The Sea of Faith is an international network of people who are interested in exploring and promoting religious faith as a wholly human creation, established in the early 1980's.

Time and Tide is a critical review of SOF from a wide range of writers who give their perspectives on the effect the Network has had on today's radical religious thinking. Paul Davies, visiting Professor of Physics at Imperial College, London, and author of the Mind of God, sees Don Cupitt as "one of the most exciting theologians of our era." Karen Armstrong, author of *A History of God* and *The Battle for God*, says that "the Sea of Faith Network was founded to meet the growing conviction that the God of Western classical theism is dead and can no longer give men and women the sense of transcendence they seek and need." Robert Ashby, Director of the British Humanist Association, comments that SOF is "profoundly important" in that it provides a "halfway house" for those who are struggling with changing beliefs. For Richard Holloway, Bishop of Edinburgh and author of Godless Morality, "the beauty of the Sea of Faith approach" is that is "celebrates the diversity of the meanings we devise for ourselves in our search for understanding". Don Cupitt, Fellow of Emmanuel College, Cambridge, believes that Sea of Faith "shows how religion might begin to grow again – and so help us to grow too."

The book will be essential reading both for questioning members of traditional faith communities, and for those who have no connection with organised religion but who refuse to abandon the search for human values to live by.

112pp, 198/128mm, paperback, £7.00.

JOURNEY TO JERUSALEM

1 903816 01 7

By Trevor Pitt

Illustrations by Linda Birch

This book is beautifully illustrated throughout with full colour pictures drawn "in situ" by Linda Birch, herself an author of several books on the art of drawing and painting.

"At once informative and meditative, thoughtful and thought-provoking, this is above all an agreeable readable book. It is just the sort of book that any pilgrim to the Holy Land will be glad to have before, during and after their pilgrimage.

Before, it will enliven anticipation of the rich possibilities of experience which lie ahead. During it can be used to check facts and – more importantly – to compare the resonance of shared experience. After, it will help consolidate and focus that experience, giving it the sort of form and cutting edge which transforms it into a truly spiritual tool: a tool which will refine their understanding of the Lord in whose footsteps they have walked and in whose company they travel still."

David Ebor

The Archbishop of York

128pp, 262/190mm, hardback with jacket, full colour, £14.99.

THE BECOMING

0 85305 473 8

Robert Fripp

A re-telling of Genesis chapter one in the light of modern science.

Robert Fripp's ingenious idea – to resurrect Genesis in the light of our present knowledge of evolutionary process – must, I suppose, count as a literary curiosity; but I have long been in favour of literary curiosities. They have a perverse habit, very often, of provoking more thought than the orthodox approach. By simplifying the complex and broadening the narrow, they spark the imagination. (Foreword by John Fowles).

The fast march of science long ago relegated the Genesis creation story to what it once was – a Bronze Age myth. But the triumph of science stole something deeper than archaic meaning: it robbed us of wonder and of that sweep of majestic vision represented in Genesis.

Robert Fripp takes an integrated approach to unfolding creation, welcoming religious thought and philosophy as partners with science at the table for discussion that is The Becoming.

174pp, 198/128mm, paperback, £7.99.